BOOKS BY KENNETH REXROTH

POEMS

The Collected Shorter Poems
The Collected Longer Poems
Sky Sea Birds Trees Earth House Beasts Flowers
New Poems
The Phoenix and the Tortoise
The Morning Star
Selected Poems

PLAYS

Beyond the Mountains

CRITICISM & ESSAYS

The Alternative Society
American Poetry in the Twentieth Century
Assays
Bird in the Bush
The Classics Revisited
Communalism, from the Neolithic to 1900
The Elastic Retort
With Eye and Ear

TRANSLATIONS

100 Poems from the Chinese
100 More Poems from the Chinese: Love and the Turning Year
Fourteen Poems of O. V. Lubicz-Milosz
Seasons of Sacred Lust: The Selected Poems of Kazuko Shiraishi
     (*with Ikuko Atsumi, John Solt, Carol Tinker, and
     Yasuyo Morita*)
The Burning Heart: Women Poets of Japan
     (*with Ikuko Atsumi*)
The Orchid Boat: The Women Poets of China
     (*with Ling Chung*)
100 French Poems
Poems from the Greek Anthology
100 Poems from the Japanese
100 More Poems from the Japanese
30 Spanish Poems of Love and Exile
Selected Poems of Pierre Reverdy
Li Ch'ing-chao: Complete Poems (*with Ling Chung*)

AUTOBIOGRAPHY

An Autobiographical Novel

EDITOR

The Continuum Poetry Series

KENNETH
REXROTH
SELECTED POEMS

Edited by Bradford Morrow

A New Directions Book

The poems in this book have been selected from *The Collected Shorter Poems of Kenneth Rexroth* (1966), *The Collected Longer Poems of Kenneth Rexroth* (1968), *New Poems* (1974), and *The Morning Star* (1979).

The editor wishes to thank Deborah Baker, Morgan Gibson, Peter Glassgold, Linda Hamalian, James Laughlin, Leslie Miller, and Carol Tinker for useful suggestions they made during the preparation of this book.

Manufactured in the United States of America
First published clothbound and as New Directions Paperbook 581 in 1984
Published simultaneously in Canada by Penguin Books Canada Limited

Library of Congress Cataloging in Publication Data
Rexroth, Kenneth, 1905–1982
    Selected poems.
    (A New Directions Book)
    Includes index.
    I. Morrow, Bradford, 1951–   .   II. Title.
PS3535.E923A6   1984   811'.52   84–9972
ISBN 0–8112–0916–4
ISBN 0–8112–0917–2 (pbk.)

New Directions Books are published for James Laughlin by New Directions Publishing Corporation, 80 Eighth Avenue, New York 10011

SECOND PRINTING

Contents

Introduction, by Bradford Morrow   ix
FROM *In What Hour* (1940)
    On What Planet   1
    Requiem for the Spanish Dead   2
    Autumn in California   3
    August 22, 1939   4
    Toward an Organic Philosophy   7
    A Lesson in Geography   11
FROM *The Phoenix and the Tortoise* (1944)
    from The Phoenix and the Tortoise   15
    When We with Sappho   25
    Lute Music   28
    Floating   29
    Another Spring   30
    The Advantages of Learning   31
    Inversely, at the Square of Their Distances
        Apart   31
    Between Two Wars   33
    Delia Rexroth   33
    Andrée Rexroth   34
FROM *The Art of Worldly Wisdom* (1949)
    The Thin Edge of Your Pride   35
FROM *The Signature of All Things* (1950)
    Between Myself and Death   41
    The Signature of All Things   42
    Lyell's Hypothesis Again   45
    Delia Rexroth   46

Andrée Rexroth 47
A Letter to William Carlos Williams 50
FROM *The Dragon and the Unicorn* (1952) 53
FROM *In Defense of the Earth* (1956)
from Seven Poems for Marthe, My Wife
The Reflecting Trees of Being and
Not Being 81
Marthe Away (She Is Away) 82
A Dialogue of Watching 83
from The Lights in the Sky Are Stars 84
A Living Pearl 87
For Eli Jacobson 89
The Bad Old Days 91
from Mary and the Seasons 92
Thou Shalt Not Kill 94
from A Bestiary 102
FROM *Natural Numbers* (1964)
Fish Peddler and Cobbler 107
from Written to Music ("Married Blues") 109
FROM *The Heart's Garden, The Garden's Heart*
(1967) 110
FROM *New Poems* (1974)
Now in the starlit moonless Spring 117
I Dream of Leslie 117
La Vie en Rose 118
Suchness 118
FROM *On Flower Wreath Hill* (1976) 119
FROM *The Silver Swan* (1978) 121
FROM *The Love Poems of Marichiko* (1978) 122

FROM *The Homestead Called Damascus*
     (1920–1925)   124
FROM *A Prolegomenon to a Theodicy*
     (1925–1927)   132
NOTES   139
INDEX OF TITLES AND FIRST LINES   151

FROM *The Homestead Called Damascus*
      (1920–1925)   124
FROM *A Prolegomenon to a Theodicy*
      (1925–1927)   132
NOTES   139
INDEX OF TITLES AND FIRST LINES   151

INTRODUCTION

In H. G. Wells' prologue to Kenneth Rexroth's favorite childhood book, *The Research Magnificent*, the idealistic, brilliant, and rather unbalanced protagonist, William Porphyry Benham, is described as a man who was led into adventure by an idea. This idea took possession of Porphyry's imagination "quite early in life, it grew with him and changed with him, it interwove at last completely with his being." The idea was simple. Life, he thought, must be lived nobly and to the utmost limits; a man must realize something out of his existence: "a flame, a jewel, a splendour." To the precocious thirteen-year-old Rexroth what a heady and marvelous blueprint for life this must have been. Unlike Porphyry, however, whose lifelong research was left crammed in bureau drawers and dozens of patent boxes, as an "indigestible aggregation" of notes for an unwritten book, Rexroth spent the nearly six decades that followed his first reading of *The Research Magnificent* amassing a polymath knowledge that would surpass that of any other American poet of the century (Pound included), while at the same time honing his writing to a simple and direct style that most resembled his own everyday speech (like Williams). As a result he is one of our most readable and yet complex poets. And, like William Porphyry Benham, there was little that didn't interest him enough to at least attempt to master it.

Peripateticism and a spirit free of prejudice, rather than a focus on the local, are the twin bases of Rexroth's fundamentally American personality. (It is a combination that would in the 1950s influence members of the Beat generation who gathered around Rexroth in San Francisco and made of him that Movement's unwilling father figure.) Born in South Bend, Indiana, on December 22, 1905, and raised in Chicago, Elkhart, Battle Creek, and Toledo, it would have been very natural for him to have developed an art whose themes derived from a pure Midwestern upbringing. But, if we are to believe the exuberant portrait of his youth set out in his *An Autobiographical Novel*, his precocity and a bohemian attitude toward life were already in full blossom by the time he was in his teens.

A pioneer brand of rational empiricism and pietistic radicalism ran deep in the family's history. Of German-American ancestry, both of Rexroth's grandfathers showed politically dissident tendencies, and descended themselves from the Schwenkfelders, a heterodox sect (whose beliefs are substantially the Quakers') that arrived in America before William Penn. While by the turn of the present century the sectarian religious cast of the Schwenkfelders had within Rexroth's family been transformed, the "radical ethical social impulse" remained, and produced in Rexroth's forefathers an inherited, almost instinctive radicalism. Indeed, his paternal grandfather George voted straight Socialist tickets and always read the Socialist papers before finally declaring himself an Anarchist in his last years. The familial climate in which Rexroth was reared nurtured self-sufficiency, self-respect, as well as a strong sense of ethical activism and "a philosophy of caste responsibility":

> I learned that other people were not as we were, but slightly demented, and demented in such a way that they could easily become dangerous. And I learned that we, as more responsible members of society who knew better, had to take care of them as though they were sick. In fact, I gained the impression then that the society which lay over against my family—*les autres*, as the French say—was a helpless and dangerous beast that we had to tend to and save from its own irrationality. I rather doubt if anything in life has ever caused me to give up this attitude.

This basic Socialist principle prompted in Rexroth the notion that all learning had inherent societal ramifications. It was a central criterion in his mother's pedagogic system that each and every bit of information her son learned must not be an abstract thing mastered for its own sake, but was studied for keeps, was a tool meant to be applied in society on a daily basis.

Rexroth's father, Charles, was a moderately successful pharmacist. His mother, Delia, oversaw most of her only son's education herself, rather than sending him to school. She instructed him in elementary arithmetic, history, astronomy, and the natural sciences, and taught him to read by the age of four, at which time she procured for him a library card. His parents helped him set up a small laboratory; even his toys were Froebellian and Montessorian, carefully selected for color and design. When he wasn't reading or studying he spent much of his time outdoors, was an avid hunter and, with his mother's help, learned the rudiments of botany and zoology. Although he has described his childhood as fundamentally Edwardian, various eccentric circumstances, such as his befriending at the age of five or six an elderly American Indian, Billy Sunlight, who lived on the Rexroth's property in a remodeled chicken coop, gave it character and quality that would elude any such rubric.

The ranging private education Rexroth received from his mother stood him in good stead after he was orphaned in 1918. His parents' marriage had begun to falter several years before this; his father's business experienced a reversal in fortune, and he began to drink heavily. Delia Rexroth died in June 1916—not three years before Charles finally suffered a miserable, painful death as a result of acute alcoholism. Upon moving in with his aunt in Chicago (see "The Bad Old Days"), Rexroth decided he would be a writer and an artist, and his education toward those ends began in earnest. He attended the Chicago Art Institute and Bush Conservatory, but soon became "a consummate master in the art of plausible hooky." An alternative educational system now insinuated itself:

> More than any of the official education and cultural institutions my favorite school was the Washington Park Bug Club . . . Here until midnight could be heard passionate exponents of every variety of human lunacy. There were Anarchist-Single-Taxers, British-Israelites, self-annointed archbishops of the American Catholic Church, Druids, Anthroposophists, and geologists who had proven the world was flat or that the surface of the earth was the inside of a hollow sphere, and people who were in communication with the inhabitants of Mars, Atlantis, and Tibet, severally and sometimes simultaneously. Besides, struggling for a hearing was the whole body of orthodox heterodoxy—Socialists, communists (still with a small "c"), IWWs, De Leonites,

Anarchists, Single Taxers (separately, not in contradictory combination), Catholic Guild Socialists, Schopenhauerians, Nietzscheans—of whom there were quite a few—Stinerites, and what were later to be called Fascists.

At the center of the Bug Club was a William Porphyry Benham come to life, one Judge Walter Freeman Cooling. Under the judge's Socratean wing came a footloose fourteen-year-old who had already digested more books than most people read in a lifetime. Cooling advanced to Rexroth a whimsical theory of the universe which tied together an intellectually rigorous bundle of sources that included the Finnish epic *Kalevala*, Migne's *Patrologia Latinae* and *Graecae*, the *Pirke Aboth*, Homer, the *Zend Avesta*, St. Bonaventura, Jacob Boehme, etc. Rexroth was not drawn into adopting the judge's bizarre polyphilosophic and cosmological system, but the experience was determinative in that it introduced him to the possibilities of autodidacticism and dissent: "With the intelligence of an Aristotle or an Aquinas, [Cooling] disagreed all along the line with all organized thought." Also, less inclined than ever to rejoin his contemporaries in school, he started reading every author the judge happened to mention, and *in toto*. He read the *Sacred Books of the East*. He tried to learn Egyptian. He wrote a play about the heretic king Ikhnaton. Tyndall, Haeckel, Clerk Maxwell, Lyell, Darwin, Mendel, and Faraday were consumed, as were Turgenev, James, Melville, Flaubert, Sainte-Beuve, Dostoevsky, Jack London. Pound's *Cathay* introduced him to Chinese literature. He read straight through the Aldine poets. As a result of this omnivorous and eccentric reading list (the student who wishes to know which books remained important to him in the end is referred to *The Classics Revisited*, in which he appraises sixty key texts) Rexroth was not "converted to the deliquescence of orthodoxy and heterodoxy, so characteristic of our time," but was inoculated against it:

> The radical disbelief which has been characteristic of all my contemporaries I shared from the beginning, but I was never led by it to embrace any of the extraordinary follies which were to become fashionable in intellectual circles in the

next thirty or forty years. I have known Socialist-Realist novelists who religiously consulted the astrology column in the daily newspapers every morning before breakfast. The whole Socialist movement after the First War, led by Frank Harris and Upton Sinclair, embraced the Abrams electronic diagnosis machine. Twenty years later, after the Second War, the reborn Anarchist movement committed suicide in the orgone boxes of Wilhelm Reich. Anyone who had taken a course in high school physics would have known that this stuff was arrant nonsense but the trouble was that these people had lost belief in high school physics along with their belief in capitalism or religion.

At the same time, he began circulating among musicians, artists, anarchists, gangsters, and the considerable human jetsam of radical bohemian Chicago. He tried his hand at numerous jobs, began to paint large abstract canvases, and followed his girlfriend Shirley Johnson to Northampton (see "When We with Sappho") and, finally, to New York. He attended classes at the New School for Social Research and the Art Students League. Living in a brownstone commune on West 13th Street in Greenwich Village, he encountered Marsden Hartley, Mark Tobey, Michael Gold, William Gropper, and others. He briefly met Sacco and Vanzetti and became involved with the Wobblies' labor movement. It is an improbable picaresque, played out against an America that was on the verge of the terrific social upheaval of the twenties, that would form a personality Whitmanesque in its all-embraciveness and Thoreauvian in its attention to detail.

A generation before it became *de rigeur* among bohemians, and two full generations before it was enshrined as a normal activity for bourgeoise collegiates, Rexroth began to hitchhike the length and breadth of the country, sampling different lifestyles, supporting himself as a workaway and occasionally even panhandling when the funds went dry. He drifted from coast to coast and worked every conceivable kind of job (see "A Living Pearl"). He shipped out of Hoboken as a mess steward and got as far as Paris (where he met Aragon, Tzara, Soupault, Cendrars, among others) and down to Buenos Aires. Thirty years before Jack Duluoz set out, he hitched and railed to Mexico City and Oaxaca. At the end of this odyssey he returned to Chicago, resolved to marry; three or four women turned him down before he met a young commercial artist, Andrée Dutcher (born Myrtle Shaefer), whom he married in 1927. Of the four books she had read with enthusiasm in her childhood, it is not surprising that one was *The Research Magnificent*.

In both his autobiography and the poetry Rexroth details the joyous first years they spent together. They painted and read; his poetry was beginning to be published in *Blues*, *Pagany*, *Morada*, and elsewhere. As an impromptu honeymoon they hitchhiked to Seattle, and proceeded to hike down the rugged Pacific Northwest coastline until they reached San Francisco, broke. It was a significant turning point in Rexroth's life, for although he found the city intellectually provincial—"Everybody we met considered George Sterling the greatest poet since Dante"—this was to become his home for the next forty years. By the time Andrée died, in October 1940, after a lifelong struggle with epilepsy, Rexroth had become an active member of its political and literary community. Within the decade that followed the outbreak of the war, Frank Norris and George Sterling would be relegated to their proper places as Rexroth laid the groundwork for what was to become the San Francisco Renaissance.

At a Nurses Union meeting he met Marie Cass, whom he married in 1941. A Conscientious Objector to the war, Rexroth worked as an attendant in a psychiatric ward. Their home became not only a meeting place for anarchist and antiwar meetings, as well as literary readings, but a secret convalescent shelter for Japanese seeking to escape internment camps:

> The whole evacuation completely disaffiliated me from the American capitalist state and from the State as such. From then on I've seen very little in American official policy and behavior to be proud of, and Hiroshima, Nagasaki and Vietnam finished the job.

In What Hour, Rexroth's first book of poems, had come out in 1940, and his long poem "The Phoenix and the Tortoise" (published in a book of the same title by New Directions in 1944) voices this same attitude of disaffiliation.

After the war, Rexroth worked off and on as a literary journalist; he wrote more poetry and worked on the series of plays in *Beyond the Mountains*. In 1949, with the appearance of a collection of juvenalia—*The Art of Wordly Wisdom* (published by James Decker)—his marriage dissolved. Shortly thereafter he married Marthe Larsen, with whom he had two daughters, Mary and Katherine. Marthe was his traveling companion through Europe, documented in *The Dragon and the Unicorn* (1952), and is the subject of some of his finest love poems, included in *In Defense of the Earth* in 1956 (see, "Marthe Away" and "A Dialogue of Watching"). Five years after his divorce in 1961 from Marthe, he moved to Montecito, just south of Santa Barbara, where he later married the poet Carol Tinker; they resided there until his death in June 1982. Always a poet of love within the relationship of holy matrimony (and, invariably, within the realm of nature), each of his four wives may be seen as touchstones through which his philosophy of sacrament and communal love is comprehended. Like burning lights, epiphanal moments passed with each served as mnemonic sparks against which he could measure his own life. Perhaps the most remarkable example of this is the beautiful "Kings River Canyon" passage in "Andrée Rexroth" (*The Signature of All Things*).

Throughout the fifties, Rexroth continued his radical political activities, though his confidence in the Anarchist movement wavered before the memories of his beloved Wobblies, whom he considered purer and more effectual. This position is evident in *The Dragon and the Unicorn*, and in several shorter poems, such as "For Eli Jacobson." Thus, more time was committed to fulfilling his self-assigned role as arbiter of the literary scene in San Francisco; his Potrero Hill rooms were quickly becoming the heart of a growing movement. With the help of Robert Duncan, Madeline Gleason, and Ruth Witt-Diamant, the San Francisco Poetry Center was founded, which for a time attracted writers as well known as Dylan Thomas, W. H. Auden, and William Carlos Williams to give readings. Through articles and on his own KPFA radio program, Rexroth tirelessly brought poets like Duncan, Lamantia, Levertov, Snyder, Ferlinghetti,

Everson, to public attention. When, in 1953, Dylan Thomas died, he wrote the remarkable "Thou Shalt Not Kill," which is widely considered to be the forerunner to, if not the model for, Allen Ginsberg's "Howl." Elegiac in its purpose, this long poem (which he read in clubs to the accompaniment of jazz—Rexroth, Patchen, and Ferlinghetti were the pioneers of this form of performance poetry) remains one of the most incriminating and relentless attacks on the destructive evils of the State ever written.

By the early sixties Rexroth had grown disenchanted with the literary scene he had helped engender: he considered the bohemian lifestyle of the Beats merely a veneer, more a sartorial, pharmaceutical, and gastronomic change than an internal, spiritual revolution. With his famous statement, "An entymologist is not a bug," he severed (though never lived down) his connection with the Beats.

While he had already translated poetry from Chinese and Japanese (as well as French, Italian, Latin, and Greek) this last period of his life is marked by five extended visits to Kyoto, and an increased interest in Buddhism. This inward turn culminated in the Marichiko poems, which were written pseudonymously as "translations" of a young Japanese woman poet; a narrative of love won and lost, these compressed poems achieve, at the end of Rexroth's life, a passionate lyricism equal to his early work, and reveal a spirit still perceptive and elastic. As his reputation as a scholar-critic grew with the publication of a series of prose books—*The Alternative Society, The Bird in the Bush, Assays, American Poetry in the Twentieth Century, Eye and Ear, The Classics Revisited*—so grew his esteem as a translator. Despite this critical output a lifetime of antiacademic pronouncements assured his being seldom taught in university classrooms and, as a consequence, his reputation as a poet drifted into a limbo. As prescient and sparkling as the criticism is, however, it is as a poet that a final assessment of his great achievement must be made.

Rexroth's art works by a technique of self-effacement. His diction and line appear to be effortless, organic, inevitable, without seam. The lack of ostentation he ascribes to his pietistic background finds as its formal companion this straightforward prosody. Still, to dissect and describe how his line, ostensibly so simple on the surface, actually works would be as difficult to do as explain Williams' variable foot: and Rexroth's was surely a less self-consciously developed art.

The longer, philosophical poems operate quite successfully within the same set of technical values as the shorter, lyrical poems. It is at least in part a function of Rexroth's antielitist politics that he never veers too far from a polished colloquial syntax—that of an experienced, unaffected, worldly man speaking. One is conducted through the seemingly spontaneous rhythms toward meaning. Like Blake, Whitman, and Lawrence, such formal directness of language functions in perfect symmetry with an embracing, mystical philosophy which thrusts the manners of that language out and away, almost into palpability. Consider the variety of cadence and verbal tone in the opening lines of "Floating":

> Our canoe idles in the idling current
> Of the tree and vine and rush enclosed
> Backwater of a torpid midwestern stream;
> Revolves slowly, and lodges in the glutted
> Waterlilies. We are tired of paddling.
> All afternoon we have climbed the weak current,
> Up dim meanders, through woods and pastures,
> Past muddy fords where the strong smell of cattle
> Lay thick across the water; singing the songs
> Of perfect, habitual motion; ski songs,
> Nightherding songs, songs of the capstan walk,
> The levee, and the roll of the voyageurs.

For all its rhythmic diversity the lines do not vary beyond nine to eleven syllables (two thirds of the passage is comprised of hendecasyllables); there are four or five stresses per line, mostly four. Yet by unstrained employment of different punctuation, enjambment, and variable balancing of syllabic stresses Rexroth invokes in the reader an actual physical feeling, the sensation of being in this idle canoe, buffeted by irregular, lazy currents, exhausted but alert. It is a remarkable achievement of form, and is carried off with effortless sanguinity. The final four lines constitute such a balance of differing weights—the second line triadic, the third of almost equal proportions mounted on the fulcrum of that comma and balanced out from the middle by the repeated "songs, songs"—they can be compared to a Calder mobile. Similarly, line-breaks are commonly intensified in Rexroth's work by intuitively perfect serializations of the various parts of speech:

California rolls into
Sleepy summer, and the air
Is full of the bitter sweet
Smoke of the grass fires burning
On the San Francisco hills.

We see in the terminal positions of these opening lines of "Delia"—each of which has exactly seven syllables—movement from preposition to noun to adjective (though at first appearance "sweet" reads curiously like a substantive, until the eye moves back to the beginning of the next line and reads "smoke"—making "sweet" adjectival) to gerundial verb to noun. Thus the various points of stress, as one moves down through the lines of the single sentence, are here accomplished less by sheer rhythm than the grammatical expectations felt in each end-word, and the consequent "weight" intuited by the reader in those words.

None of these effects is possible, of course, in a verse that suppresses linear syntax. It is for this reason, as much as any other, that Rexroth abandoned the asyntactical techniques (cubist in origin) of the "half decade of foreboding—1927–1932," most of which were published in *The Art of Worldly Wisdom* in 1949. Although he proposed that the elements of his cubist verse (see "Prolegomenon to a Theodicy") "are as simple as the elementary shapes of a cubist painting and the total poem is as definite and apprehensible as the finished picture," it was the measured, syntactical line of "Floating" and "Delia" he was to develop and largely use from the thirties on. Even in the later poems in *The Heart's Garden, The Garden's Heart, On Flower Wreath Hill,* and *The Silver Swan*—so thoroughly influenced by Japanese and Chinese models (after Waley and Pound, Rexroth was the great bringer of East Asian poetry into our culture)—he maintains much the same voice and cadences and line of the earlier work.

The simplicity of exact pronouncement may allow for particularly complex thought. Precision of fact in observation, as well as in syntax or form, is perhaps nowhere more evident than in Rexroth's crucial booklength poem, *The Dragon and the Unicorn*. That this poem is now so seldom read, even by Rexroth aficionados and practitioners of the craft of poetry, troubled Rexroth, and depressed him. For in *The Dragon and the Unicorn* we find the most complete formulation of his personal, mystical philosophy, the most extensive indictment of Western civilization (comparable to, if not as fiery and incantatory as "Thou Shalt Not Kill"), and perhaps the closest approximation to his speaking voice there is in his poetical works. (*An Autobiographical Novel* is the most perfect mirror to Rexroth's spoken word, as it was dictated, and edited only enough to get it past Doubleday's libel lawyers.) Set as a running travelog of his year-long journey through Wales, England, France, Italy, Switzerland, and back to America, *The Dragon and the Unicorn* is a meditation on the nature of love, of time and knowledge, of will and the responsibilities of the self-defining individual, of community (the moral opposite of the collective, the State), and ethics. Juxtapositions are abrupt; the life of the traveler's mind is pingponged against crisply drawn episodes on the road—the latter of which are in turn ribald, poignant, engaging, scientific, very opinionately lived moments. Together the contemplation and the travelog comprise what Rexroth himself has suggested is a Whitmanesque "interior autobiography." And nowhere in his work is the dictum "Epistomology is moral" more intricately played out than this poem.

However important *The Dragon and the Unicorn* may be for one hoping to gain some understanding of Rexroth's general philosophy, there is little doubt that his reputation as a poet rests, at least for the present, more on his love and nature poems (too, on his translations from Chinese and Japanese which, for lack of space, I was unable to include in this selection).

Clearly, he has written some of the most beautiful love poems in the century. His lyric celebrates not merely the disembodied metaphysic nor simply the corporeal erotic, but a synthetic and human whole, composed of both these elements. As a religious poet, Rexroth's love poems are primarily of conjugal love:

Let me celebrate you. I
Have never known anyone
More beautiful than you. I
Walking beside you, watching
You move beside me, watching
That still grace of hand and thigh.
Watching your face change with words
You do not say, watching your
Solemn eyes as they turn to me,
Or turn inward, full of knowing,
Slow or quick, watching your full
Lips part and smile or turn grave,
Watching your narrow waist, your
Proud buttocks in their grace . . .

Fundamentally sacramental, seldom does the poet's contemplation of his love of his wife distinguish between body and soul. In the above passage from "A Dialogue of Love" (written for Rexroth's third wife, Marthe) the usual dichotomy between the observing mind and the tactile flesh is consciously played down: each reflects the other. In an earlier poem, "Between Myself and Death," the dichotomy is altogether erased:

It is wonderful to watch you,
A living woman in a room
Full of frantic sterile people,
And think of your arching buttocks
Under your velvet evening dress,
And the beautiful fire spreading
From your sex, burning flesh and bone,
The unbelievably complex
Tissues of your brain all alive
Under your coiling, splendid hair.

——————

I like to think of you naked.
I put your naked body
Between myself alone and death.

It is the most original and persuasive synthesis of transcendent metaphysical and erotic verse written by an American poet this century.

As a constant backdrop to most of Rexroth's poems, whether travelog, amatory, or meditative, is the immutable presence of nature. Majestic constellations, always wheeling yet always locked in set patterns, embody as heavenly analogues a philosophy of a universe in which all things are ineluctable, unending, linked in a certain process of generation, collapse, rebirth. The moon in its phases is a salient and predominant symbol-charged globe, so often encountered as it walks across the night sky, above the mountains, in many of these poems. Rexroth was a skilled camper and rock-climber, and spent every moment he could manage up in the Sierras, away from the feverish meetings, the readings, the work of the city. Indeed, in the thirties he wrote a full-length book about the subject, *Camping in the Western Mountains*, which was never published. The mountains were his refuge, and it was by the refreshing and, for him, mystical communion with nature that his spirit, and access to his linguistic gift, was most freed.

The poems I have selected represent nearly sixty years' work. For the most part I have followed chronological publication of the poems in books, beginning with the selection from *In What Hour* and ending with work from *The Morning Star*, which collected three shorter books: *The Silver Swan*, *On Flower Wreath Hill*, and *The Love Poems of Marichiko*. Textually the poems follow the versions given in *The Collected Longer Poems* and *The Collected Shorter Poems*, although I have restored the original title of one of the "Marthe poems" from *In Defense of the Earth*.

The exceptions to this chronological ordering are from two long early poems which are included at the end of this selection. "The Homestead Called Damascus" Rexroth composed in his late teens; it remained unpublished until 1957 when *The Quarterly Review of Literature* brought it out accompanied by an illuminating essay by Lawrence Lipton. Indeed, it wasn't finally published in book form until 1962, when New Directions included it in its World Poets Series. Similarly, his long cubist poem, "A Prolegomenon to a Theodicy," was written in the late 1920s, and was published in an abridged and bowdlerized version in Louis Zukofsky's *An "Objectivists" Anthology* in 1932. The piece was to have appeared in textually complete form in the 1942 Decker edition of *The Art of Worldly Wisdom*, but only a few dozen copies got into circulation. A reissue by The Golden Goose Press in 1957 added Rexroth's lively introduction but due to a small press run and poor distribution it gained few new readers for the poem. Again, it was not until *The Collected Longer Poems* came out in 1966 that this juvenile work truly enjoyed a general circulation. Shorter poems, such as "The Thin Edge of Your Pride," which were also written during this early period but not collected in book form until later, are presented within the context of collections in which they first appeared.

Bradford Morrow
New York City, March 1984

from IN WHAT HOUR (1940)

ON WHAT PLANET

Uniformly over the whole countryside
The warm air flows imperceptibly seaward;
The autumn haze drifts in deep bands
Over the pale water;
White egrets stand in the blue marshes;
Tamalpais, Diablo, St. Helena
Float in the air.
Climbing on the cliffs of Hunter's Hill
We look out over fifty miles of sinuous
Interpenetration of mountains and sea.

Leading up a twisted chimney,
Just as my eyes rise to the level
Of a small cave, two white owls
Fly out, silent, close to my face.
They hover, confused in the sunlight,
And disappear into the recesses of the cliff.

All day I have been watching a new climber,
A young girl with ash blond hair
And gentle confident eyes.
She climbs slowly, precisely,
With unwasted grace.
While I am coiling the ropes,
Watching the spectacular sunset,
She turns to me and says, quietly,
"It must be very beautiful, the sunset,
On Saturn, with the rings and all the moons."

REQUIEM FOR THE SPANISH DEAD

The great geometrical winter constellations
Lift up over the Sierra Nevada,
I walk under the stars, my feet on the known round earth.
My eyes following the lights of an airplane,
Red and green, growling deep into the Hyades.
The note of the engine rises, shrill, faint,
Finally inaudible, and the lights go out
In the southeast haze beneath the feet of Orion.

As the sound departs I am chilled and grow sick
With the thought that has come over me. I see Spain
Under the black windy sky, the snow stirring faintly,
Glittering and moving over the pallid upland,
And men waiting, clutched with cold and huddled together,
As an unknown plane goes over them. It flies southeast
Into the haze above the lines of the enemy,
Sparks appear near the horizon under it.
After they have gone out the earth quivers
And the sound comes faintly. The men relax for a moment
And grow tense again as their own thoughts return to them.

I see the unwritten books, the unrecorded experiments,
The unpainted pictures, the interrupted lives,
Lowered into the graves with the red flags over them.
I see the quick gray brains broken and clotted with blood,
Lowered each in its own darkness, useless in the earth.
Alone on a hilltop in San Francisco suddenly
I am caught in a nightmare, the dead flesh
Mounting over half the world presses against me.

Then quietly at first and then rich and full-bodied,
I hear the voice of a young woman singing.
The emigrants on the corner are holding
A wake for their oldest child, a driverless truck

Broke away on the steep hill and killed him,
Voice after voice adds itself to the singing.
Orion moves westward across the meridian,
Rigel, Bellatrix, Betelgeuse, marching in order,
The great nebula glimmering in his loins.

AUTUMN IN CALIFORNIA

Autumn in California is a mild
And anonymous season, hills and valleys
Are colorless then, only the sooty green
Eucalyptus, the conifers and oaks sink deep
Into the haze; the fields are plowed, bare, waiting;
The steep pastures are tracked deep by the cattle;
There are no flowers, the herbage is brittle.
All night along the coast and the mountain crests
Birds go by, murmurous, high in the warm air.
Only in the mountain meadows the aspens
Glitter like goldfish moving up swift water;
Only in the desert villages the leaves
Of the cottonwoods descend in smoky air.
   Once more I wander in the warm evening
Calling the heart to order and the stiff brain
To passion. I should be thinking of dreaming, loving, dying,
Beauty wasting through time like draining blood,
And me alone in all the world with pictures
Of pretty women and the constellations.
But I hear the clocks in Barcelona strike at dawn
And the whistles blowing for noon in Nanking.
I hear the drone, the snapping high in the air
Of planes fighting, the deep reverberant
Grunts of bombardment, the hasty clamor
Of anti-aircraft.
                    In Nanking at the first bomb,
A moon-faced, willowy young girl runs into the street,
Leaves her rice bowl spilled and her children crying,
And stands stiff, cursing quietly, her face raised to the sky.

3

Suddenly she bursts like a bag of water,
And then as the blossom of smoke and dust diffuses,
The walls topple slowly over her.
                                    I hear the voices
Young, fatigued and excited, of two comrades
In a closed room in Madrid. They have been up
All night, talking of trout in the Pyrenees,
Spinoza, old nights full of riot and sherry,
Women they might have had or almost had,
Picasso, Velasquez, relativity.
The candlelight reddens, blue bars appear
In the cracks of the shutters, the bombardment
Begins again as though it had never stopped,
The morning wind is cold and dusty,
Their furloughs are over. They are shock troopers,
They may not meet again. The dead light holds
In impersonal focus the patched uniforms,
The dog-eared copy of Lenin's Imperialism,
The heavy cartridge belt, holster and black revolver butt.
     The moon rises late over Mt. Diablo,
Huge, gibbous, warm; the wind goes out,
Brown fog spreads over the bay from the marshes,
And overhead the cry of birds is suddenly
Loud, wiry, and tremulous.

AUGUST 22, 1939

"... when you want to distract your mother from the discouraging
soulness, I will tell you what I used to do. To take her for a long walk
in the quiet country, gathering wildflowers here and there, resting under
the shade of trees, between the harmony of the vivid stream and the
tranquillity of the mother-nature, and I am sure she will enjoy this
very much, as you surely will be happy for it. But remember always,
Dante, in the play of happiness, don't use all for yourself only, but
down yourself just one step, at your side and help the weak ones that
cry for help, help the prosecuted and the victim; because they are
your friends; they are the comrades that fight and fall as your father
and Bartolo fought and fell yesterday, for the conquest of the joy of

freedom for all and the poor workers. In this struggle of life you will find more love and you will be loved."

Nicola Sacco to his son Dante, Aug. 18, 1927.

Angst und Gestalt und Gebet — Rilke

What is it all for, this poetry,
This bundle of accomplishment
Put together with so much pain?
Twenty years at hard labor,
Lessons learned from Li Po and Dante,
Indian chants and gestalt psychology;
What words can it spell,
This alphabet of one sensibility?
The pure pattern of the stars in orderly progression,
The thin air of fourteen-thousand-foot summits,
Their Pisgah views into what secrets of the personality,
The fire of poppies in eroded fields,
The sleep of lynxes in the noonday forest,
The curious anastomosis of the webs of thought,
Life streaming ungovernably away,
And the deep hope of man.
The centuries have changed little in this art,
The subjects are still the same.
"For Christ's sake take off your clothes and get into bed,
We are not going to live forever."
"Petals fall from the rose,"
We fall from life,
Values fall from history like men from shellfire,
Only a minimum survives,
Only an unknown achievement.
They can put it all on the headstones,
In all the battlefields,
"Poor guy, he never knew what it was all about."
Spectacled men will come with shovels in a thousand years,
Give lectures in universities on cultural advances, cultural lags.
A little more garlic in the soup,
A half-hour more in bed in the morning,
Some of them got it, some of them didn't;
The things they dropped in their hurry
Are behind the glass cases of dusky museums.

This year we made four major ascents,
Camped for two weeks at timberline,
Watched Mars swim close to the earth,
Watched the black aurora of war
Spread over the sky of a decayed civilization.
These are the last terrible years of authority.
The disease has reached its crisis,
Ten thousand years of power,
The struggle of two laws,
The rule of iron and spilled blood,
The abiding solidarity of living blood and brain.
They are trapped, beleaguered, murderous,
If they line their cellars with cork
It is not to still the pistol shots,
It is to insulate the last words of the condemned.
"Liberty is the mother
Not the daughter of order."
"Not the government of men
But the administration of things."
"From each according to his ability,
Unto each according to his needs."
We could still hear them,
Cutting steps in the blue ice of hanging glaciers,
Teetering along shattered arêtes.
The cold and cruel apathy of mountains
Has been subdued with a few strands of rope
And some flimsy iceaxes,
There are only a few peaks left.
Twenty-five years have gone since my first sweetheart.
Back from the mountains there is a letter waiting for me.
"I read your poem in the New Republic.
Do you remember the undertaker's on the corner,
How we peeped in the basement window at a sheeted figure
And ran away screaming? Do you remember?
There is a filling station on the corner,
A parking lot where your house used to be,
Only ours and two other houses are left.
We stick it out in the noise and carbon monoxide."
It was a poem of homesickness and exile,
Twenty-five years wandering around

In a world of noise and poison.
She stuck it out, I never went back,
But there are domestic as well as imported
Explosions and poison gases.
Dante was homesick, the Chinese made an art of it,
So was Ovid and many others,
Pound and Eliot amongst them,
Kropotkin dying of hunger,
Berkman by his own hand,
Fanny Baron biting her executioners,
Mahkno in the odor of calumny,
Trotsky, too, I suppose, passionately, after his fashion.
Do you remember?
What is it all for, this poetry,
This bundle of accomplishment
Put together with so much pain?
Do you remember the corpse in the basement?
What are we doing at the turn of our years,
Writers and readers of the liberal weeklies?

TOWARD AN ORGANIC PHILOSOPHY

SPRING, COAST RANGE

The glow of my campfire is dark red and flameless,
The circle of white ash widens around it.
I get up and walk off in the moonlight and each time
I look back the red is deeper and the light smaller.
Scorpio rises late with Mars caught in his claw;
The moon has come before them, the light
Like a choir of children in the young laurel trees.
It is April; the shad, the hot headed fish,
Climbs the rivers; there is trillium in the damp canyons;
The foetid adder's tongue lolls by the waterfall.
There was a farm at this campsite once, it is almost gone now.
There were sheep here after the farm, and fire
Long ago burned the redwoods out of the gulch,
The Douglas fir off the ridge; today the soil

Is stony and incoherent, the small stones lie flat
And plate the surface like scales.
Twenty years ago the spreading gully
Toppled the big oak over onto the house.
Now there is nothing left but the foundations
Hidden in poison oak, and above on the ridge,
Six lonely, ominous fenceposts;
The redwood beams of the barn make a footbridge
Over the deep waterless creek bed;
The hills are covered with wild oats
Dry and white by midsummer.
I walk in the random survivals of the orchard.
In a patch of moonlight a mole
Shakes his tunnel like an angry vein;
Orion walks waist deep in the fog coming in from the ocean;
Leo crouches under the zenith.
There are tiny hard fruits already on the plum trees.
The purity of the apple blossoms is incredible.
As the wind dies down their fragrance
Clusters around them like thick smoke.
All the day they roared with bees, in the moonlight
They are silent and immaculate.

SPRING, SIERRA NEVADA

Once more golden Scorpio glows over the col
Above Deadman Canyon, orderly and brilliant,
Like an inspiration in the brain of Archimedes.
I have seen its light over the warm sea,
Over the coconut beaches, phosphorescent and pulsing;
And the living light in the water
Shivering away from the swimming hand,
Creeping against the lips, filling the floating hair.
Here where the glaciers have been and the snow stays late,
The stone is clean as light, the light steady as stone.
The relationship of stone, ice and stars is systematic and enduring
Novelty emerges after centuries, a rock spalls from the cliffs,
The glacier contracts and turns grayer,
The stream cuts new sinuosities in the meadow,
The sun moves through space and the earth with it,

The stars change places.
                    The snow has lasted longer this year,
Than anyone can remember. The lowest meadow is a lake,
The next two are snowfields, the pass is covered with snow,
Only the steepest rocks are bare. Between the pass
And the last meadow the snowfield gapes for a hundred feet,
In a narrow blue chasm through which a waterfall drops,
Spangled with sunset at the top, black and muscular
Where it disappears again in the snow.
The world is filled with hidden running water
That pounds in the ears like ether;
The granite needles rise from the snow, pale as steel;
Above the copper mine the cliff is blood red,
The white snow breaks at the edge of it;
The sky comes close to my eyes like the blue eyes
Of someone kissed in sleep.
                    I descend to camp,
To the young, sticky, wrinkled aspen leaves,
To the first violets and wild cyclamen,
And cook supper in the blue twilight.
All night deer pass over the snow on sharp hooves,
In the darkness their cold muzzles find the new grass
At the edge of the snow.

FALL, SIERRA NEVADA

This morning the hermit thrush was absent at breakfast,
His place was taken by a family of chickadees;
At noon a flock of humming birds passed south,
Whirling in the wind up over the saddle between
Ritter and Banner, following the migration lane
Of the Sierra crest southward to Guatemala.
All day cloud shadows have moved over the face of the mountain,
The shadow of a golden eagle weaving between them
Over the face of the glacier.
At sunset the half-moon rides on the bent back of the Scorpion,
The Great Bear kneels on the mountain.
Ten degrees below the moon
Venus sets in the haze arising from the Great Valley.
Jupiter, in opposition to the sun, rises in the alpenglow

Between the burnt peaks. The ventriloquial belling
Of an owl mingles with the bells of the waterfall.
Now there is distant thunder on the east wind.
The east face of the mountain above me
Is lit with far off lightnings and the sky
Above the pass blazes momentarily like an aurora.
It is storming in the White Mountains,
On the arid fourteen-thousand-foot peaks;
Rain is falling on the narrow gray ranges
And dark sedge meadows and white salt flats of Nevada.
Just before moonset a small dense cumulus cloud,
Gleaming like a grape cluster of metal,
Moves over the Sierra crest and grows down the westward
    slope.
Frost, the color and quality of the cloud,
Lies over all the marsh below my campsite.
The wiry clumps of dwarfed whitebark pines
Are smoky and indistinct in the moonlight,
Only their shadows are really visible.
The lake is immobile and holds the stars
And the peaks deep in itself without a quiver.
In the shallows the geometrical tendrils of ice
Spread their wonderful mathematics in silence.
All night the eyes of deer shine for an instant

As they cross the radius of my firelight.
In the morning the trail will look like a sheep driveway,
All the tracks will point down to the lower canyon.
"Thus," says Tyndall, "the concerns of this little place
Are changed and fashioned by the obliquity of the earth's
    axis,
The chain of dependence which runs through creation,
And links the roll of a planet alike with the interests
Of marmots and of men."

A LESSON IN GEOGRAPHY

*"of Paradys ne can not I speken
propurly ffor I was not there"*
Mandeville

The stars of the Great Bear drift apart
The Horse and the Rider together northeastward
Alpha and Omega asunder
The others diversely
There are rocks
On the earth more durable
Than the configurations of heaven
Species now motile and sanguine
Shall see the stars in new clusters
The beaches changed
The mountains shifted
Gigantic
Immobile
Floodlit
The faces appear and disappear
Chewing the right gum
Smoking the right cigarette
Buying the best refrigerator
The polished carnivorous teeth
Exhibited in approval
The lights
Of the houses
Draw together
In the evening dewfall on the banks
Of the Wabash
Sparkle discreetly
High on the road to Provo
Above the Salt Lake Valley
And
The mountain shaped like a sphinx
And
The mountain shaped like a finger
Pointing
On the first of April at eight o'clock
Precisely at Algol

There are rocks on the earth
And one who sleepless
Throbbed with the ten
Nightingales in the plum trees
Sleepless as Boötes stood over him
Gnawing the pillow
Sitting on the bed's edge smoking
Sitting by the window looking
One who rose in the false
Dawn and stoned
The nightingales in the garden
The heart pawned for wisdom
The heart
Bartered for knowledge and folly
The will troubled
The mind secretly aghast
The eyes and lips full of sorrow
The apices of vision wavering
As the flower spray at the tip of the windstalk
The becalmed sail
The heavy wordless weight
And now
The anguishing and pitiless file
Cutting away life
Capsule by capsule biting
Into the heart
The coal of fire
Sealing the lips
There are rocks on earth

And

In the Japanese quarter
A phonograph playing
"Moonlight on ruined castles"
Kojo n'suki
And
The movement of the wind fish
Keeping time to the music
Sirius setting behind it

(The Dog has scented the sun)
Gold immense fish
Squirm in the trade wind
"Young Middle Western woman
In rut
Desires correspondent"
The first bright flower
Cynoglossum
The blue hound's tongue
Breaks on the hill
"The tide has gone down
Over the reef
I walk about the world
There is great
Wind and then rain"
"My life is bought and paid for
So much pleasure
For so much pain"
The folded fossiliferous
Sedimentary rocks end here
The granite batholith
Obtrudes abruptly
West of the fault line
Betelgeuse reddens
Drawing its substance about it
It is possible that a process is beginning
Similar to that which lifted
The great Sierra fault block
Through an older metamorphic range

(The Dog barks on the sun's spoor)

Now
The thought of death
Binds fast the flood of light
Ten years ago the snow falling
All a long winter night
I had lain waking in my bed alone
Turning my heavy thoughts
And no way might
Sleep

Remembering divers things long gone
Now
In the long day in the hour of small shadow
I walk on the continent's last western hill
And lie prone among the iris in the grass
My eyes fixed on the durable stone
That speaks and hears as though it were myself

from THE PHOENIX AND THE TORTOISE
(1944)

I

Webs of misery spread in the brain,
In the dry Spring in the soft heat.
Dirty cotton bolls of cloud hang
At the sky's edge; vague yellow stratus
Glimmer behind them. It is storming
Somewhere far out in the ocean.
All night vast rollers exploded
Offshore; now the sea has subsided
To a massive, uneasy torpor.
Fragments of its inexhaustible
Life litter the shingle, sea hares,
Broken starfish, a dead octopus,
And everywhere, swarming like ants,
Innumerable hermit crabs,
Hungry and efficient as maggots.

This is not the first time this shingle
Has been here. These cobbles are washed
From ancient conglomerate beds,
Beaches of the Franciscan series,
The immense layer cake of grey strata
That hangs without top or bottom
In the geological past
Of the California Coast Ranges.
There are no fossils in them. Their
Dates are disputed—thousands of feet,
Thousands and thousands of years, of bays,
Tidemarshes, estuaries, beaches,
Where time flowed eventless as silt.
Further along the beach the stones
Change; the cliffs are yellow with black
Bands of lignite; and scattered amongst
The sand dollars in the storm's refuse

Are fossil sand dollars the sea
Has washed from stone, as it has washed
These, newly dead, from life.

                    And I,
Walking by the viscid, menacing
Water, turn with my heavy heart
In my baffled brain, Plutarch's page—
The falling light of the Spartan
Heroes in the late Hellenic dusk—
Agis, Cleomenes—this poem
Of the phoenix and the tortoise—
Of what survives and what perishes,
And how, of the fall of history
And waste of fact—on the crumbling
Edge of a ruined polity
That washes away in an ocean
Whose shores are all washing into death.

A group of terrified children
Has just discovered the body
Of a Japanese sailor bumping
In a snarl of kelp in a tidepool.
While the crowd collects, I stand, mute
As he, watching his smashed ribs breathe
Of the life of the ocean, his white
Torn bowels braid themselves with the kelp;
And, out of his drained grey flesh, he
Watches me with open hard eyes
Like small indestructible animals—
Me—who stand here on the edge of death,
Seeking the continuity,
The germ plasm, of history,
The epic's lyric absolute.

What happened, and what is remembered—
Or—history is the description
Of those forms of man's activity
Where value survives at the lowest
Level necessary to insure

Temporal continuity.
Or "as the Philosopher says,"
The historian differs from
The poet in this: the historian
Presents what did happen, the poet,
What might happen. For this reason
Poetry is more philosophic
Than history, and less trivial.
Poetry presents generalities,
History merely particulars.
So action is generalized
Into what an essential person
Must do by virtue of his essence—
Acting in an imaginary
Order of being, where existence
And essence, as in the Deity
Of Aquinas, fuse in pure act.
What happens in the mere occasion
To human beings is recorded
As an occurrence in the gulf
Between essence and existence—
An event of marginal content.

. . . .

II

I am cold in my folded blanket,
Huddled on the ground in the moonlight.

The crickets cry in congealing frost;
Field mice run over my body;
The frost thickens and the night goes by.

North of us lies the vindictive
Foolish city asleep under its guns;
Its rodent ambitions washing out
In sewage and unwholesome dreams.
Behind the backs of drowsy sentries

The moonlight shines through frosted glass—
On the floors of innumerable
Corridors the mystic symbols
Of the bureaucrats are reversed—
Mirrorwise, as Leonardo
Kept the fever charts of one person.
Two Ptahs, two Muhammad's coffins,
We float in the illimitable
Surgery of moonlight, isolate
From each other and the turning earth;
Motionless; frost on our faces;
Eyes by turns alive, dark in the dark.

The State is the organization
Of the evil instincts of mankind.
History is the penalty
We pay for original sin.
In the conflict of appetite
And desire, the person finally
Loses; either the technology
Of the choice of the lesser evil
Overwhelms him; or a universe
Where the stars in their courses move
To ends that justify their means
Dissolves him in its elements.
He cannot win, not on this table.
The World, the Flesh, and the Devil—
The Tempter offered Christ mastery
Of the three master institutions,
Godparents of all destruction—
"Miracle, Mystery, and Authority—"
The systematization of
Appetitive choice to obtain
Desire by accumulation.

History continuously
Bleeds to death through a million secret
Wounds of trivial hunger and fear.
Its stockholders' private disasters
Are amortized in catastrophe.

War is the health of the State? Indeed!
War is the State. All personal
Anti-institutional values
Must be burnt out of each generation.
If a massive continuum
Of personality endured
Into grandchildren, history
Would stop.

IV

Dark within dark I cling to sleep,
The heart's capsule closed in the fist
Of circumstance; prison within
Prison, inseparably dark,
I struggle to hold oblivion
As Jacob struggled in a dream,
And woke touched and with another name.
And on the thin brainpan of sleep
The mill of Gaza grinds;
The heart condenses; and beyond
The world's lip the sun to me is dark
And silent as the moon that falls
Through the last degrees of night into
The unknown antipodes. I lie
At random, carelessly diffused,
Stone and amoeba on the verge
Of partition; and beyond the reach
Of my drowsy integrity,
The race of glory and the race
Of shame, just or unjust, alike
Miserable, both come to evil end.

Eventually history
Distills off all accumulated
Values but one. Babies are more
Durable than monuments, the rose
Outlives Ausonius, Ronsard,

And Waller, and Horace's pear tree
His immortal column. Once more
Process is precipitated
In the tirelessly receptive womb.
In the decay of the sufficient
Reasonableness of sacraments
Marriage holds by its bona fides.

Beneath what shield and from what flame.

The darkness gathers about Lawrence
Dying by the dead Mediterranean—
Catullus is psychoanalyzed
Between wars in lickerish London.
Another aging précieux
Drinks cognac, dreams of rutting children
In the Mississippi Valley,
Watches the Will destroy the logic
Of Christopher Wren and Richelieu.
Schweitzer plays Bach in the jungle.
It is all over—just and unjust.
The seed leaks through the gravel.

The light grows stronger and my lids
That were black turn red; the blood turns
To the coming sun. I sit up
And look out over the bright quiet
Sea and the blue and yellow cliffs
And the pure white tatters of fog
Dissolving on the black fir ridges.
The world is immovable
And immaculate. The argument
Has come to an end; it is morning,
And in the isolating morning
The problem hangs suspended, lucid
In a crystal cabinet of air
And angels where only bird song wakes.

"Value is the elastic ether
Of quality that fills up the gaps

In the continuum of discreet
Quality—the prime togetherness."
The assumption of order,
The principle of parsimony,
Remain mysteries; fact and logic
Meet only in catastrophe.
So long ago they discovered that
Each new irrational is the start
Of a new series of numbers;
Called God the source of systematic
Irrationalization of given
Order—the organism that
Geometricizes. And that vain
Boy, systematically deranging
Himself amongst the smoky cannoneers
Of the Commune, finding a bronze
Apotheosis as the perfect
Provincial French merchant who made good.
The statistical likelihood
Of being blown to pieces.

"Value is the reflection
Of satisfied appetite."
The State organizes ecstasy.
The dinosaur wallows in the chilling
Marsh. The bombs fall on the packed dance halls.
The sperm seeks the egg in the gravel.
"Novelty is, by definition,
Value-positive."

                    "Value
Is a phase change in the relations
Of events." Does that mean anything?

Morning. It is Good Friday Morning;
Communion has past to Agony
And Agony is gone and only
Responsibility remains; doom
Watches with its inorganic eyes,

The bright, blind regiments, hidden
By the sun-flushed sky, the remote
Indestructible animals.

Value, causality, being,
Are reducible to the purest
Act, the self-determining person,
He who discriminates structure
In contingency, he who assumes
All the responsibility
Of ordered, focused, potential—
Sustained by all the universe,
Focusing the universe in act—
The person, the absolute price,
The only blood defiance of doom.

Whymper, coming down the Matterhorn,
After the mountain had collected
Its terrible, casual fee,
The blackmail of an imbecile beauty:
"About 6 PM we arrived
Upon the ridge descending towards
Zermatt, and all peril was over.
We frequently looked, but in vain,
For traces of our unfortunate
Companions; we bent over the ridge
And cried to them, but no sound returned.
Convinced at last that they were neither
Within sight nor hearing we ceased;
And, too cast down for speech, silently
Gathered up our things and the little
Effects of those who were lost
And prepared to continue
The descent. When, lo! a mighty arch
And beneath it a huge cross of light
Appeared, rising above the Lyskamm
High into the sky. Pale, colorless,
And noiseless, but perfectly sharp
And defined, except where it was lost
In the clouds, this unearthly

Apparition seemed like a vision
From another world; and appalled,
We watched with amazement the gradual
Development of two vast crosses
One on either side . . . Our movements
Had no effect on it, the spectral
Forms remained motionless. It was
A fearful and wonderful sight;
Unique in my experience,
And impressive beyond description,
Coming at such a moment."

Nude, my feet in the cold shallows,
The motion of the water surface
Barely perceptible, and the sand
Of the bottom in fine sharp ridges
Under my toes, I wade out, waist deep
And swim seaward down the narrow inlet.
In the distance, beyond the sand bar,
The combers are breaking, and nearer,
Like a wave crest escaped and frozen,
One white egret guards the harbor mouth.
The immense stellar phenomenon
Of dawn focuses in the egret
And flows out, and focuses in me
And flows infinitely away
To touch the last galactic dust.

This is the prime reality—
Bird and man, the individual
Discriminate, the self evalued
Actual, the operation
Of infinite, ordered potential.
Birds, sand grains, and souls bleed into being;
The past reclaims its own, "I should have,
I could have—It might have been different—"
Sunsets on Saturn, desert roses,
Corruptions of the will, quality—

The determinable future, fall
Into quantity, into the
Irreparable past, history's
Cruel irresponsibility.

This is the minimum negative
Condition, the "Condition humaine,"
The tragic loss of value into
Barren novelty, the condition
Of salvation; out of this alone
The person emerges as complete
Responsible act—this lost
And that conserved—the appalling
Decision of the verb "to be."
Men drop dead in the ancient rubbish
Of the Acropolis, scholars fall
Into self-dug graves, Jews are smashed
Like heroic vermin in the Polish winter.
This is my fault, the horrible term
Of weakness, evasion, indulgence,
The total of my petty fault—
No other man's.

        And out of this
Shall I reclaim beauty, peace of soul,
The perfect gift of self-sacrifice,
Myself as act, as immortal person?

I walk back along the sandspit,
The horizon cuts the moon in half,
And far out at sea a path of light,
Violent and brilliant, reflected
From high stratus clouds and then again
On the moving sea, the invisible
Sunrise spreads its light before the moon.

My wife has been swimming in the breakers,
She comes up the beach to meet me, nude,
Sparkling with water, singing high and clear
Against the surf. The sun crosses

The hills and fills her hair, as it lights
The moon and glorifies the sea
And deep in the empty mountains melts
The snow of Winter and the glaciers
Of ten thousand thousand years.

WHEN WE WITH SAPPHO

"... about the cool water
the wind sounds through sprays
of apple, and from the quivering leaves
slumber pours down ..."

We lie here in the bee filled, ruinous
Orchard of a decayed New England farm,
Summer in our hair, and the smell
Of summer in our twined bodies,
Summer in our mouths, and summer
In the luminous, fragmentary words
Of this dead Greek woman.
Stop reading. Lean back. Give me your mouth.
Your grace is as beautiful as sleep.
You move against me like a wave
That moves in sleep.
Your body spreads across my brain
Like a bird filled summer;
Not like a body, not like a separate thing,
But like a nimbus that hovers
Over every other thing in all the world.
Lean back. You are beautiful,
As beautiful as the folding
Of your hands in sleep.

We have grown old in the afternoon.
Here in our orchard we are as old
As she is now, wherever dissipate
In that distant sea her gleaming dust
Flashes in the wave crest

Or stains the murex shell.
All about us the old farm subsides
Into the honey bearing chaos of high summer.
In those far islands the temples
Have fallen away, and the marble
Is the color of wild honey.
There is nothing left of the gardens
That were once about them, of the fat
Turf marked with cloven hooves.
Only the sea grass struggles
Over the crumbled stone,
Over the splintered steps,
Only the blue and yellow
Of the sea, and the cliffs
Red in the distance across the bay.
Lean back.
Her memory has passed to our lips now.
Our kisses fall through summer's chaos
In our own breasts and thighs.

Gold colossal domes of cumulus cloud
Lift over the undulant, sibilant forest.
The air presses against the earth.
Thunder breaks over the mountains.
Far off, over the Adirondacks,
Lightning quivers, almost invisible
In the bright sky, violet against
The grey, deep shadows of the bellied clouds.
The sweet virile hair of thunder storms
Brushes over the swelling horizon.
Take off your shoes and stockings.
I will kiss your sweet legs and feet
As they lie half buried in the tangle
Of rank scented midsummer flowers.
Take off your clothes. I will press
Your summer honeyed flesh into the hot
Soil, into the crushed, acrid herbage
Of midsummer. Let your body sink
Like honey through the hot
Granular fingers of summer.

Rest. Wait. We have enough for a while.
Kiss me with your mouth
Wet and ragged, your mouth that tastes
Of my own flesh. Read to me again
The twisting music of that language
That is of all others, itself a work of art.
Read again those isolate, poignant words
Saved by ancient grammarians
To illustrate the conjugations
And declensions of the more ancient dead.
Lean back in the curve of my body,
Press your bruised shoulders against
The damp hair of my body.
Kiss me again. Think, sweet linguist,
In this world the ablative is impossible.
No other one will help us here.
We must help ourselves to each other.
The wind walks slowly away from the storm;
Veers on the wooded crests; sounds
In the valleys. Here we are isolate,
One with the other; and beyond
This orchard lies isolation,
The isolation of all the world.
Never let anything intrude
On the isolation of this day,
These words, isolate on dead tongues,
This orchard, hidden from fact and history,
These shadows, blended in the summer light,
Together isolate beyond the world's reciprocity.

Do not talk any more. Do not speak.
Do not break silence until
We are weary of each other.
Let our fingers run like steel
Carving the contours of our bodies' gold.
Do not speak. My face sinks
In the clotted summer of your hair.
The sound of the bees stops.
Stillness falls like a cloud.
Be still. Let your body fall away

Into the awe filled silence
Of the fulfilled summer—
Back, back, infinitely away—
Our lips weak, faint with stillness.

See. The sun has fallen away.
Now there are amber
Long lights on the shattered
Boles of the ancient apple trees.
Our bodies move to each other
As bodies move in sleep;
At once filled and exhausted,
As the summer moves to autumn,
As we, with Sappho, move towards death.
My eyelids sink toward sleep in the hot
Autumn of your uncoiled hair.
Your body moves in my arms
On the verge of sleep;
And it is as though I held
In my arms the bird filled
Evening sky of summer.

LUTE MUSIC

The earth will be going on a long time
Before it finally freezes;
Men will be on it; they will take names,
Give their deeds reasons.
We will be here only
As chemical constituents—
A small franchise indeed.
Right now we have lives,
Corpuscles, ambitions, caresses,
Like everybody had once—
All the bright neige d'antan people,
"Blithe Helen, white Iope, and the rest,"
All the uneasy, remembered dead.

Here at the year's end, at the feast
Of birth, let us bring to each other
The gifts brought once west through deserts—
The precious metal of our mingled hair,
The frankincense of enraptured arms and legs,
The myrrh of desperate, invincible kisses—
Let us celebrate the daily
Recurrent nativity of love,
The endless epiphany of our fluent selves,
While the earth rolls away under us
Into unknown snows and summers,
Into untraveled spaces of the stars.

FLOATING

Our canoe idles in the idling current
Of the tree and vine and rush enclosed
Backwater of a torpid midwestern stream;
Revolves slowly, and lodges in the glutted
Waterlilies. We are tired of paddling.
All afternoon we have climbed the weak current,
Up dim meanders, through woods and pastures,
Past muddy fords where the strong smell of cattle
Lay thick across the water; singing the songs
Of perfect, habitual motion; ski songs,
Nightherding songs, songs of the capstan walk,
The levee, and the roll of the voyageurs.
Tired of motion, of the rhythms of motion,
Tired of the sweet play of our interwoven strength,
We lie in each other's arms and let the palps
Of waterlily leaf and petal hold back
All motion in the heat thickened, drowsing air.
Sing to me softly, Westron Wynde, Ah the Syghes,
Mon coeur se recommend à vous, Phoebi Claro;
Sing the wandering erotic melodies
Of men and women gone seven hundred years,
Softly, your mouth close to my cheek.
Let our thighs lie entangled on the cushions,

Let your breasts in their thin cover
Hang pendant against my naked arms and throat;
Let your odorous hair fall across our eyes;
Kiss me with those subtle, melodic lips.
As I undress you, your pupils are black, wet,
Immense, and your skin ivory and humid.
Move softly, move hardly at all, part your thighs,
Take me slowly while our gnawing lips
Fumble against the humming blood in our throats.
Move softly, do not move at all, but hold me,
Deep, still, deep within you, while time slides away,
As this river slides beyond this lily bed,
And the thieving moments fuse and disappear
In our mortal, timeless flesh.

ANOTHER SPRING

The seasons revolve and the years change
With no assistance or supervision.
The moon, without taking thought,
Moves in its cycle, full, crescent, and full.

The white moon enters the heart of the river;
The air is drugged with azalea blossoms;
Deep in the night a pine cone falls;
Our campfire dies out in the empty mountains.

The sharp stars flicker in the tremulous branches;
The lake is black, bottomless in the crystalline night;
High in the sky the Northern Crown
Is cut in half by the dim summit of a snow peak.

O heart, heart, so singularly
Intransigent and corruptible,
Here we lie entranced by the starlit water,
And moments that should each last forever

Slide unconsciously by us like water.

THE ADVANTAGES OF LEARNING

I am a man with no ambitions
And few friends, wholly incapable
Of making a living, growing no
Younger, fugitive from some just doom.
Lonely, ill-clothed, what does it matter?
At midnight I make myself a jug
Of hot white wine and cardamon seeds.
In a torn grey robe and old beret,
I sit in the cold writing poems,
Drawing nudes on the crooked margins,
Copulating with sixteen year old
Nymphomaniacs of my imagination.

INVERSELY, AS THE SQUARE OF
THEIR DISTANCES APART

It is impossible to see anything
In this dark; but I know this is me, Rexroth,
Plunging through the night on a chilling planet.
It is warm and busy in this vegetable
Darkness where invisible deer feed quietly.
The sky is warm and heavy, even the trees
Over my head cannot be distinguished,
But I know they are knobcone pines, that their cones
Endure unopened on the branches, at last
To grow imbedded in the wood, waiting for fire
To open them and reseed the burned forest.
And I am waiting, alone, in the mountains,
In the forest, in the darkness, and the world
Falls swiftly on its measured ellipse.

It is warm tonight and very still.
The stars are hazy and the river—
Vague and monstrous under the fireflies—
Is hardly audible, resonant
And profound at the edge of hearing.
I can just see your eyes and wet lips.
Invisible, solemn, and fragrant,
Your flesh opens to me in secret.
We shall know no further enigma.
After all the years there is nothing
Stranger than this. We who know ourselves
As one doubled thing, and move our limbs
As deft implements of one fused lust,
Are mysteries in each other's arms.

At the wood's edge in the moonlight
We dropped our clothes and stood naked,
Swaying, shadow mottled, enclosed
In each other and together
Closed in the night. We did not hear
The whip-poor-will, nor the aspen's
Whisper; the owl flew silently
Or cried out loud, we did not know.
We could not hear beyond the heart.
We could not see the moving dark
And light, the stars that stood or moved,
The stars that fell. Did they all fall
We had not known. We were falling
Like meteors, dark through black cold
Toward each other, and then compact,
Blazing through air into the earth.

I lie alone in an alien
Bed in a strange house and morning

More cruel than any midnight
Pours its brightness through the window—
Cherry branches with the flowers
Fading, and behind them the gold
Stately baubles of the maple,
And behind them the pure immense
April sky and a white frayed cloud,
And in and behind everything,
The inescapable vacant
Distance of loneliness.

BETWEEN TWO WARS

Remember that breakfast one November—
Cold black grapes smelling faintly
Of the cork they were packed in,
Hard rolls with hot, white flesh,
And thick, honey sweetened chocolate?
And the parties at night; the gin and the tangos?
The torn hair nets, the lost cuff links?
Where have they all gone to,
The beautiful girls, the abandoned hours?
They said we were lost, mad and immoral,
And interfered with the plans of the management.
And today, millions and millions, shut alive
In the coffins of circumstance,
Beat on the buried lids,
Huddle in the cellars of ruins, and quarrel
Over their own fragmented flesh.

DELIA REXROTH

Died June, 1916

Under your illkempt yellow roses,
Delia, today you are younger
Than your son. Two and a half decades—

The family monument sagged askew,
And he overtook your half-a-life.
On the other side of the country,
Near the willows by the slow river,
Deep in the earth, the white ribs retain
The curve of your fervent, careful breast;
The fine skull, the ardor of your brain.
And in the fingers the memory
Of Chopin études, and in the feet
Slow waltzes and champagne twosteps sleep.
And the white full moon of midsummer,
That you watched awake all that last night,
Watches history fill the deserts
And oceans with corpses once again;
And looks in the east window at me,
As I move past you to middle age
And knowledge past your agony and waste.

ANDREE REXROTH

Died October, 1940

Now once more gray mottled buckeye branches
Explode their emerald stars,
And alders smoulder in a rosy smoke
Of innumerable buds.
I know that spring again is splendid
As ever, the hidden thrush
As sweetly tongued, the sun as vital—
But these are the forest trails we walked together,
These paths, ten years together.
We thought the years would last forever,
They are all gone now, the days
We thought would not come for us are here.
Bright trout poised in the current—
The raccoon's track at the water's edge—
A bittern booming in the distance—
Your ashes scattered on this mountain—
Moving seaward on this stream.

from THE ART OF WORDLY WISDOM (1949)

THE THIN EDGE OF YOUR PRIDE

1922-1926

Poems for Leslie Smith

I

Later when the gloated water
Burst with red lotus; when perfect green
Enameled grass and tree, "I most solitary,
Boating," rested thoughtful on the moated water;
Where the low sun spread crimson
Interstices in the glowing lotus; aware
Of the coming, deep in the years, of a time
When these lagoons and darkening trees,
This twilight sliding mirror where we have floated,
Would surge hugely out of memory
Into some distant, ordinary evening—
Hugely, in vertigo and awe.

II

Six months as timeless as dream,
As impotent . . .
You pause on the subway stairs,
Wave and smile and descend.
Was it an instant between waking
And waking,
That you smile and wave again,
Two blocks away on a smoky
Chicago boulevard?
How many dynasties decayed
Meanwhile, how many
Times did the second hand
Circumvent its dial?

III

Indigenes of furnished rooms,
Our best hours have been passed
At the taxpayers' expense
In the public parks of four cities.
It could be worse, the level
Well-nurtured lawns, the uplifted
Rhythmic arms of children,
A bright red ball following
A graph of laughter,
The dresses of the little girls
Blossoming like hyacinths
In early August, the fountains,
The tame squirrels, pigeons
And sparrows, and other
Infinitely memorable things.

IV

Chill and abandoned, the pavilion
In Jackson Park stands like a sightless
Lighthouse beside the lake.
It is very dark, there would be no moon
Even if the night were not thickly overcast.
The wind moans in the rustic carpentry,
But the rain returns silently to the water,
Without even a hiss or a whisper.
We have the shadows to ourselves,
The lovers, the psychopathic, the lonely,
Have gone indoors for the winter.
We have been here in other autumns,
Nights when the wind stirred this inland water
Like the sea, piled the waves over the breakwater,
And onto the highway, tore apart tall clouds,
And revealed the moon, rushing dead white
Over the city.

V

The absorbent, glimmering night
Receives a solitary nighthawk cry;
Marshalls its naked housefronts;
And waits.
The lights of a passing yacht
Jewel for a moment your windblown hair.
The shadows of the lombardy poplars
Tilt like planks on water.
The sea breeze smells faintly of hospitals.
Far off,
On the desert coasts of the Antipodes,
Mountains slide silently into the sea.

VI

Paradise Pond

The minute fingers of the imperceptible air
Arrange a shadow tracery of leaf and hair
About your face.
Downstream a group of Hungarians from the mill,
Stiff with unaccustomed ease,
Catch insignificant fish.
A row of brown ducklings jerks itself across the water,
Moving like furry cartridges
Into some beneficent machine gun.
We shall arise presently, having said nothing,
And hand in vibrating hand walk back the way we came.

VII

I think these squalid houses are the ghosts
Of dinosaur and mammoth and all
The other giants now long rotted from the earth.
I think that on lonely nights when we,
Disparate, distraught, half a continent between us,
Walk the deserted streets,
They take their ancient forms again,
And shift and move ahead of us
For elbow room; and as we pass

They touch us here and there,
Softly, awestruck, curious;
And then with lurching step
Close in upon our heels.

VIII

"Whether or not, it is no question now,
Of time or place, or even how,
It is not time for questions now,
Nor yet the place."
The soft lights of your face
Arrange themselves in memories
Of smiles and frowns.
You are reading,
Propped up in the window seat;
And I stand hesitant at the rug's edge . . .
Whether or not . . . it is no question now.
I wonder what we have done
To merit such ironic lives.
Hesitant on the rug's edge,
I study the kaleidoscope
Before my toes, where some long
Dead Persian has woven
A cynical, Levantine prayer.

IX

After an hour the mild
Confusion of snow
Amongst the lamplights
Has softened and subdued
The nervous lines of bare
Branches etched against
The chill twilight.
Now behind me, upon the pallid
Expanse of empty boulevard,
The snow reclaims from the darkened
Staring shop windows,
One by one, a single
Line of footprints.

X

Out of the westborne snow shall come a memory
Floated upon it by my hands,
By my lips that remember your kisses.
It shall caress your hands, your lips,
Your breasts, your thighs, with kisses,
As real as flesh, as real as memory of flesh.
I shall come to you with the spring,
Spring's flesh in the world,
Translucent narcissus, dogwood like a vision,
And phallic crocus,
Spring's flesh in my hands.

XI

Someone has cast an unwary match
Into the litter of the tamarack woodlot.
A herd of silent swine watch the long flames
Blend into the sunset.
By midnight the fire is cold,
But long streamers of grey smoke
Still drift between the blackened trees,
And mingle with the mist and fireflies
Of the marsh.
I shall not sleep well tonight.
Tomorrow three days will have passed
Since I have heard your voice.

XII

After a hundred years have slept above us
Autumn will still be painting the Berkshires;
Gold and purple storms will still
Climb over the Catskills.
They will have to look a long time
For my name in the musty corners of libraries;
Utter forgetfulness will mock
Your uncertain ambitions.
But there will be other lovers,
Walking along the hill crests,

Climbing, to sit entranced
On pinnacles in the sunset,
In the moonrise.
The Catskills,
The Berkshires,
Have good memories.

XIII

This shall be sufficient,
A few black buildings against the dark dawn,
The bands of blue lightless streets,
The air splotched with the gold,
Electric, coming day.

XIV

You alone,
A white robe over your naked body,
Passing and repassing
Through the dreams of twenty years.

from THE SIGNATURE OF ALL THINGS
(1950)

BETWEEN MYSELF AND DEATH

To Jimmy Blanton's Music:
Sophisticated Lady, Body and Soul

A fervor parches you sometimes,
And you hunch over it, silent,
Cruel, and timid; and sometimes
You are frightened with wantonness,
And give me your desperation.
Mostly we lurk in our coverts,
Protecting our spleens, pretending
That our bandages are our wounds.
But sometimes the wheel of change stops;
Illusion vanishes in peace;
And suddenly pride lights your flesh—
Lucid as diamond, wise as pearl—
And your face, remote, absolute,
Perfect and final like a beast's.
It is wonderful to watch you,
A living woman in a room
Full of frantic, sterile people,
And think of your arching buttocks
Under your velvet evening dress,
And the beautiful fire spreading
From your sex, burning flesh and bone,
The unbelievably complex
Tissues of your brain all alive
Under your coiling, splendid hair.

I like to think of you naked.
I put your naked body
Between myself alone and death.

41

If I go into my brain
And set fire to your sweet nipples,
To the tendons beneath your knees,
I can see far before me.
It is empty there where I look,
But at least it is lighted.

I know how your shoulders glisten,
How your face sinks into trance,
And your eyes like a sleepwalker's,
And your lips of a woman
Cruel to herself.
                    I like to
Think of you clothed, your body
Shut to the world and self contained,
Its wonderful arrogance
That makes all women envy you.
I can remember every dress,
Each more proud then a naked nun.
When I go to sleep my eyes
Close in a mesh of memory.
Its cloud of intimate odor
Dreams instead of myself.

THE SIGNATURE OF ALL THINGS

My head and shoulders, and my book
In the cool shade, and my body
Stretched bathing in the sun, I lie
Reading beside the waterfall—
Boehme's "Signature of all Things."
Through the deep July day the leaves
Of the laurel, all the colors
Of gold, spin down through the moving
Deep laurel shade all day. They float
On the mirrored sky and forest
For a while, and then, still slowly

Spinning, sink through the crystal deep
Of the pool to its leaf gold floor.
The saint saw the world as streaming
In the electrolysis of love.
I put him by and gaze through shade
Folded into shade of slender
Laurel trunks and leaves filled with sun.
The wren broods in her moss domed nest.
A newt struggles with a white moth
Drowning in the pool. The hawks scream,
Playing together on the ceiling
Of heaven. The long hours go by.
I think of those who have loved me,
Of all the mountains I have climbed,
Of all the seas I have swum in.
The evil of the world sinks.
My own sin and trouble fall away
Like Christian's bundle, and I watch
My forty summers fall like falling
Leaves and falling water held
Eternally in summer air.

Deer are stamping in the glades,
Under the full July moon.
There is a smell of dry grass
In the air, and more faintly,
The scent of a far off skunk.
As I stand at the wood's edge,
Watching the darkness, listening
To the stillness, a small owl
Comes to the branch above me,
On wings more still than my breath.
When I turn my light on him,
His eyes glow like drops of iron,
And he perks his head at me,
Like a curious kitten.
The meadow is bright as snow.

My dog prowls the grass, a dark
Blur in the blur of brightness.
I walk to the oak grove where
The Indian village was once.
There, in blotched and cobwebbed light
And dark, dim in the blue haze,
Are twenty Holstein heifers,
Black and white, all lying down,
Quietly together, under
The huge trees rooted in the graves.

When I dragged the rotten log
From the bottom of the pool,
It seemed heavy as stone.
I let it lie in the sun
For a month; and then chopped it
Into sections, and split them
For kindling, and spread them out
To dry some more. Late that night,
After reading for hours,
While moths rattled at the lamp—
The saints and the philosophers
On the destiny of man—
I went out on my cabin porch,
And looked up through the black forest
At the swaying islands of stars.
Suddenly I saw at my feet,
Spread on the floor of night, ingots
Of quivering phosphorescence,
And all about were scattered chips
Of pale cold light that was alive.

LYELL'S HYPOTHESIS AGAIN

An Attempt to Explain the Former
Changes of the Earth's Surface by
Causes Now in Operation
Subtitle of Lyell: Principles of Geology

The mountain road ends here,
Broken away in the chasm where
The bridge washed out years ago.
The first scarlet larkspur glitters
In the first patch of April
Morning sunlight. The engorged creek
Roars and rustles like a military
Ball. Here by the waterfall,
Insuperable life, flushed
With the equinox, sentient
And sentimental, falls away
To the sea and death. The tissue
Of sympathy and agony
That binds the flesh in its Nessus' shirt;
The clotted cobweb of unself
And self; sheds itself and flecks
The sun's bed with darts of blossom
Like flagellant blood above
The water bursting in the vibrant
Air. This ego, bound by personal
Tragedy and the vast
Impersonal vindictiveness
Of the ruined and ruining world,
Pauses in this immortality,
As passionate, as apathetic,
As the lava flow that burned here once;
And stopped here; and said, 'This far
And no further.' And spoke thereafter
In the simple diction of stone.

Naked in the warm April air,
We lie under the redwoods,
In the sunny lee of a cliff.
As you kneel above me I see
Tiny red marks on your flanks
Like bites, where the redwood cones
Have pressed into your flesh.
You can find just the same marks
In the lignite in the cliff
Over our heads. *Sequoia
Langsdorfii* before the ice,
And *sempervirens* afterwards,
There is little difference,
Except for all those years.

Here in the sweet, moribund
Fetor of spring flowers, washed,
Flotsam and jetsam together,
Cool and naked together,
Under this tree for a moment,
We have escaped the bitterness
Of love, and love lost, and love
Betrayed. And what might have been,
And what might be, fall equally
Away with what is, and leave
Only these ideograms
Printed on the immortal
Hydrocarbons of flesh and stone.

DELIA REXROTH

California rolls into
Sleepy summer, and the air
Is full of the bitter sweet
Smoke of the grass fires burning
On the San Francisco hills.
Flesh burns so, and the pyramids

Likewise, and the burning stars.
Tired tonight, in a city
Of parvenus, in the inhuman
West, in the most blood drenched year,
I took down a book of poems
That you used to like, that you
Used to sing to music I
Never found anywhere again —
Michael Field's book, *Long Ago*.
Indeed it's long ago now —
Your bronze hair and svelte body.
I guess you were a fierce lover,
A wild wife, an animal
Mother. And now life has cost
Me more years, though much less pain,
Than you had to pay for it.
And I have bought back, for and from
Myself, these poems and paintings,
Carved from the protesting bone,
The precious consequences
Of your torn and distraught life.

ANDREE REXROTH

MT. TAMALPAIS

The years have gone. It is spring
Again. Mars and Saturn will
Soon come on, low in the West,
In the dusk. Now the evening
Sunlight makes hazy girders
Over Steep Ravine above
The waterfalls. The winter
Birds from Oregon, robins
And varied thrushes, feast on
Ripe toyon and madroñe
Berries. The robins sing as

The dense light falls.
                            Your ashes
Were scattered in this place. Here
I wrote you a farewell poem,
And long ago another,
A poem of peace and love,
Of the lassitude of a long
Spring evening in youth. Now
It is almost ten years since
You came here to stay. Once more,
The pussy willows that come
After the New Year in this
Outlandish land are blooming.
There are deer and raccoon tracks
In the same places. A few
New sand bars and cobble beds
Have been left where erosion
Has gnawed deep into the hills.
The rounds of life are narrow.
War and peace have past like ghosts.
The human race sinks towards
Oblivion. A bittern
Calls from the same rushes where
You heard one on our first year
In the West; and where I heard
One again in the year
Of your death.

KINGS RIVER CANYON

My sorrow is so wide
I cannot see across it;
And so deep I shall never
Reach the bottom of it.
The moon sinks through deep haze,
As though the Kings River Canyon
Were filled with fine, warm, damp gauze.
Saturn gleams through the thick light
Like a gold, wet eye; nearby,
Antares glows faintly,

Without sparkle. Far overhead,
Stone shines darkly in the moonlight —
Lookout Point, where we lay
In another full moon, and first
Peered down into this canyon.
Here we camped, by still autumnal
Pools, all one warm October.
I baked you a bannock birthday cake.
Here you did your best paintings —
Innocent, wondering landscapes.
Very few of them are left
Anywhere. You destroyed them
In the terrible trouble
Of your long sickness. Eighteen years
Have passed since that autumn.
There was no trail here then.
Only a few people knew
How to enter this canyon.
We were all alone, twenty
Miles from anybody;

A young husband and wife,
Closed in and wrapped about
In the quiet autumn,
In the sound of quiet water,
In the turning and falling leaves,
In the wavering of innumerable
Bats from the caves, dipping
Over the odorous pools
Where the great trout drowsed in the evenings.

Eighteen years have been ground
To pieces in the wheels of life.
You are dead. With a thousand
Convicts they have blown a highway
Through Horseshoe Bend. Youth is gone,
That only came once. My hair
Is turning grey and my body
Heavier. I too move on to death.
I think of Henry King's stilted

But desolated *Exequy,*
Of Yuan Chen's great poem,
Unbearably pitiful;
Alone by the Spring river
More alone than I had ever
Imagined I would ever be,
I think of Frieda Lawrence,
Sitting alone in New Mexico,
In the long drought, listening
For the hiss of the milky Isar,
Over the cobbles, in a lost Spring.

A LETTER TO
WILLIAM CARLOS WILLIAMS

Dear Bill,

When I search the past for you,
Sometimes I think you are like
St. Francis, whose flesh went out
Like a happy cloud from him,
And merged with every lover —
Donkeys, flowers, lepers, suns —
But I think you are more like
Brother Juniper, who suffered
All indignities and glories
Laughing like a gentle fool.
You're in the *Fioretti*
Somewhere, for you're a fool, Bill,
Like the Fool in Yeats, the term
Of all wisdom and beauty.
It's you, stands over against
Helen in all her wisdom,
Solomon in all his glory.

Remember years ago, when
I told you you were the first

Great Franciscan poet since
The Middle Ages? I disturbed
The even tenor of dinner.
Your wife thought I was crazy.
It's true, though. And you're 'pure', too,
A real classic, though not loud
About it—a whole lot like
The girls of the Anthology.
Not like strident Sappho, who
For all her grandeur, must have
Had endemetriosis,
But like Anyte, who says
Just enough, softly, for all
The thousands of years to remember.

It's a wonderful quiet
You have, a way of keeping
Still about the world, and its
Dirty rivers, and garbage cans,
Red wheelbarrows glazed with rain,
Cold plums stolen from the icebox,
And Queen Anne's lace, and day's eyes,
And leaf buds bursting over
Muddy roads, and splotched bellies
With babies in them, and Cortes
And Malinche on the bloody
Causeway, the death of the flower world.

Nowadays, when the press reels
With chatterboxes, you keep still,
Each year a sheaf of stillness,
Poems that have nothing to say,
Like the stillness of George Fox,
Sitting still under the cloud
Of all the world's temptation,
By the fire, in the kitchen,
In the Vale of Beavor. And
The archetype, the silence
Of Christ, when he paused a long
Time and then said, 'Thou sayest it'.

Now in a recent poem you say,
'I who am about to die.'
Maybe this is just a tag
From the classics, but it sends
A shudder over me. Where
Do you get that stuff, Williams?
Look at here. The day will come
When a young woman will walk
By the lucid Williams River,
Where it flows through an idyllic
News from Nowhere sort of landscape,
And she will say to her children,
'Isn't it beautiful? It
Is named after a man who
Walked here once when it was called
The Passaic, and was filthy
With the poisonous excrements
Of sick men and factories.
He was a great man. He knew
It was beautiful then, although
Nobody else did, back there
In the Dark Ages. And the
Beautiful river he saw
Still flows in his veins, as it
Does in ours, and flows in our eyes,
And flows in time, and makes us
Part of it, and part of him.
That, children, is what is called
A sacramental relationship.
And that is what a poet
Is, children, one who creates
Sacramental relationships
That last always.'
   With love and admiration,
   Kenneth Rexroth.

from THE DRAGON AND THE UNICORN
(1952)

I

"And what is love?" said Pilate,
And washed his hands.

All night long
The white snow falls on the white
Peaks through the quiet darkness.
The overland express train
Drives through the night, through the snow.
In the morning the land slopes
To the Atlantic, the sky
Is thicker, Spring stirs, smelling
Like old wet wood, new life speaks
In pale green fringes of marsh
Marigolds on the edges
Of the mountain snow drifts. Spring
Is only a faint green haze
On the high plains, only haze
And the fences that disappear
Over the horizon, and the
Rails, and the telegraph
Poles and the pale singing wires
Going on and on forever.

All things are made new by fire.
The plow in the furrow, Burns
Or Buddha, the first call to
Vocation, the severed worms,
The shattered mouse nest, the seed
Dripping from the bloody sword.
The sleepers chuckle under
The wheels, mocking the heartbeat.

We think of time as serial
And atomic, the expression
By mechanical means of a
Philosophical notion,
Regular divisibility
With a least common divisor
Of motion by motion, so
Many ticks to a century.
Such a thing does not exist.
Actually, the concept
Of time arose from the weaving
Together of the great organic
Cycles of the universe,
Sunrise and sunset, the moon
Waxing and waning, the changing
Stars and seasons, the climbing
And declining sun in heaven,
The round of sowing and harvest,
And the life and death of man.

The doom of versifying—
Orpheus was torn to pieces
By the vindictiveness of
Women or struck down by the
Jealousy of heaven.

The doom of the testicles—
Chiron's masculinity
Was so intense that all his
Children were adopted and
Later destroyed by the gods.

The deed done, Orestes draws
His steel penis like a snake
From its hole. The sun and moon
In Capricorn, Electra,
The little she goat, bleats and squirms,
Her brother between her thighs.
From whose wounds pour forth both blood
And water, the wine of whose

Maidenhead turns to water
Of baptism, the fiery
Mixture of being and not being.
The artist is his own mother.

Chicago, the train plunges through
A vast dome of electric gloom.
Cold wind, deepening dark, miles
Of railroad lights, 22nd
And Wentworth. The old Chinese
Restaurants now tourist joints.
Gooey Sam where we once roared
And taught the waiters to say
Fellow Worker, is now plush.
As the dark deepens I walk
Out Wentworth, grit under my feet.
The smell of frying potatoes
Seeps through the dirty windows.
The old red light district is
Mostly torn down, vacant lots
Line the railroad tracks. I know
What Marvell meant by desarts
Of vast eternitie. Man
Gets daily sicker and his
Ugliness knots his bowels.
On the sight of several
Splendid historical brothels
Stands the production plant of
Time-Luce Incorporated.
Die Ausrottung der Besten.

Do not cut a hole in the
Side of a boat to mark the
Place where your sword dropped and sank.

. . . .

II

Discursive knowledge, knowledge by
Indirection passes away
And love, knowledge by direction,
Directly of another, grows
In its place. There exists a point
At which the known passes through
A sort of occultation,
A zero between plus and
Minus in which knower and known
And their knowledge cease to exist.
Perfect love casts out knowledge.

The Pont du Gard as beautiful
As ever. Why can't a culture
Of businessmen and engineers
Make beautiful things? I walk
Across on top and then back
Under the small arches with
Idyllic frames of Provence
Slipping past me and suddenly
I notice the shells in the rock—
With my head full of the
Fossils of a million years,
Standing on this fossilized
Roman engineering, built of
Mudflats of fossil seas, springing
From cliffs with caves of fossil man—
Half-naked jeunesse with golden
Bodies scamper over golden
Stone, the air is full of swallows
Whirling above flowing water.

There are three ways of loving,
Modes of communication,
The realization via
The ground of possibility,

We touch each other through the
Material of love, the earth
Center which all share; or by means
Of ultimate inclusive
Action, the empyrean
Shared by all persons where the
Mythology and drama
Of the person is realized
In pure archetype; or face
To face in the act of love,
Which for most men is the way
In which the other modes are
Raised into consciousness and
Into a measure of control.

Provence hot, the hills grey with heat,
Miles of olive trees, silver green,
The color of Sung celadon,
The houses peach colored, over
Each doorway a grape vine, around
It the wall stained pale blue-green with
Copper sulphate spray. Avignon,
Beautiful across the river
But with a god damned visite;
(The legends and chauvinism
Of an ancien combattant,
Permitted, because he has given
A leg or arm to France to beg
In this tedious way. Splendid
Fellows, salty and wise, as who
Wouldn't have to be if this
Was all he got from a grateful
People, but hardly the screen
Through which to absorb The Past.)
And over all the lingering
Stink of the Papacy and
The present stink of English tourists.

The vélos roll down hill, mile
After mile beside rushing
Water into Aix. We go for
A swim in the cold piscine at
The Roman baths and on into
That city of small splendors.

Seldom has man made so perfect
A work of art of light and shade.
The Fromentins are fine in the
Cathedral, but they can't compare
With the green submarine light
Of the Cours Mirabeau broken
By pools of clarity at the
Small fountains at the crossings,
The dark gloom and black statue
Of King René at one end,
The white glare of the Fountain
Of Culture at the other.
Certainly the most civilized
Man ever to get mixed up
With a revolution has
An elegant monument.

The author of *Le Rideau levé*,
Approached as a colleague by
Sade in prison, repulsed him
Succinctly, "Mon Sieur, je ne suis
Pas ici pour avoir donné des
Confits empoisonnés aux femmes
De chambre." The existentialistes
Don't like him very much.

Granet painting in Rome, never
Forgot that light and shade. In
The museum his paintings with
Their stereoscopic values
Hang by his two portraits—
The famous Ingres, more handsome
Than Byron, and another
Of an old, old, dying man.

Lots of Cézanne watercolors
Full of peach blossoms and leaf flicker.

Milhaud, Cendrars, Tal-Coat, a place
Where men with balls can escape
The maggots of the Deux Magots.

Dinner at the Café Mistral,
Plover's eggs and tomatillos
In aspic, écrevisse, raw tuna
With chives, thick noodles with saffron,
Duckling with truffles and cèpes,
Fricassée of guinea hen,
A local wine, not still, not
Sparkling, but volatile like
The chiantis of Florence,
A dark blue cheese, and black, black
Coffee and Rémy Martin
And thick layers of cream—
And then like all the world we
Promenade on Mirabeau's
Fine street and eat glaces and
Drink more cognac and coffee.
At last the strange malady
Of France has vanished and the
Women once more are mammals.

At last the ability to
Know directly becomes a
Habit of the soul and the
Dominant mode in which
Possibility is presented
To the developing person.
As such it ceases to appear
As consequence and becomes
Conscious communion with a
Person. A duality
Is established which focuses
The reflection of the mountain
As an illuminating ray

On the mountain itself,
The moon dissolves in the water
Held in the palm of the hand.

. . . .

III

. . . .

Boswell: "Sir, what is the chief
Virtue?" Johnson: "Courage, Sir,
Without it, opportunity
To exercise the others
Will often be found wanting."

On his first visit to the States,
Wells was asked what most impressed him.
He said, "The female schoolteachers.
In two generations they will
Destroy the country." It took one.

In the Uffizi I prefer
To spend most of my time with the
Even tempered Greeks and Romans.
Pictures in galleries always
Look to me like dressed meat in
Butcher shops. From Cimabue
And Simone Martini,
Arrows point across the river
To Bronzino, and via
Raphael, to Picasso.
Without Florence, there isn't
Really any modern painting,
But just the same, it looks cooked.
Straight through, from beginning to end,
It is all Mannerism.

In the churches you get tired
Of all the Taddis and Gaddis.
Why does no one ever point out
That the great Masaccios are
Compounded of the elements
Of Roman painting, and no
Others at all, and that each figure
Is derived from classic sculpture?
There is the same knowledge of
Good and evil, and in the face
Of it, the same serenity.

God is that person who
Satisfies all love, with whom
Indwelling encompasses
All reality. It is
Impossible to say if there
Exists only one god, the
Ultimate beloved of all
Persons. It would seem rather,
Since the relationship is
Reciprocal and progressive,
That there are as many gods
As lovers. Theoretically
One infinite god could
Satisfy all finite lovers—
But this concept comes from the
Insoluble residues of
The quantitative mathematics
Of infinitudes. It really
Has no place in the discussion
Of the love relationship,
Which knows neither finite nor
Infinite. The Shekinah
And Jehovah are only
An enlarged mirror image
Of the terrestrial embrace.
The sephiroth of the Kabbalah
Are the chakras of the Tantra.
The records of Hafidh, Rumi,

St. Theresa, even the crazed
Augustine, seem to be the
Records in each case of a
Unique duality. The
Object of love is a person
Like the lover, and the demands
On the definition of
A monotheistic god
Made by other philosophical
Considerations, largely
Of an arithmetical
Nature, make it unlikely
That such an entity could be
Also a person. There is here a
Collision of two exclusive
Modes of viewing reality.
Hence perhaps the peculiar
Subjective tension of the
Monotheistic mystic,
The reason why he always feels
His love as incomplete and
Destructive of his person.

Agathias Scholasticus:
Restless and discontent
I lie awake all night long.
And as I drowse in the dawn,
The swallows stir in the eaves,
And wake me weeping again.
I press my eyes close tight, but
Your face rises before me.
O birds, be quiet with
Your tittering accusations.
I did not cut that dead girl's tongue.
Go weep for her lover in the hills,
Cry by the hoopoe's nest in the rocks.
Let me sleep for a while, and dream
I lie once more in my girl's arms.

Under a lattice of leaves
Her white thighs in cloth of gold
That casts a glittering shade.
She turned to her left and stared at
The sun. My imagination
Was moved by her gesture, and as
I turned, I saw the sun
Sparkle all round, like iron
Pulled molten from the furnace.

Bright petals of evening
Shatter, fall, drift over Florence,
And flush your cheeks a redder
Rose and gleam like fiery flakes
In your eyes. All over Florence
The swallows whirl between the
Tall roofs, under the bridge arches,
Spiral in the zenith like larks,
Sweep low in crying clouds above
The brown river and the white
River bed. Your moist, quivering
Lips are like the wet scarlet wings
Of a reborn butterfly who
Trembles on the rose petal as
Life floods his strange body.
Turn to me. Part your lips. My dear,
Some day we will be dead.

I feel like Pascal often felt.

About the mid houre of the nicht

FIRE

The air is dizzy with swallows.

Sunset comes on the golden
Towers, on the Signoría.
In the Badía, the light goes
From the face of Filippino's

Weary lady, exhausted with
The devotion of her worshipper.
Across the face of the Duomo
The Campanile's blue shadow
Marks the mathematics of beauty.
In San Miniato the gold
Mosaics still glitter through
The smoky gloom. At the end
Of the Way of the Cross, the dense
Cypress wood, full of lovers,
Shivering with impatience.
As the dark thickens, two by two
They take each other. Nightfall, all
The wood is filled with soft moaning,
As though it were filled with doves.

. . . .

Michelangelo was surely
A noisy man, and terribly
Conceited. After all, nothing
Ever happened to him that
Doesn't happen to all of us.
If you have tragedy to
Portray, you should be humble
About it, you are serving
The bread of communion.
"Too many nakeds for a chapel,"
Said Evelyn. But I don't think it
Was the exposed privates of the
Mother of God made the Pope faint.
That's an arrogant, perverse, pride
Soaked wall, a good thing to look down
On the election of the Popes.
Maybe he intended it for
A portrait of the Papacy.
But the Moses was beautiful
Just before the church shut, looking
Like oiled ivory against
The wavering blackness in
The light of the vigil lamps.

The worship of art, the attempt
To substitute it for religion,
Is the blindest superstition
Of them all. Almost all works of
Art are failures. The successes
Occur hardly once in a
Lifetime even in periods
Of great cultural flowering;
And then they are likely to be
Unpretentious perfections,
Of modest scope, exquisite
As a delicate wine and
Often no more significant.
Better lump them all together—
"A good judge of wine, women,
And horseflesh"—than go posting
For the Absolute in the
Galleries of Fifty-seventh Street—
Or the Louvre—or the Uffizi.
The World's Masterpieces are
Too often by Vasari,
Benjamin West, Picasso,
Or Diego Rivera.

The Pope was once content to rule
The rulers, the masses were
Allowed their old worship under
A new nomenclature. Feudal
Methods of exploitation
Required a homogeneous
Society, a "natural"
Religion. New methods,
New cadres. Capitalism
Revived all the paranoid
Compulsions of rabbinical
Judaism, coupled with
A schizophrenic doctrine
Of the person as utterly
Alone, subsistent as a pure
Integer at the will of a

Uniquely self subsistent
Commander (hardly a lover),
Two things with wills. It required
The total atomization
Of society. The family
Hierarchy disappeared and the
Monogamous couple was
Substituted. Not a vehicle
Of mystic love, but an iron
Necessity for survival.

Says Evelyn, "Turning to the right
Out of the Porta del Popolo,
We came to Justinian's
Gardens, near the Muro Torto,
So prominently built as to
Threaten to fall any moment,
Yet standing so these thousand years.
Under this is the burying
Place of the common prostitutes,
Where they are put into the ground
Sans ceremony." In the
Rotonda Sant' Agostino,
A sign, "Whores will refrain
From hustling the customers
During their devotions." From the
Albergo Inghilterra
To the Piazza di Spagna
Stretches a solid tide wall
Of crew-cut American fairies,
Elderly nymphomaniacs,
Double breasted, gabardined
Artisti. The latter have reduced
Hemingway to a formula.
"Let's go," Bill said. "Let's go," Pete said.
"OK, let's go," Joe said. It's like
Dante's terza rima, and the
Triad of the dialectic.
Honest. They write books about it.
Everybody on the prowl

For Cineasti and Milioni
Of any sex. The Via
Vittorio Veneto
After dark is strictly graded.
On the terrace of the Doni
Sit the condottieri of
The Marshall Plan like Rameses.
The Cineasti and Milioni
Lounge over their highballs.
The artisti stand and bow.
The more expensive whores walk
The sidewalks. The poorer whores work
The side streets. The most expensive
Sit. At the entrance to the
Park are whores from Masereel
And Félicien Rops. Inside are
Italian boys who get paid.
Further inside are beringed
Cigar smoking Italians, who
All look like Mussolini's
Grandfather. They will pay you.
At the beginning of the street
Is the American Embassy.
Midway is an ESSO pump.
At the end is the devouring dark.

"La mauvaise conscience des
Bourgeois, ai-je dit, a paralysé
Tout le mouvement intellectuel
Et moral de la bourgeoisie.
Je me corrige, et je remplace
Ce mot 'paralysé' par
Cet autre: 'dénaturé.' "
So Bakunin says, and Marx,
"The bourgeoisie, wherever
It has got the upper hand,
Has put an end to all feudal,
Patriarchal, idyllic
Relations. It has pitilessly
Torn asunder the motley

Feudal ties that bound man to
His 'natural superiors,'
And has left no other nexus
Between man and man than naked
Self interest, than callous
Cash payment. It has drowned the
Most heavenly ecstasies
Of religious fervor, of
Chivalrous enthusiasm,
Of philistine sentimentalism,
In the icy water of
Egotistical calculation.
It has resolved personal worth
Into exchange value, and in
Place of the numberless
Indefeasible chartered freedoms,
Has set up that single
Unconscionable freedom,
Free trade. In a word, for
Exploitation veiled by
Religious and political
Illusions, it has substituted
Naked, shameless, direct, brutal
Exploitation."
For Dante,
Usury was the ultimate
Form of pederasty, in which
Buggery attempts to make
Its turds its heirs.

Sexual fulfillment was robbed
Of all meaning. The sex act became
A nervous stimulant and
Anodyne outside of the
Productive process, but still
Necessary to it as an
Insatiable, irrational
Drive, without which the struggle
For meaningless abstractions,
Commodities, would collapse.

This is the ultimate in
Human self alienation.
This is what the revolution
Is about. In a society
Ruled only by the cash nexus
The sexual relationship
Must be a continual struggle
Of each to obtain security
From the other, a kind of
Security, a mass of
Commodities, which has no
Meaning for love, and today in
America, no meaning at all.
The greater the mass of things,
The greater the insecurity.
The security of love lies
In the state of indwelling rest.
It is its own security.
This is what free love is, freedom
From the destructive power
Of a society coerced
Into the pursuit of insane
Objectives. Until men learn
To administer things, and are
No longer themselves organized
And exploited as things, there can
Be no love except by intense
Effort directed against
The whole pressure of the world.
In other words, love becomes,
As it was with the Gnostics,
The practice of a kind of cult.
Against it are arrayed all
The consequences of a
Vast systematic delusion,
Without intelligence or
Mercy or even real being,
But with the power to kill.

. . . .

America is today a
Nation profoundly deranged,
Demented, and sick, because
Americans with very few
Exceptions believe, or when
They doubt are terrified to
Be discovered doubting, that
Love is measured entirely
In an interchange of
Commodities. The wife provides
Pop-up toast, synthetic coffee,
Frozen orange juice, two eggs of
Standard color, size, and flavor,
In the morning, at night the
Fantastic highly-colored canned
Poisons which grace the cooking
And advertising pages
Of the women's magazines.
In exchange the husband provides
Her with the clothes and cosmetics
Of a movie courtesan,
A vast array of "labor"
Saving devices, all streamlined,
Presumably so they can be
Thrown, a car, never more than
Two years old, engineered with
Great skill to their social status,
A television set, a dream
House, designed by a fairy,
And built of glass and cardboard,
A bathroom full of cramped, pastel
Tinted plumbing. When they wish
To satisfy their passions,
They go to a movie. The
Sexual relation is
A momentary lapse from
The routine fulfillment of
This vision, which is portrayed
As love and marriage by thousands
Of decorticated and

Debauched intellectuals,
Who enjoy the incomes of princes.
Almost all advertising
In America today
Is aimed at the young married
Couple. Billions are consciously
And deliberately spent
To destroy love at its source.
Like the "fiends" who are picked up
In parks, an advertising
Man is a professional
Murderer of young lovers—
On an infinitely vaster scale.

You will find more peace and more
Communion, more love, in an hour
In the arms of a pickup in
Singapore or Reykjavik,
Than you will find in a lifetime
Married to a middle class
White American woman.

It feels like it's made of plastic.
It smells like it's perfumed with
Coal tar. It tastes like it's made
Of soybeans. It looks like an
Abandoned pee-wee golf course.
It is still and sterile
As a crater on the moon.

Sitting there, reading this in your
Psychoanalyst's waiting room,
Thirty-five years old, faintly
Perfumed, expensively dressed,
Sheer nylons strapped to freezing thighs,
Brain removed at Bennington
Or Sarah Lawrence, dutiful
Reader of the *Partisan*
Review's Book of the Month, target
Of my highbrow publisher, you

Think this is all just Art—contrast—
Naples—New York. It is not. Every time
You open your frigidaire
A dead Neapolitan baby
Drops out. Your world is not crazy.
But dead. It can only mimic
Life with the economics of
Murder. "War production and
Colonialization of
The former imperialist
Centers." This is the definition
Of Fascism. You are not just
Responsible. You are the dead
Neapolitan baby,
The other side of the coin.
I don't wonder you've never
Been the same since you left the
Tickets to *Don Giovanni*
In the orgone collector.

. . . .

Paestum, the apex of the trip,
And the zenith of our years.

Helen's jewel, the Schethya,
The Taoist uncut block,
The stone of the alchemist,
The footstool of Elohim's throne,
Which they hurled into the Abyss,
On which stands the queen and sacred
Whore, Malkuth, the stone which served
Jacob for pillow and altar.

"And what is truth?" said Pilate,
"A,E,I,O,U—the spheres
Of the planets, the heavens'
Pentachord. A noir, E blanc,
I rouge, O bleu, U vert."

When in Japan, the goddess
Of the sun, attracted by
The obscene gestures of the flesh,
Came out from eclipse, she spoke
The first and oldest mystery,
"1, 2, 3, 4, 5, 6, 7,
8, 9, 10."

All things have a name.
Every mote in the sunlight has
A name, and the sunlight itself
Has a name, and the spirit who
Troubles the waters has a name.

As the Philosopher says,
"The Pythagoreans are
Of the opinion that the shapes
Of the Greek vase are reflections
Of the irrational numbers
Thought by the Pure Mind. On the
Other hand, the Epicureans
Hold them to be derived
From the curves of a girl's
Breasts and thighs and buttocks."

The doctrine of Signatures—
The law by which we must make
Use of things is written in
The law by which they were made.
It is graven upon each
As its unique character.
The forms of being are the
Rules of life.

The Smaragdine Tablet
Says, "That which is above is
Reflected in that which is below."

Paestum of the twice blooming
Roses, the sea god's honey-

Colored stone still strong against
The folly of the long decline
Of man. The snail climbs the Doric
Line, and the empty snail shell
Lies by the wild cyclamen.
The sandstone of the Roman
Road is marked with sun wrinkles
Of prehistoric beaches,
But no time at all has touched
The deep constant melodies
Of space as the columns swing
To the moving eye. The sea
Breathes like a drowsy woman.
The sun moves like a drowsy hand.
Poseidon's pillars have endured
All tempers of the sea and sun.
This is the order of the spheres,
The curve of the unwinding fern,
And the purple shell in the sea;
These are the spaces of the notes
Of every kind of music.
The world is made of number
And moved in order by love.
Mankind has risen to this point
And can only fall away,
As we can only turn homeward
Up Italy, through France, to life
Always pivoted on this place.

Sweet Anyte of Tegea—
"The children have put purple
Reins on you, he goat, and a
Bridle in your bearded mouth.
And they play at horse races
Round a temple where a god
Gazes on their childish joy."

Finally the few tourists go,
The German photographers, the
Bevy of seminarians,

And we are left alone. We eat
In the pronaos towards the sea.
Greek food, small white loaves, smoked cheese,
Pickled squid, black figs, and honey
And olive oil, the common food
Of Naples, still, for those who eat.
An ancient dog, Odysseus' dog,
Spawned before there were breeds of dogs,
Appears, begs, eats, and disappears—
The exoteric proxy of
The god. And we too grow drowsy with
White wine, tarry from the wineskin.
The blue and gold shafts interweave
Across our nodding eyes. The sea
Prepares to take the sun. We go
Into the naos, open to the
Sky and make love, where the sea god
And the sea goddess, wet with sperm,
Coupled in the incense filled dark,
As the singing rose and was still.

Mist comes with the sunset. (The Yanks
Killed the mosquitoes.) Long lines of
Umber buffalo, their backs a
Rippling congruence, as in the
Paintings of Krishna, file across
The brilliant green sea meadows,
Under banners of white mist.
The fires of the bivouacs of
Spartacus twinkle in the hills.
Our train comes with the first stars.
Venus over the wine dark sea.

All the way back the train fills
And fills up, and fills again,
With girls from the fish canneries,
And girls from the lace factories,
And girls from the fields, who have been
Working twelve hours for nothing,
Or at the best a few pennies.

They laugh and sing, all the way
Back to Naples, like broad bottomed,
Deep bosomed angels, wet with sweat.

Only in a secret place
May human love perfect itself.

. . . .

V

I come back to the cottage in
Santa Monica Canyon where
Andrée and I were poor and
Happy together. Sometimes we
Were hungry and stole vegetables
From the neighbors' gardens.
Sometimes we went out and gathered
Cigarette butts by flashlight.
But we went swimming every day,
All year round. We had a dog
Called Proclus, a vast yellow
Mongrel, and a white cat named
Cyprian. We had our first
Joint art show, and they began
To publish my poems in Paris.
We worked under the low umbrella
Of the acacia in the dooryard.
Now I get out of the car
And stand before the house in the dusk.
The acacia blossoms powder the walk
With little pills of gold wool.
The odor is drowsy and thick
In the early evening.
The tree has grown twice as high
As the roof. Inside, an old man
And woman sit in the lamplight.
I go back and drive away
To Malibu Beach and sit
With a grey-haired childhood friend and

Watch the full moon rise over the
Long rollers wrinkling the dark bay.

"It is those who are married
Who should live the contemplative
Life together. In the world
There is the long day of
Destruction to go by. But
Let those who are single, man
Torn from woman, woman from
Man, men altogether, women
Altogether, separate
Deathly fragments, each returning
And adhering to its own kind,
The body of life torn in two,
Let these finish the day of
Destruction, and those who have
United go into the
Wilderness to know a new
Heaven and a new earth."

There are those who spend all their lives
Whirling in the love and hate
Of the deities they create.

Contemplation is direct
Knowledge, beyond consequence,
Ignorance, appetite, grasping
Of possibility. The
Contemplative knows himself
As the focus of the others,
And he knows the other, the
Dual, as the mirror of
Himself and all the others,
The others as the mirror
Of himself and the dual.

. . . .

As long as we are lost
In the world of purpose
We are not free. I sit
In my ten foot square hut.
The birds sing. The bees hum.
The leaves sway. The water
Murmurs over the rocks.
The canyon shuts me in.
If I moved, Bashō's frog
Would splash in the pool.
All Summer long the gold
Laurel leaves fell through space.
Today I was aware
Of a maple leaf floating
On the pool. In the night
I stare into the fire.
Once I saw fire cities,
Towns, palaces, wars,
Heroic adventures,
In the campfires of youth.
Now I see only fire.
My breath moves quietly.
The stars move overhead.
In the clear darkness
Only a small red glow
Is left in the ashes.
On the table lies a cast
Snakeskin and an uncut stone.

There is no need to assume
The existence of a god
Behind the community
Of persons, the community
Is the absolute. There is no
Future life because there is
No future. Reality
Is not conditioned by time,
Space, ignorance, grasping.
The shift from possibility
To consequence gives rise to

The convention of time. At
The heart of being is the act of
Contemplation, it is timeless.

Since Isis and Osiris
Many gods and goddesses
Have ridden the boats of
The sun and the moon. I stand
On the hill above my hut
And watch the sun set in the
Fog bank over the distant
Ocean. Shortly afterward
The moon rises, transparent
In the twilight above the
Mountain. There is nobody
In them this evening. I
Am sure they are empty, that
I am alone in the great
Void, where they journey, empty
Through the darkness and the light.

Deep in myself arise the rays
Called Artemis and Apollo,
Helios, Luna, Sun and Moon,
Flowing forever out into
The void, towards the unknown others.

The heavens and hells of man,
The gods and demons, the ghosts of
Superstition, are crude attempts;
The systems of philosophers,
The visions of religion,
Are more or less successful
Mythological descriptions
Of knowing, acting, loving—
You are Shiva, but you dream.

It is the dark of the moon.
Late at night, the end of Summer,
The Autumn constellations

Glow in the arid heaven.
The air smells of cattle, hay,
And dust. In the old orchard
The pears are ripe. The trees
Have sprouted from old rootstocks
And the fruit is inedible.
As I pass them I hear something
Rustling and grunting and turn
My light into the branches.
Two raccoons with acrid pear
Juice and saliva drooling
From their mouths, stare back at me,
Their eyes deep sponges of light.
They know me and do not run
Away. Coming up the road
Through the black oak shadows, I
See ahead of me, glinting
Everywhere from the dusty
Gravel, tiny points of cold
Blue light, like the sparkle of
Iron snow. I suspect what it is,
And kneel to see. Under each
Pebble and oak leaf is a
Spider, her eyes shining at
Me with my reflected light
Across immeasurable distance.

from IN DEFENSE OF THE EARTH (1956)

from SEVEN POEMS FOR MARTHE, MY WIFE

THE REFLECTING TREES
OF BEING AND NOT BEING

In my childhood when I first
Saw myself unfolded in
The triple mirrors, in my
Youth, when I pursued myself
Wandering on wandering
Nightbound roads like a roving
Masterless dog, when I met
Myself on sharp peaks of ice,
And tasted myself dissolved
In the lulling heavy sea,
In the talking night, in the
Spiraling stars, what did I
Know? What do I know now,
Of myself, of the others?
Blood flows out to the fleeing
Nebulae, and flows back, red
With all the worn space of space,
Old with all the time of time.
It is my blood. I cannot
Taste in it as it leaves me
More of myself than on its
Return. I can see in it
Trees of silence and fire.
In the mirrors on its waves
I can see faces. Mostly
They are your face. On its streams
I can see the soft moonlight
On the Canal du Midi.
I can see the leaf shadows
Of the plane trees on the deep
Fluids of your eyes, and the
Golden fires and lamps of years.

MARTHE AWAY (SHE IS AWAY)

All night I lay awake beside you,
Leaning on my elbow, watching your
Sleeping face, that face whose purity
Never ceases to astonish me.
I could not sleep. But I did not want
Sleep nor miss it. Against my body,
Your body lay like a warm soft star.
How many nights I have waked and watched
You, in how many places. Who knows?
This night might be the last one of all.
As on so many nights, once more I
Drank from your sleeping flesh the deep still
Communion I am not always strong
Enough to take from you waking, the peace of love.
Foggy lights moved over the ceiling
Of our room, so like the rooms of France
And Italy, rooms of honeymoon,
And gave your face an ever changing
Speech, the secret communication
Of untellable love. I knew then,
As your secret spoke, my secret self,
The blind bird, hardly visible in
An endless web of lies. And I knew
The web too, its every knot and strand,
The hidden crippled bird, the terrible web.
Towards the end of night, as trucks rumbled
In the streets, you stirred, cuddled to me,
And spoke my name. Your voice was the voice
Of a girl who had never known loss
Of love, betrayal, mistrust, or lie.
And later you turned again and clutched
My hand and pressed it to your body.
Now I know surely and forever,
However much I have blotted our
Waking love, its memory is still
There. And I know the web, the net,
The blind and crippled bird. For then, for
One brief instant it was not blind, nor

Trapped, nor crippled. For one heart beat the
Heart was free and moved itself. O love,
I who am lost and damned with words,
Whose words are a business and an art,
I have no words. These words, this poem, this
Is all confusion and ignorance.
But I know that coached by your sweet heart,
My heart beat one free beat and sent
Through all my flesh the blood of truth.

A DIALOGUE OF WATCHING

Let me celebrate you. I
Have never known anyone
More beautiful than you. I
Walking beside you, watching
You move beside me, watching
That still grace of hand and thigh,
Watching your face change with words
You do not say, watching your
Solemn eyes as they turn to me,
Or turn inward, full of knowing,
Slow or quick, watching your full
Lips part and smile or turn grave,
Watching your narrow waist, your
Proud buttocks in their grace, like
A sailing swan, an animal,
Free, your own, and never
To be subjugated, but
Abandoned, as I am to you,
Overhearing your perfect
Speech of motion, of love and
Trust and security as
You feed or play with our children.
I have never known any
One more beautiful than you.

from THE LIGHTS IN THE SKY ARE STARS

for Mary

HALLEY'S COMET

When in your middle years
The great comet comes again
Remember me, a child,
Awake in the summer night,
Standing in my crib and
Watching that long-haired star
So many years ago.
Go out in the dark and see
Its plume over water
Dribbling on the liquid night,
And think that life and glory
Flickered on the rushing
Bloodstream for me once, and for
All who have gone before me,
Vessels of the billion-year-long
River that flows now in your veins.

THE GREAT NEBULA OF ANDROMEDA

We get into camp after
Dark, high on an open ridge
Looking out over five thousand
Feet of mountains and mile
Beyond mile of valley and sea.
In the star-filled dark we cook
Our macaroni and eat
By lantern light. Stars cluster
Around our table like fireflies.
After supper we go straight
To bed. The night is windy
And clear. The moon is three days
Short of full. We lie in bed
And watch the stars and the turning

Moon through our little telescope.
Late at night the horses stumble
Around camp and I awake.
I lie on my elbow watching
Your beautiful sleeping face
Like a jewel in the moonlight.
If you are lucky and the
Nations let you, you will live
Far into the twenty-first
Century. I pick up the glass
And watch the Great Nebula
Of Andromeda swim like
A phosphorescent amoeba
Slowly around the Pole. Far
Away in distant cities
Fat-hearted men are planning
To murder you while you sleep.

A SWORD IN A CLOUD OF LIGHT

Your hand in mine, we walk out
To watch the Christmas Eve crowds
On Fillmore Street, the Negro
District. The night is thick with
Frost. The people hurry, wreathed
In their smoky breaths. Before
The shop windows the children
Jump up and down with spangled
Eyes. Santa Clauses ring bells.
Cars stall and honk. Street cars clang.
Loud speakers on the lampposts
Sing carols, on juke boxes
In the bars Louis Armstrong
Plays *White Christmas*. In the joints
The girls strip and grind and bump
To *Jingle Bells*. Overhead
The neon signs scribble and
Erase and scribble again

Messages of avarice,
Joy, fear, hygiene, and the proud
Names of the middle classes.
The moon beams like a pudding.
We stop at the main corner
And look up, diagonally
Across, at the rising moon,
And the solemn, orderly
Vast winter constellations.
You say, "There's Orion!"
The most beautiful object
Either of us will ever
Know in the world or in life
Stands in the moonlit empty
Heavens, over the swarming
Men, women, and children, black
And white, joyous and greedy,
Evil and good, buyer and
Seller, master and victim,
Like some immense theorem,
Which, if once solved would forever
Solve the mystery and pain
Under the bells and spangles.
There he is, the man of the
Night before Christmas, spread out
On the sky like a true god
In whom it would only be
Necessary to believe
A little. I am fifty
And you are five. It would do
No good to say this and it
May do no good to write it.
Believe in Orion. Believe
In the night, the moon, the crowded
Earth. Believe in Christmas and
Birthdays and Easter rabbits.
Believe in all those fugitive
Compounds of nature, all doomed
To waste away and go out.
Always be true to these things.
They are all there is. Never

Give up this savage religion
For the blood-drenched civilized
Abstractions of the rascals
Who live by killing you and me.

A LIVING PEARL

At sixteen I came West, riding
Freights on the Chicago, Milwaukee
And St. Paul, the Great Northern,
The Northern Pacific. I got
A job as helper to a man
Who gathered wild horses in the
Mass drives in the Okanogan
And Horse Heaven country. The best
We culled out as part profit from
The drive, the rest went for chicken
And dog feed. We took thirty head
Up the Methow, up the Twisp,
Across the headwaters of Lake
Chelan, down the Skagit to
The Puget Sound country. I
Did the cooking and camp work.
In a couple of weeks I
Could handle the stock pretty well.
Every day we saddled and rode
A new horse. Next day we put a
Packsaddle on him. By the
Time we reached Marblemount
We considered them well broken.
The scissorbills who bought them
Considered them untamed mustangs
Of the desert. In a few weeks
They were peacefully pulling
Milk wagons in Sedro-Wooley.
We made three trips a season

And did well enough for the
Post-war depression.
Tonight,
Thirty years later, I walk
Out of the deserted miner's
Cabin in Mono Pass, under
The full moon and the few large stars.
The sidehills are piebald with snow.
The midnight air is suffused
With moonlight. As Dante says,
"It is as though a cloud enclosed
Me, lucid, dense, solid, polished,
Like a diamond forged by the sun.
We entered the eternal pearl,
Which took us as water takes
A ray of light, itself uncleft."
Fifteen years ago, in this place,
I wrote a poem called "Toward
An Organic Philosophy."
Everything is still the same,
And it differs very little
From the first mountain pass I
Crossed so long ago with the
Pintos and zebra duns and
Gunmetal roans and buckskins,
And splattered lallapaloosas,
The stocky wild ponies whose
Ancestors came with Coronado.
There are no horse bells tonight,
Only the singing of frogs
In the snow-wet meadows, the shrill
Single bark of a mountain
Fox, high in the rocks where the
Wild sheep move silently through the
Crystal moonlight. The same feelings
Come back. Once more all the awe
Of a boy from the prairies where
Lanterns move through the comfortable
Dark, along a fence, through a field,
Home; all the thrill of youth

Suddenly come from the flat
Geometrical streets of
Chicago, into the illimitable
And inhuman waste places
Of the Far West, where the mind finds
Again the forms Pythagoras
Sought, the organic relations
Of stone and cloud and flower
And moving planet and falling
Water. Marthe and Mary sleep
In their down bags, cocoons of
Mutual love. Half my life has
Been passed in the West, much of it
On the ground beside lonely fires
Under the summer stars, and in
Cabins where the snow drifted through
The pines and over the roof.
I will not camp here as often
As I have before. Thirty years
Will never come for me again.
"Our campfire dies out in the
Lonely mountains. The transparent
Moonlight stretches a thousand miles.
The clear peace is without end."
My daughter's deep blue eyes sleep
In the moon shadow. Next week
She will be one year old.

FOR ELI JACOBSON

December, 1952

There are few of us now, soon
There will be none. We were comrades
Together, we believed we
Would see with our own eyes the new
World where man was no longer
Wolf to man, but men and women

Were all brothers and lovers
Together. We will not see it.
We will not see it, none of us.
It is farther off than we thought.
In our young days we believed
That as we grew old and fell
Out of rank, new recruits, young
And with the wisdom of youth,
Would take our places and they
Surely would grow old in the
Golden Age. They have not come.
They will not come. There are not
Many of us left. Once we
Marched in closed ranks, today each
Of us fights off the enemy,
A lonely isolated guerrilla.
All this has happened before,
Many times. It does not matter.
We were comrades together.
Life was good for us. It is
Good to be brave — nothing is
Better. Food tastes better. Wine
Is more brilliant. Girls are more
Beautiful. The sky is bluer
For the brave — for the brave and
Happy comrades and for the
Lonely brave retreating warriors.
You had a good life. Even all
Its sorrows and defeats and
Disillusionments were good,
Met with courage and a gay heart.
You are gone and we are that
Much more alone. We are one fewer,
Soon we shall be none. We know now
We have failed for a long time.
And we do not care. We few will
Remember as long as we can,
Our children may remember,
Some day the world will remember.
Then they will say, "They lived in

The days of the good comrades.
It must have been wonderful
To have been alive then, though it
Is very beautiful now."
We will be remembered, all
Of us, always, by all men,
In the good days now so far away.
If the good days never come,
We will not know. We will not care.
Our lives were the best. We were the
Happiest men alive in our day.

THE BAD OLD DAYS

The summer of nineteen eighteen
I read *The Jungle* and *The
Research Magnificent*. That fall
My father died and my aunt
Took me to Chicago to live.
The first thing I did was to take
A streetcar to the stockyards.
In the winter afternoon,
Gritty and fetid, I walked
Through the filthy snow, through the
Squalid streets, looking shyly
Into the people's faces,
Those who were home in the daytime.
Debauched and exhausted faces,
Starved and looted brains, faces
Like the faces in the senile
And insane wards of charity
Hospitals. Predatory
Faces of little children.
Then as the soiled twilight darkened,
Under the green gas lamps, and the
Sputtering purple arc lamps,
The faces of the men coming

Home from work, some still alive with
The last pulse of hope or courage,
Some sly and bitter, some smart and
Silly, most of them already
Broken and empty, no life,
Only blinding tiredness, worse
Than any tired animal.
The sour smells of a thousand
Suppers of fried potatoes and
Fried cabbage bled into the street.
I was giddy and sick, and out
Of my misery I felt rising
A terrible anger and out
Of the anger, an absolute vow.
Today the evil is clean
And prosperous, but it is
Everywhere, you don't have to
Take a streetcar to find it,
And it is the same evil.
And the misery, and the
Anger, and the vow are the same.

from MARY AND THE SEASONS

SPRING RAIN

The smoke of our campfire lowers
And coagulates under
The redwoods, like low-lying
Clouds. Fine mist fills the air. Drops
Rattle down from all the leaves.
As the evening comes on
The treetops vanish in fog.
Two saw-whet owls utter their
Metallic sobbing cries high
Overhead. As it gets dark
The mist turns to rain. We are

All alone in the forest.
No one is near us for miles.
In the firelight mice scurry
Hunting crumbs. Tree toads cry like
Tiny owls. Deer snort in the
Underbrush. Their eyes are green
In the firelight like balls of
Foxfire. This morning I read
Mei Yao Chen's poems, all afternoon
We walked along the stream through
Woods and meadows full of June
Flowers. We chased frogs in the
Pools and played with newts and young
Grass snakes. I picked a wild rose
For your hair. You brought
New flowers for me to name.
Now it is night and our fire
Is a red throat open in
The profound blackness, full of
The throb and hiss of the rain.

THOU SHALT NOT KILL

A Memorial for Dylan Thomas

I

They are murdering all the young men.
For half a century now, every day,
They have hunted them down and killed them.
They are killing them now.
At this minute, all over the world,
They are killing the young men.
They know ten thousand ways to kill them.
Every year they invent new ones.
In the jungles of Africa,
In the marshes of Asia,
In the deserts of Asia,
In the slave pens of Siberia,
In the slums of Europe,
In the nightclubs of America,
The murderers are at work.

They are stoning Stephen,
They are casting him forth from every city in the world.
Under the Welcome sign,
Under the Rotary emblem,
On the highway in the suburbs,
His body lies under the hurling stones.
He was full of faith and power.
He did great wonders among the people.
They could not stand against his wisdom.
They could not bear the spirit with which he spoke.
He cried out in the name
Of the tabernacle of witness in the wilderness.
They were cut to the heart.
They gnashed against him with their teeth.
They cried out with a loud voice.
They stopped their ears.

They ran on him with one accord.
They cast him out of the city and stoned him.
The witnesses laid down their clothes
At the feet of a man whose name was your name —
You.

You are the murderer.
You are killing the young men.
You are broiling Lawrence on his gridiron.
When you demanded he divulge
The hidden treasures of the spirit,
He showed you the poor.
You set your heart against him.
You seized him and bound him with rage.
You roasted him on a slow fire.
His fat dripped and spurted in the flame.
The smell was sweet to your nose.
He cried out,
"I am cooked on this side,
Turn me over and eat,
You
Eat of my flesh."

You are murdering the young men.
You are shooting Sebastian with arrows.
He kept the faithful steadfast under persecution.
First you shot him with arrows.
Then you beat him with rods.
Then you threw him in a sewer.
You fear nothing more than courage.
You who turn away your eyes
At the bravery of the young men.

You,
The hyena with polished face and bow tie,
In the office of a billion dollar
Corporation devoted to service;
The vulture dripping with carrion,
Carefully and carelessly robed in imported tweeds,
Lecturing on the Age of Abundance;
The jackal in double-breasted gabardine,

Barking by remote control,
In the United Nations;
The vampire bat seated at the couch head,
Notebook in hand, toying with his decerebrator;
The autonomous, ambulatory cancer,
The Superego in a thousand uniforms;
You, the finger man of behemoth,
The murderer of the young men.

II

What happened to Robinson,
Who used to stagger down Eighth Street,
Dizzy with solitary gin?
Where is Masters, who crouched in
His law office for ruinous decades?
Where is Leonard who thought he was
A locomotive? And Lindsay,
Wise as a dove, innocent
As a serpent, where is he?
    Timor mortis conturbat me.

What became of Jim Oppenheim?
Lola Ridge alone in an
Icy furnished room? Orrick Johns,
Hopping into the surf on his
One leg? Elinor Wylie
Who leaped like Kierkegaard?
Sara Teasdale, where is she?
    Timor mortis conturbat me.

Where is George Sterling, that tame fawn?
Phelps Putnam who stole away?
Jack Wheelwright who couldn't cross the bridge?
Donald Evans with his cane and
Monocle, where is he?
    Timor mortis conturbat me.

John Gould Fletcher who could not
Unbreak his powerful heart?
Bodenheim butchered in stinking
Squalor? Edna Millay who took
Her last straight whiskey? Genevieve
Who loved so much; where is she?
     Timor mortis conturbat me.

Harry who didn't care at all?
Hart who went back to the sea?
     Timor mortis conturbat me.

Where is Sol Funaroff?
What happened to Potamkin?
Isidor Schneider? Claude McKay?
Countee Cullen? Clarence Weinstock?
Who animates their corpses today?
     Timor mortis conturbat me.

Where is Ezra, that noisy man?
Where is Larsson whose poems were prayers?
Where is Charles Snider, that gentle
Bitter boy? Carnevali,
What became of him?
Carol who was so beautiful, where is she?
     Timor mortis conturbat me.

III

Was their end noble and tragic,
Like the mask of a tyrant?
Like Agamemnon's secret golden face?
Indeed it was not. Up all night
In the fo'c'sle, bemused and beaten,
Bleeding at the rectum, in his
Pocket a review by the one
Colleague he respected, "If he
Really means what these poems
Pretend to say, he has only

One way out —." Into the
Hot acrid Caribbean sun,
Into the acrid, transparent,
Smoky sea. Or another, lice in his
Armpits and crotch, garbage littered
On the floor, gray greasy rags on
The bed. "I killed them because they
Were dirty, stinking Communists.
I should get a medal." Again,
Another, Simenon foretold,
His end at a glance. "I dare you
To pull the trigger." She shut her eyes
And spilled gin over her dress.
The pistol wobbled in his hand.
It took them hours to die.
Another threw herself downstairs,
And broke her back. It took her years.
Two put their heads under water
In the bath and filled their lungs.
Another threw himself under
The traffic of a crowded bridge.
Another, drunk, jumped from a
Balcony and broke her neck.
Another soaked herself in
Gasoline and ran blazing
Into the street and lived on
In custody. One made love
Only once with a beggar woman.
He died years later of syphilis
Of the brain and spine. Fifteen
Years of pain and poverty,
While his mind leaked away.
One tried three times in twenty years
To drown himself. The last time
He succeeded. One turned on the gas
When she had no more food, no more
Money, and only half a lung.
One went up to Harlem, took on
Thirty men, came home and
Cut her throat. One sat up all night

Talking to H. L. Mencken and
Drowned himself in the morning.
How many stopped writing at thirty?
How many went to work for *Time?*
How many died of prefrontal
Lobotomies in the Communist Party?
How many are lost in the back wards
Of provincial madhouses?
How many on the advice of
Their psychoanalysts, decided
A business career was best after all?
How many are hopeless alcoholics?
René Crevel!
Jacques Rigaud!
Antonin Artaud!
Mayakofsky!
Essenin!
Robert Desnos!
Saint Pol Roux!
Max Jacob!
All over the world
The same disembodied hand
Strikes us down.
Here is a mountain of death.
A hill of heads like the Khans piled up.
The first-born of a century
Slaughtered by Herod.
Three generations of infants
Stuffed down the maw of Moloch.

IV

He is dead.
The bird of Rhiannon.
He is dead.
In the winter of the heart.
He is Dead.
In the canyons of death,
They found him dumb at last,

In the blizzard of lies.
He never spoke again.
He died.
He is dead.
In their antiseptic hands,
He is dead.
The little spellbinder of Cader Idris.
He is dead.
The sparrow of Cardiff.
He is dead.
The canary of Swansea.
Who killed him?
Who killed the bright-headed bird?
You did, you son of a bitch.
You drowned him in your cocktail brain.
He fell down and died in your synthetic heart.
You killed him,
Oppenheimer the Million-Killer,
You killed him,
Einstein the Gray Eminence.
You killed him,
Havanahavana, with your Nobel Prize.
You killed him, General,
Through the proper channels.
You strangled him, Le Mouton,
With your *mains étendues*.
He confessed in open court to a pince-nezed skull.
You shot him in the back of the head
As he stumbled in the last cellar.
You killed him,
Benign Lady on the postage stamp.
He was found dead at a Liberal Weekly luncheon.
He was found dead on the cutting room floor.
He was found dead at a *Time* policy conference.
Henry Luce killed him with a telegram to the Pope.
Mademoiselle strangled him with a padded brassiere.
Old Possum sprinkled him with a tea ball.
After the wolves were done, the vaticides
Crawled off with his bowels to their classrooms
    and quarterlies.
When the news came over the radio

You personally rose up shouting, "Give us Barabbas!"
In your lonely crowd you swept over him.
Your custom-built brogans and your ballet slippers
Pummeled him to death in the gritty street.
You hit him with an album of Hindemith.
You stabbed him with stainless steel by Isamu Noguchi,
He is dead.
He is Dead.
Like Ignacio the bullfighter,
At four o'clock in the afternoon.
At precisely four o'clock.
I too do not want to hear it.
I too do not want to know it.
I want to run into the street,
Shouting, "Remember Vanzetti!"
I want to pour gasoline down your chimneys.
I want to blow up your galleries.
I want to burn down your editorial offices.
I want to slit the bellies of your frigid women.
I want to sink your sailboats and launches.
I want to strangle your children at their finger paintings.
I want to poison your Afghans and poodles.
He is dead, the little drunken cherub.
He is dead,
The effulgent tub thumper.
He is Dead.
The ever living birds are not singing
To the head of Bran.
The sea birds are still
Over Bardsey of Ten Thousand Saints.
The underground men are not singing
On their way to work.
There is a smell of blood
In the smell of the turf smoke.
They have struck him down,
The son of David ap Gwilym.
They have murdered him,
The Baby of Taliessin.
There he lies dead,

By the Iceberg of the United Nations.
There he lies sandbagged,
At the foot of the Statue of Liberty.
The Gulf Stream smells of blood
As it breaks on the sand of Iona
And the blue rocks of Canarvon.
And all the birds of the deep sea rise up
Over the luxury liners and scream,
"You killed him! You killed him.
In your God damned Brooks Brothers suit,
You son of a bitch."

from A BESTIARY

for my daughters, Mary and Katharine

Aardvark

The man who found the aardvark
Was laughed out of the meeting
Of the Dutch Academy.
Nobody would believe him.
The aardvark had its revenge —
It returned in dreams, in smoke,
In anonymous letters.
One day somebody found out
It was in Hieronymus
Bosch all the time. From there it
Had sneaked off to Africa.

Cat

There are too many poems
About cats. Beware of cat
Lovers, they have a hidden
Frustration somewhere and will
Stick you with it if they can.

Fox

The fox is very clever.
In England people dress up
Like a movie star's servants
And chase the fox on horses.
Rather, they let dogs chase him,
And they come along behind.
When the dogs have torn the fox
To pieces they rub his blood
On the faces of young girls.
If you are clever do not
Let anybody know it,
But especially Englishmen.

Goat

G stands for goat and also
For genius. If you are one,
Learn from the other, for he
Combines domestication,
Venery, and independence.

Herring

The herring is prolific.
There are plenty of herrings.
Some herrings are eaten raw.
Many are dried and pickled.
But most are used for manure.
See if you can apply this
To your history lessons.

I

Take care of this. It's all there is.
You will never get another.

Lion

The lion is called the king
Of beasts. Nowadays there are
Almost as many lions
In cages as out of them.
If offered a crown, refuse.

Man

Someday, if you are lucky,
You'll each have one for your own.
Try it before you pick it.
Some kinds are made of soybeans.
Give it lots to eat and sleep.
Treat it nicely and it will
Always do just what you want.

Raccoon

The raccoon wears a black mask,
And he washes everything
Before he eats it. If you
Give him a cube of sugar,
He'll wash it away and weep.
Some of life's sweetest pleasures
Can be enjoyed only if
You don't mind a little dirt.
Here a false face won't help you.

Uncle Sam

Like the unicorn, Uncle
Sam is what is called a myth.
Plato wrote a book which is
An occult conspiracy
Of gentlemen pederasts.
In it he said ideas

Are more nobly real than
Reality, and that myths
Help keep people in their place.
Since you will never become,
Under any circumstances,
Gentlemen pederasts, you'd
Best leave these blood-soaked notions
To those who find them useful.

Unicorn

The unicorn is supposed
To seek a virgin, lay
His head in her lap, and weep,
Whereupon she steals his horn.
Virginity is what is
Known as a privation. It is
Very difficult to find
Any justification for
Something that doesn't exist.
However, in your young days
You might meet a unicorn.
There are not many better
Things than a unicorn horn.

Vulture

St. Thomas Aquinas thought
That vultures were lesbians
And fertilized by the wind.
If you seek the facts of life,
Papist intellectuals
Can be very misleading.

Wolf

Never believe all you hear.
Wolves are not as bad as lambs.
I've been a wolf all my life,
And have two lovely daughters
To show for it, while I could
Tell you sickening tales of
Lambs who got their just deserts.

FISH PEDDLER AND COBBLER

Always for thirty years now
I am in the mountains in
August. For thirty Augusts
Your ghosts have stood up over
The mountains. That was nineteen
Twenty seven. Now it is
Nineteen fifty seven. Once
More after thirty years I
Am back in the mountains of
Youth, back in the Gros Ventres,
The broad park-like valleys and
The tremendous cubical
Peaks of the Rockies. I learned
To shave hereabouts, working
As cookee and night wrangler.
Nineteen twenty two, the years
Of revolutionary
Hope that came to an end as
The iron fist began to close.
No one electrocuted me.
Nothing happened. Time passed.
Something invisible was gone.
We thought then that we were the men
Of the years of the great change,
That we were the forerunners
Of the normal life of mankind.
We thought that soon all things would
Be changed, not just economic
And social relationships, but
Painting, poetry, music, dance,
Architecture, even the food
We ate and the clothes we wore
Would be ennobled. It will take
Longer than we expected.

These mountains are unchanged since
I was a boy wandering
Over the West, picking up
Odd jobs. If anything they are
Wilder. A moose cow blunders
Into camp. Beavers slap their tails
On their sedgy pond as we fish
From on top of their lodge in the
Twilight. The horses feed on bright grass
In meadows full of purple gentian,
And stumble through silver dew
In the full moonlight.
The fish taste of meadow water.
In the morning on far grass ridges
Above the red rim rock wild sheep
Bound like rubber balls over the
Horizon as the noise of camp
Begins. I catch and saddle
Mary's little golden horse,
And pack the first Decker saddles
I've seen in thirty years. Even
The horse bells have a different sound
From the ones in California.
Canada jays fight over
The last scraps of our pancakes.
On the long sandy pass we ride
Through fields of lavender primrose
While lightning explodes around us.
For lunch Mary catches a two pound
Grayling in the whispering river.
No fourteen thousand foot peaks
Are named Sacco and Vanzetti.
Not yet. The clothes I wear
Are as unchanged as the Decker
Saddles on the pack horses.
America grows rich on the threat of death.
Nobody bothers anarchists anymore.
Coming back we lay over
In Ogden for ten hours.
The courthouse square was full

Of miners and lumberjacks and
Harvest hands and gandy dancers
With broken hands and broken
Faces sleeping off cheap wine drunks
In the scorching heat, while tired
Savage eyed whores paraded the street.

from WRITTEN TO MUSIC

Married Blues

I didn't want it, you wanted it.
Now you've got it you don't like it.
You can't get out of it now.

Pork and beans, diapers to wash,
Too poor for the movies, too tired to love.
There's nothing we can do.

Hot stenographers on the subway.
The grocery boy's got a big one.
We can't do anything about it.

You're only young once.
You've got to go when your time comes.
That's how it is. Nobody can change it.

Guys in big cars whistle.
Freight trains moan in the night.
We can't get away with it.

That's the way life is.
Everybody's in the same fix.
It will never be any different.

from THE HEART'S GARDEN, THE GARDEN'S HEART (1967)

II

Pausing in my sixth decade
At the end of a journey
Around the earth—where am I?
I am sitting on a rock
Close beside a waterfall
Above Kurama Hot Springs
In the hills above Kyoto.
So I have sat by hundreds,
In the Adirondacks and
The Green Mountains of Vermont,
In the Massif Central, Alps,
Cascades, Rockies, Sierras,
Even Niagara long, long
Ago in a night of snow.
The water speaks the same language.
It should have told me something
All these years, all these places,
Always saying the same thing.
I should have learned more than I did,
My wit ought to have been more.
I am now older than I was,
In Winters and in lore.
What can I see before me
In the water's smoke and mist?
I should have learned something. "Who
Am I? What can I do? What can I
Hope?" Kant on Euler's bridges
Of dilemma in Koenigsberg.
Somewhere in some topology
The knots untie themselves,
The bridges are all connected.
Is that true? How do you know?
"What is love?" said jesting Pilate
And would not stay for an answer.

I have asked many idle
Questions since the day I could speak.
Now I have many Winters
But very few answers.
Age has me bestolen on
Ere I it wist.
Ne might I see before me
For smoke nor for mist. The smoke
And mist of the waterfall
Shifts and billows. The double
Rainbow remains constant.
There are more years behind me
Than years ahead, and have been
For a very long time. What
Remains in either pan of
The unstable balances of time?
Childbirth, love, and ecstasy
Activate nerves otherwise
Never used and so are hard
To recall, and visions are
The measure of the defect
Of vision. I loved. I saw.
All the way down to Kyoto,
And high above me on all
The ridges are temples full of
Buddhas. This village of stone
Carvers and woodcutters is
Its own illimitable Buddha world.
The illuminated live
Always in light and so do
Not know it is there as fishes
Do not know they live in water.
Under the giant cypresses
Amongst the mossy stones and
Bamboo grass there are white stars
Of dwarf iris everywhere.
The forest is filled with incense.
Boys' Day, the giant wind carp
Float in the breeze of early
Summer over all the houses

Of this mountain village.
The light, cheap, paper ones do.
The more durable cloth ones
Hardly lift and sway at all.
There are rocks on the earth
More durable than the
Constellations of heaven.
Gold leaves of feather bamboo
Fall through the warm wind of May
On to the white rectangle
Of raked gravel in the temple
Garden. Why does the bamboo shed
Its leaves at this time of year?
Smoky, oppressively hot,
The evening comes to an end.
An uguisu sings in the gnarled pine.
The cuckoos call in the ginko trees,
Just like they do in the old poems.
Swallows mate on the telephone wires.
A wood pigeon, speckled like
A quail, drinks from the dew basin.
The new leaves are just coming in.
The bamboos look like green gold smoke.
In the weavers' quarter
Beyond the temple walls,
As the noises of the day cease
I can hear the throb and clack
Of thousands of home looms.
Nishikigi—but no ghosts rise.
Gold fish swim in the moat, red
As fire, they burn in the brown
Water. The moat guards the scriptures
From fire, but the Buddha word
Is burning like the dry grass on
The Indian hills and like the stars.
How easy it is for men
To do right—the submarine
Green of young maple leaves on moss,
Fourteen trees and some earth bare
Of all but moss, and the light

Like Cours Mirabeau in Aix
Before greed destroyed it.
The turtle is the symbol
Of obscenity, but all
The moats that guard the scriptures
Are planted with honorable
Turtles. Turtle-san, protect
The Three Jewels, as the lewd
Pigeons in the air protect
The Great Void. When they rut and beg
In the gravel garden, they fill
Their craws with uncut stones.
"Vectors of reticulation."
We are defined by the webs
Of ten thousand lines of force.
Rocks surrounded by currents
Of raked gravel. Stripes of tigers
Playing in the bamboo shade.
Lichens on ruined dragon stones.
"When I see the wild chrysanthemum
Blooming in the crannies
Of the cliff, I try to forget
The glories of the capital."
The water ouzel walks on
The bottom under the torrent
And builds her nest behind the
Waterfall. Kurama River,
Kaweah River, it is
The same water ouzel although
It is a different species.

VI

The Eve of Ch'ing Ming—Clear Bright,
A quail's breast sky and smoky hills,
The great bronze gong booms in the
Russet sunset. Late tonight

It will rain. Tomorrow will
Be clear and cool once more. One more
Clear, bright day in this floating life.
The slopes of Mt. Hiei are veiled
In haze for the last day of Spring.
Spring mist turns to Summer haze
And hides the distant mountains,
But the first evening breeze
Brings the scent of their flowers.
I say a few words and the haze
Lifts from Mt. Hiei and trees
And temples and climbing people
Stand out as sharp as glass.
Three red pigeons on the sunbaked
Gravel, murmuring like the
Far off voices of people
I loved once. The turtles sleep
On the surface of the moat.
If belief and anxiety,
Covetousness and grasping,
Be banished from experience
Of any object whatever,
Only its essence remains,
Only its ultimate being.
He who lives without grasping
Lives always in experience
Of the immediate as the
Ultimate. The solution
Of the problem of knowing
And being is ethical.
Epistemology is moral.
The rutting cock pigeons fill
Their craws with cob from the wall.
Each has his territory,
Where, already this season,
He has dug a hole as big
As a tea cup. They defend
The holes against intrusion
Like they quarrel over the hens.
The knot tied without a rope

Cannot be untied. The seven
Bridges of Koenigsberg cannot
Be crossed but you can always
Go for a swim in the river.
The lower leaves of the trees
Tangle the sunset in dusk.
Awe perfumes the warm twilight.
St. John of the Cross said it,
The desire for vision is
The sin of gluttony.
The bush warbler sings in the
Ancient white pine by the temple
Of the Buddha of Healing.

X

The sound of gongs, the songs of birds,
The chanting of men, floating wisps
Of incense, drifting pine smoke,
Perfume of the death of Spring—
The warm breeze clouds the mirror
With the pollen of the pines,
And thrums the strings of the lute.
Higher in the mountains the
Wild cherry is still blooming.
The driving mist tears away
And scatters the last petals,
And tears the human heart. Altair
and Vega climb to the zenith.
A long whistling wail on the flute,
The drummer makes a strangling cry.
And to the clacking of the sticks,
The weaving girl dances for
Her cowboy far across the
Cloudy River. Wings waver
And break. Pine boughs sigh in the
Dark. The water of life runs
Quick through dry reeds.

Under the full moon, a piercing
Fragrance spreads through the white night
Like the perfume of new snow.
An unknown tree has blossomed
Outside my cabin window.
In the warm night cold air drains
Down the mountain stream and fills
The summer valley with the
Incense of early Spring. I
Remember a grass hut on
A rainy night, dreaming of
The past, and my tears starting
At the cry of a mountain cuckoo.
Her bracelets tinkle, her anklets
Clink. She sways at her clattering
Loom. She hurries to have a new
Obi ready when he comes—
On the seventh day of the seventh
Month when the pachinko balls
Fall like meteor swarms.
 Click clack click click clack click
Cho Cho
 Click clack click click clack click
Cho Cho
 Toak. tolk. tock. toak. toik. tok. tok.
Chidori. Chidori.
Kannon. Kannon.
The great hawk went down the river
In the twilight. The belling owl
Went up the river in the
Moonlight. He returns to
Penelope, the wanderer
Of many devices, to
The final woman who weaves,
And unweaves, and weaves again.
In the moon drenched night the floating
Bridge of dreams breaks off. The clouds
Banked against the mountain peak
Dissipate in the clear sky.

from NEW POEMS (1974)

Now the starlit moonless Spring

Now the starlit moonless Spring
Night stands over the Fontaine
De Medicis, and the gold
Fish swim in the cold, starlit
Water. Yesterday, in the
New sunshine, lovers sat by
The water, and talked, and fed
The goldfish, and kissed each other.
I am in California
And evening is coming on.
Now it is morning in Paris
By the Fontaine de Medicis.
And the lovers will come today,
And talk and kiss, and feed the fish,
After they have had their coffee.

I DREAM OF LESLIE

You entered my sleep,
Come with your immense,
Luminous eyes,
And light brown hair,
Across fifty years,
To sing for me again that song
Of Campion's we loved so once.
I kissed your quivering throat.
There was no hint in the dream
That you were long, long since
A new arrivéd guest,
With blithe Helen, white Iope and the rest—
Only the peace
Of late afternoon

In a compassionate autumn
In youth.
And I forgot
That I was old and you a shade.

LA VIE EN ROSE

Fog fills the little square
Between Avenue du Maine
And the Gaité Montparnasse.
I walk around and around,
Waiting for my girl.
My footsteps echo
From the walls
Of the second storeys.
Deep in the future
My ghost follows me,
Around and around.

SUCHNESS

In the theosophy of light,
The logical universal
Ceases to be anything more
Than the dead body of an angel.
What is substance? Our substance
Is whatever we feed our angel.
The perfect incense for worship
Is camphor, whose flames leave no ashes.

from ON FLOWER WREATH HILL (1976)

I

An aging pilgrim on a
Darkening path walks through the
Fallen and falling leaves, through
A forest grown over the
Hilltop tumulus of a
Long dead princess, as the
Moonlight grows and the daylight
Fades and the Western Hills turn
Dim in the distance and the
Lights come on, pale green
In the streets of the hazy city.

I V

No leaf stirs. I am alone
In the midst of a hundred
Empty mountains. Cicadas,
Locusts, katydids, crickets,
Have fallen still, one after
Another. Even the wind
Bells hang motionless. In the
Blue dusk, widely spaced snowflakes
Fall in perfect verticals.
Yet, under my cabin porch,
The thin, clear Autumn water
Rustles softly like fine silk.

V

This world of ours, before we
Can know its fleeting sorrows,
We enter it through tears.
Do the reverberations
Of the evening bell of
The mountain temple ever
Totally die away?
Memory echoes and reechoes
Always reinforcing itself.
No wave motion ever dies.
The white waves of the wake of
The boat that rows away into
The dawn, spread and lap on the
Sands of the shores of all the world.

from THE SILVER SWAN (1978)

I V

Under the half moon
The field crickets are silent.
Only the cricket
Of the hearth still sings, louder
Still, behind the gas heater.

XIV

Hototogisu—horobirete

The cuckoo's call, though
Sweet in itself, is hard to
Bear, for it cries,
"Perishing! Perishing!"
Against the Spring.

XIX

The drowned moon plunges
Through a towering surf
Of storm clouds, and momently
The wet leaves glitter.
Moment by moment an owl cries.
Rodents scurry, building
Their winter nests, in the moments of dark.

from THE LOVE POEMS OF MARICHIKO
(1978)

VII

Making love with you
Is like drinking sea water.
The more I drink
The thirstier I become,
Until nothing can slake my thirst
But to drink the entire sea.

IX

You wake me,
Part my thighs, and kiss me.
I give you the dew
Of the first morning of the world.

XXV

Your tongue thrums and moves
Into me, and I become
Hollow and blaze with
Whirling light, like the inside
Of a vast expanding pearl.

XXVII

As I came from the
Hot bath, you took me before

The horizontal mirror
Beside the low bed, while my
Breasts quivered in your hands, my
Buttocks shivered against you.

XXXI

Some day in six inches of
Ashes will be all
That's left of our passionate minds,
Of all the world created
By our love, its origin
And passing away.

XXXII

I hold your head tight between
My thighs, and press against your
Mouth, and float away
Forever, in an orchid
Boat on the River of Heaven.

XXXIII

I cannot forget
The perfumed dusk inside the
Tent of my black hair,
As we awoke to make love
After a long night of love.

from THE HOMESTEAD CALLED DAMASCUS
(1920–1925)

I

Heaven is full of definite stars
And crowded with modest angels, robed
In tubular, neuter folds of pink and blue.
Their feet tread doubtless on that utter
Hollowness, with never a question
Of the "ineluctable modality"
Of the invisible; busy, orderly,
Content to ignore the coal pockets
In the galaxy, dark nebulae,
And black broken windows into space.
Youthful minds may fret infinity,
Moistly dishevelled, poking in odd
Corners for unsampled vocations
Of the spirit, while the flesh is strong.
Experience sinks its roots in space—
Euclidean, warped, or otherwise.
The will constructs rhomboids, nonagons,
And paragons in time to suit each taste.
Or, if not the will, then circumstance.
History demands satisfaction,
And never lacks, with or without help
From the subjects of its curious science.

Thomas Damascan and the mansion,
A rambling house with Doric columns
On the upper Hudson in the Catskills,
Called Damascus. We were walking there
Once in early Spring; his brother Sebastian
Said, staring into the underbrush,
"If you'll look close you'll see the panthers
In there eating the crocus." And Thomas said,
"Panthers are always getting into
The crocus. Every spring. There were too many
Panthers about the courts in my father's time."

They had an odd wry sort of family humor
That startled idle minds and plagued your
Memory for years afterwards.
We sat up late that night drinking wine,
Playing chess, arguing—Plato and Leibnitz,
Einstein, Freud and Marx, and woke at noon.
The next day was grey and rained till twilight,
And ice from somewhere in the Adirondacks
Drifted soggily down the river.
In the afternoon Sebastian read
The Golden Bough, and Thomas said,
"Remember, in school, after we read Frazer,
I insisted on signing myself Tammuz,
To the horror of all our teachers?"
"And now," he said, "We're middle aged, wise,"
(They were very far from middle aged.)
"And what we thought once was irony
Is simple fact, simple, sensuous,
And so forth. Fate is a poor scholar."
We said nothing, and the three of us
Watched the rain fall through the budding trees,
Until at last Thomas rose and took
A bow from the rack, sprung it, and said,
"I wish we could shoot these things in the rain."
Sebastian said, "I'd much rather shoot
In the sunshine, and besides it spoils
The arrows. I'm going for a hike."
So we went off through the hanging woods,
Single file, and up the steep meadow,
Scratched by thistles, in a thistle wind—
Last year's thistles, and a pungent wind.
Thomas said, "We've got to move the goats
Before they ruin all the pasture.
There'll be nothing but thistles next year."
Sebastian said, "Thistles or blue grass,
Goats or cattle, what does it matter,
We'll have to die quick to be buried here."
The goats hurried ahead up the slope,
Stopped among the rocks and there gave us
Their clinical goatish regard.

We climbed to the top of the Pope's Nose
And stood looking out at the river,
Slaty in the rain, and the traffic
Wallowing on the muddy highway,
And beneath us in the closed hollow,
The swollen carp ponds, the black water
Flowing through the clattering rushes,
And, poised each on one cold leg, two herons,
Staring over their puckered shoulders
At a hieroglyph of crows in the distance.

. . . .

II

THE AUTUMN OF MANY YEARS
. . . .

How short a time for a life to last.
So few years, so narrow a space, so
Slight a melody, a handful of
Notes. Most of it dreams and dreamless sleep,
And solitary walks in empty
Parks and foggy streets. Or all alone,
In the midst of nightstruck, excited
Crowds. Once in a while one of them
Spoke, or a face smiled, but not often.
One or two could recall the tune if asked.
Now she is gone. Hooded candles in
The Spring wind tilt and move down the
Narrow columned aisle. Incense plumes whirl.
Thuribles clink. The last smoke dissolves
Above the rain soaked hills, the black pines,
Broken by a flock of migrating birds.

Thomas climbed the ice and crossed the pass.
Coneys whistled in the shrill air. Ice
And rock and indigo sky—Enoch
Walked the hills and waged war on substance

In the vertical. Is it best to
Remember always the same memory,
To see the world always in the same hour?
Good Friday, incense and hooded candles.
Sebastian descends the wet hillside
Into the coiling river fog. He
Sinks from sight into the hidden world.
And on the mountain crest the tattered
Crows wheel like an apparition
In a fog as serpentine and cold,
And much more opaque, and unseen caw
And caw. This hour the sacramental
Man was broken on the height, in dark
Opacity rent with caw and caw.

Thomas, called Tammuz, the first
Of twins, "the beloved one," the one
Called Didymus in the upper room—
The involuntary active man—
Peers in the black wounds, hammers the frame
That squeezes the will. The arrow breaks.
He breaks the gold arrow in the gold
Light. The arrow breaks the brittle flesh,
Breaking upon it. Baldur in the
Autumn, the image of the twin.
The Autumn light, the level lawn.
Modred, Iscariot, Loki cross
Beyond the Catskills. Sebastian drinks
Cold astringent tea in the damp
Summer house above the hazy river.

III

THE DOUBLE HELLAS

> *Claret enim claris quod clare concopulator*

. . . .

The world is composed of a pair of
Broken pillars, a round sun in a

Rigid sky, a sea, and in the great
Distance, a red line of cliffs. The world
Is composed of a pair of broken
Pillars, of pillars, of a suave line
Conceived in a mind infinitely
Refined by edges infinitely
Sharp. The world is composed. There is a
Little boat upon the sea, a striped
Sail. They raise a net from the bright sea
And go away rowing with the wind.
Recently awe and precision hung
In this landscape, the keen edge of pride,
The suave line, the Doric mind. Voices
Of children come up the steep valley.
A blur of smoke smudges the skyline.
"Come back, baby, I miss your little
Brown body and your childish ways."
"Hush, Chloris, heed not the stars
Narcissistically parading
There above the mannered pools."
You can always find pity
And terror amongst the broken
Statuary. Whose profiles
Coin the wind? The Bactrian
Kings. Pisanello's courtesans.
The whole sky is made of gold.
The dancing master in a
Castled wig, Priapus in
The vines. The soft sliding eyes.
"Ah, Chloris, heed not the stars,
The smoky shattering fountains
In the teeming night."

My parents had their life, it was not
Your soft dark tragedy. It was not
Anything like it. Saffron twilights
Over the gas lit horse drawn city.
Purple and gold above the desert.
When they were sad, they shut their mouths tight.
When God spoke to Job from the whirlwind

He refused to answer his questions—
On the advice of his attorney.
The rainbow mountains glitter in
The breaking prism. Within the mirror
Of ice, pain speaks to sorrow outside.
And now the sun has set and the strange
Blake-like forms fade from our memories.
The sky was deeper than a ruby.
The hoarfrost spreads over the marshes
Like a mandolin note over water.
Between the mountains a candle burned.
A narrow leaf of flame casting no
Light about it. The epic hero
Came, in full armor, making a huge
Clatter, and fell, struck down from behind,
And lay in the barren eternal
Dawn, geometrically prostrate,
As the clock ticks measured out his death—
As the spouting flame leaped from roof to
Roof and all the houses full of ticking
Clocks caught fire one after another.

. . . .

IV

THE STIGMATA OF FACT
. . . .

Morphology repeats ontology.
Thomas drank all night and read John of the Cross.
He was drunk and forsaken before
Dawn. At daylight he went out through the
Lion Gate and bought a ticket for
Knossos, where the women paint their breasts
And the men use perfume and the girls
Mate with bulls. The crowd boiled around him,
Lonely as beasts in a slaughter house.
The period grew blackly backward
Across its sentence. Theseus died

129

At last in a vulgar brawl. The priests,
Stinking of perfume, got him ready.
Why these overstained contortionist
Tricks? Archaeologists have proved
The Minotaur a lie, the labyrinth
A vast grocery store, Knossos so mild
It went unwalled. Even the Easter
Island anthropoliths were harmless
Statues of the royal kinfolks. Near
To us, nearer than the lamps that lit
The ceilings of Altamira and Dordogne,
The uncanny geomorphous companions wait—
Maybe, but today his theromorphs
Have outlasted every Pharaoh.

Saturday night, rain falls in the slums.
Rain veils the tired hurrying faces,
Sordid and beautiful in the rain.
Sebastian walks, puzzled, in the rain.
This is the macrocosm, on these
Materials it subsists. And the
Microcosm—This is the very thing.
There is no self that suffers rebirth.
Few trigliths of Stonehenge still stand there
In that immense windy nightbound plain.
It is cold after the summer rain.
"This is the place," she says, "Let's eat here."
She turns against him, warm and firm, rain
On her brown cheeks and odorous hair.
When he got home his cheeks were bronze, too,
As though with fever rather than sun,
His beard grizzled, his hair thinner.
The old dog discovered him and died.
The evil rivals died. The web flew wide.
And this was the little brother, the
Holy comedian, offering
Him the password at which all rusted
Hinges fall. This is the place where knowledge
Was so close to poplars and to stones.

Thomas looks out over the valley.
Far off in the low mists and fireflies
The lights along the railroad track change.
Then the whistle comes as distant as
A star and finally the distant
Roar and like a diamond necklace falling
Through the long somber valley the lighted
Cars, pulsating and slipping away
And the headlight twisting into the
Dimness like a cold needle. All so
Far away, not like a toy train but
Like some bright micro organism,
The night train to Omaha goes by.
Then Thomas quiets the zebra dun,
Tends the bannock and the tea and turns
The bacon. Grey low shapes of night bulk
Slow and make their own horizon. White
Ash flakes fall from the heart of the fire.
Now far, now near, the chuck-will's-widows
Call. Thomas smokes and spits into the
Fire. Bats cry, the creaking of the hundred,
Tiny, closing doors of silence.

from A PROLEGOMENON TO A THEODICY*
(1925–1927)

II

We were interested in ways of being
We saw lives
We saw animals
We saw agile rodents
Scala rodent
The harmonic pencil
Scala rodent
Emits its fundamental
The stricken plethora
A bottle of water against a very blue sky
A toppling shutter
The final peninsulas of space
Germinate in the secret ovoid perimeter
e.g.: scholia
The white hill
Elastic fatigue
The white lax hill and immediately the iced antelope
The line warps
The meridian of least resistance ascends the sky
The brain ferments
The curdled brain
The repercussion
The bullweaver
Obsessed by an ideograph
A mechanical bracelet
A small diesel engine
First one and then the other
Air congeals in water
The mural rift
A kind of going

*A long excerpt from this poem was originally published in *An "Objectivists" Anthology* (Le Beausset: To Publishers, 1932).

The little block falls
The little wooden block
That long snarl of coast on the Mediterranean
The heart inclines
The four triangles
The fifth
The fingers jerk
The green cheek
The fourth
The image in the portal
The resin curls
The soggy mitten
The third
The cleaved cough
The second
The closing ribs
The first
The double envoi
The grackle breaks
Sweat
The diverse arrows
The anagogic eye

III

This is the winter of the hardest year
And did you dream
The white the large
The slow movement
The type of dream
The terror
The stumble stone
The winter the snow that was there
The neck and the hand
The head
The snow that was in the air
The long sun
The exodus of thought
The enervated violin

The oiled temples
The singing song and the sung
The lengthy home
The trundling endless stairs
The young stone
Homing and the song
The air that was there
Flayed jaws piled on the steps
The twirling rain
And laying they repeat the horizon
Ineffably to know how it goes swollen and then not swollen
Cold and then too warm
So many minor electrocutions
So many slaps of nausea
The keen eyelids
The abrupt diastole
That leaves you wondering
Why it was ever despite their assurances unlocked
Stars like lice along the scalp
The brain pan bitten burning
And dull on one foot
And dull on one foot
O cry aloud
O teeth unbound
Don't you know that the stone walk alone
Do you know the shredded brow
Are you aware
Do you take this forever concentric bland freezing to touch
Let the scarlet rustle
Let the globes come down
Let the oblate spheroids fall infinitely away
Forever away always falling but you can always see them
The creak
The squeak that makes you so slightly open your mouth
Patiently to be strangled
It is gone away somewhere
It is Winter
Reason
Winter
Ache

IX

a

The bell
Too softly and too slowly tolled
And the first wave was snow
The second ice
The third fire
The fourth blood
The fifth adders
The sixth smother
The seventh foul stink
And unnumbered beasts swam in the sea
Some feather footed
Some devoid of any feet
And all with fiery eyes
And phosphorescent breath
The enduring bell
The wash of wave
The wiry cranes that stagger in the air
The hooded eyes struggling in the confused littoral
The smoky cloak
Those who walk
Those who are constrained
Those who watch the hole of wavering dark
There is no order in expectation
The feet fall
Even the enemy of cold labor
Of the mighty tongue
The gull matted on the sand
Worms spilling out of the beak
The cervical agony
Unplumbed and unforgotten caves
A cry sent up in expectation
A mouth filling the sky
Shaping the words of the victor
The bell
A voice
Blessed are the dead who die
The generations of generations

b

They were in an unstable condition
Floating about in a putrid fog
Throughout the tangled forest
Between the charred trunks
Over the yellow marshes
Some squirmed after the manner of lizards
Some were upright with their arms held up
Some lay with their knees partly drawn up
Some lay on their sides
Some lay stretched at full length
Some lay on their backs
Some were stooping
Some held their heads bent down
Some drew up their legs
Some embraced
Some kicked out with arms and legs
Some were kneeling
Some stood and inhaled deep breaths
Some crawled
Some walked
Some felt about in the dark
Some arose
Some gazed, sitting still

d

Light
Light
The sliver in the firmament
The stirring horde
The rocking wave
The name breaks in the sky
Why stand we
Why go we nought
They broken seek the cleaving balance
The young men gone
Lux lucis
The revolving company

The water flowing from the right side
Et fons luminis
The ciborium of the abyss
The bread of light
The chalice of the byss
The wine of flaming light
The wheeling multitude
The rocking cry
The reverberant scalar song lifts up
The metric finger aeon by aeon
And the cloud of memory descends
The regnant fruitful vine
The exploding rock
The exploding mountain cry
Tris agios
The sapphire snow
Hryca hryca nazaza

NOTES

The following notes are intended as a guide to some of the more difficult references in the poems included in this volume and not as comprehensive commentary.

from IN WHAT HOUR (1940)

August 22, 1939
Nicola Sacco: Nicola Sacco and Bartolomeo Vanzetti, both immigrants and radicals, were arrested for robbery and the murder of two employees of a shoe factory in South Braintree, Massachusetts, in April 1920. Their conviction stirred a public outcry joined by many prominent writers and intellectuals. They were executed on August 23, 1937.

Angst und Gestalt und Gebet: The last line of the poem "Erinnerung" ("Remembering") by Rainer Marie Rilke (1875–1926) translates from the German, "Anguish and form and prayer."

Pisgah: Mountain at the northern end of the Dead Sea (highest elevation, 2,644 ft.) from which Moses viewed the promised land but could not enter (Deut. 3:27, 4:29).

"From each according to . . . need": Karl Marx, *Critique of the Gotha Program,* I.

Kropotkin: Pyotr Kropotkin (1842–1921), Russian revolutionary, a leader and theorist of the anarchist movement, died disenchanted with the Bolsheviks.

Berkman: Alexander Berkman (1870–1936), American anarchist, who attempted to assassinate Henry Clay Frick. Eventually he was deported in 1919 with Emma Goldman for agitation against conscription and traveled to Russia, but left in 1921 disillusioned with the Bolshevik revolution. He committed suicide when he learned he had cancer.

Fanny Baron: Fanya Baron, Russian anarchist, executed by the Bolsheviks on September 30, 1921.

Mahkno: Nester Mahkno (1889–1935), Russian anarchist, who led the revolt against the German occupation of the Ukraine during World War I. The Bolsheviks eventually purged Mahnko and exiled in Paris he died in poverty, obscurity, and bitterness.

A *Lesson in Geography*
"of Paradys ne can I speken . . .": From *The Travels of Sir John Mandeville*, a mid-fourteenth century account of the East. Originally written in French, it was translated into English, Latin, and German.

Boötes: the "plowman," a constellation.

"Moonlight on ruined castles" / Kojo n'suki: Title in English and Japanese of a poem by Doi Bansui (1871–1952), pseudonym of Tsuchii Rinkichi. It was set to music by Taki Rentarō and made famous.

from THE PHOENIX AND THE TORTOISE (1944)

Plutarch's page . . . Agis, Cleomenes: Plutarch (*c.* A.D. 46–c. *120*), Greek biographer and moral philosopher. His *Parallel Lives* relates the lives of eminent Greek and Roman statesmen and soldiers. Agis and Cleomenes were kings of Sparta in the second century B.C., and they are usually paired nineteenth in Plutarch's *Lives*.

existence / And essence . . . Of Aquinas: St. Thomas Aquinas (*c.* 1225–74), Italian scholastic, Dominican friar, and Christian theologian.

Ptahs: Ptah in Egyptian mythology is the creator and chief god of Memphis, and the father of Ra, the sun.

Jacob struggled . . . another name: Jacob, having wrestled with an angel, was given the name of Israel (Gen. 32:24–28).

the rose / Outlives Ausonius, Ronsard, / And Waller: Decimus Magnus Ausonius (*c.* 310–95), Roman poet born in Bordeaux; Pierre de Ronsard (1524–85), French lyric poet, the principal figure in the "Pléiade"; Edmund Waller (1606–87), English poet. The rose is a frequent image in their poetry, but see especially, Ausonius, *De rosis nascentibus*; Ronsard's sonnets "Comme on voit sur la branch au mois de May la rose" (*Les Amours*), "Quand vous serez bien vielle, au soir à la chandelle" (*Sonnets pour Hélène*), and *Ode à Cassandre*; Waller's "Go, lovely Rose!"

Horace: (65–8 B.C.), Roman poet. Cf. "I have built me a monument more lasting than bronze" (*Odes*, Book III, XXX, line 1).

Christopher Wren: (1631–1723), English architect, designer of St. Paul's Cathedral.

Richelieu: Armand Jean du Plessi, Duc de Richelieu (1585–1642), French statesman and chief minister to Louis XIII.

Whymper . . . "About 6 PM . . .": Edward Whymper (1840–1911) was the first to climb the Matterhorn in 1865. During the descent four members of the climb fell to their deaths. Account quoted by Rexroth is from Whymper's book, *Scrambles Among the Alps in the Years 1860–69.*

When We With Sappho
". . . about the cool waters . . .": Rexroth's translation of Sappho's apple tree fragment.

Lute Music
All the bright neige d'antan people: The refrain to François Villon's (1431–c. 1463) "Ballade des dames du temps jadis" ("Ballad of the Ladies of Bygone Times") in *The Testament* is "Mais ou sont les neiges d'antan?" ("But where are the snows of yesteryear?").

"Blithe Helen, white Iope, and the rest": Iope is the wife of Theseus or Aeolus' daughter.

from THE SIGNATURE OF ALL THINGS (1950)

Lyell's Hypothesis Again
Lyell, *Principles of Geology:* Sir Charles Lyell (1797–1875), leading geologist of early to midVictorian Britain. His greatest contribution to the field was to prove that the landscape of Earth's surface (e.g., mountains) is produced over millions of years, often imperceptibly, by natural processes, thus refuting the "catastrophic" theory of change. His work influenced Darwin. *The Principles of Geology* was published in 1830–33.

Nessus' shirt: The shirt dipped in the blood of the centaur Nessus, which when worn by Hercules caused him unbearable pain, and led to his death.

Delia Rexroth
Michael Field's book, *Long Ago:* Michael Field is the psuedonym of Katharine Harris Bradley (1846–1914) and Edith Emma Cooper (1862–1913). *Long Ago* (1889) is a volume of poetry in which fragments by Sappho were expanded into poems.

Andrée Rexroth
Henry King's *Exequy:* Henry King (1592–1669), bishop of Chichester and author of verses sacred and profane. "An Exequy to his Matchlesse never to be forgotten Friend" was written on the occasion of the death of Ann King, his wife.

Yuan Chen's great poem: Possibly an allusion to "Three Dreams at Chiang-ling" by the Chinese poet Yuan Chen (779–831), which describes the dreams of a husband for his dead wife, usually understood as referring to the poet and his wife.

Isar: River in Austria and Germany, which bisects Munich and flows into the Danube.

A Letter to William Carlos Williams
Brother Juniper: One of the original followers of St. Francis of Assisi (1182–1226).

The girls of the Anthology: *The Greek Anthology* is a collection of approximately 6,000 short elegiac poems, epigrams, etc., by more than 300 writers from the 7th century B.C. to the 10th century A.D.

Anyte: Greek poetess, active *c.* 290 B.C., whose verses are included in *The Greek Anthology.*

George Fox: (1624–91), founder of the Society of Friends, or Quakers. His *Journal*, published in 1694, narrates his spiritual experiences and the persecutions of his followers.

from THE DRAGON AND THE UNICORN (1952)

The plow in the furrow, Burns: Robert Burns (1759–96), Scottish poet. See "To a Mouse: On Turning her up in her Nest with the Plough, November 1785."

Chiron: Centaur who taught Achilles and many other heroes of Greek mythology.

What Marvell meant by desarts . . . : Andrew Marvell (1621–78), English metaphysical poet. See "To His Coy Mistress."

Die Ausrottung der Besten: German; "the extermination of the best."

Stink of Papacy: The curia resided in Avignon beginning with Pope Clement V in 1309, until Gregory XI re-established it in Rome in 1377. During the papal schism (1378–1417), two anti-popes, Clement VII and Benedict XII, resided in Avignon.

Fromentin: Eugene Fromentin (1820–76), French painter and novelist, best known for his pictorial scenes of Algeria and his novel, *Dominique*.

King René: René of Provence (1408–80), known as "le bon Roi René," son of Louis II, duke of Anjou, and titular king of Naples, the Two Sicilies, and Jerusalem.

author of *Le Rideau levé* / Approached . . . by / Sade: Honoré-Gabriel de Riqueti, comte de Mirabeau (1749–91), orator and statesman in the National Assembly, and author of *Le Rideau levé ou l'Education de Laure* (*The Raised Curtain or the Education of Laura*). Mirabeau was jailed in Vincennes in 1777, where he quarreled with the Marquis de Sade (1740–1814), who had been jailed for having given prostitutes candy laced with the aphrodisiac Spanish fly.

Granet painting in Rome: François Marius Granet (1775–1849), French painter, born and died in Aix-en-Provence, went to Rome in 1802. Granet established a museum in Aix which bears his name, and in which hangs his portrait of Ingres (French painter, 1780–1867) and his *Un quart-d'heure avant l'office* of a dying man.

Milhaud: Darius Milhaud (1892–1974), born in Aix-en-Provence, French composer, one of "Les Six," and especially known for his development of polytonality and uses of American jazz.

Deux Magots: Literary and artistic café in Paris on the Boulevard Saint-Germain, since the 1920s.

Boswell: "Sir, what is the chief / Virtue?" . . . : Adapted from James Boswell's *Life of Johnson* (Wednesday, April 5, 1775): "Johnson: . . . Whereas, Sir, you know courage is reckoned the greatest of all virtues; because, unless a man has that virtue, he has no security for preserving any other."

Simone Martini: (*c.* 1284–1344), Sienese painter.

Bronzino: Agnolo Bronzino (1503–72), Florentine painter, court painter to Cosimo I de' Medici and important Mannerist portrait painter.

Taddis and Gaddis: Taddeo Gaddi (*c.* 1300–*c.* 1366), Florentine painter. There is no painter by the name of Taddi, though there is another contemporary painter of the name Bernardo Daddi (*c.* 1290–1349). Both were pupils of Giotto.

Masaccio: Tómmaso di Giovanni di Simone Guidi, known as Masaccio (1401–*c.* 1428), Florentine painter, who advanced the art of perspective.

Shekinah: A word used frequently in Jewish mysticism to mean the immanent principle, feminine aspect of God. (Hebrew meaning, "that which dwells or resides.")

The sephiroth of the Kabbalah: The sephiroth are the ten attributes or emanations by means of which the Infinite enters into relation with the finite.

the chakras of the Tantra: The *Tantras*, Sanskrit religious books (6th and 7th centúries A.D.), form the basis of a Hindu cult whose adherents worship Shiva's wife, Parvati, the female spirit. The *Tantras* are mostly in the form of dialogues between Shiva and Parvati and contain one of the most elaborate spiritual systems in the whole of Hindu tradition. *Tantra* is Sanskrit for thread or warp, and *chakra* a spinning wheel.

Hafidh: Hafiz (1325–89), Persian lyric poet.

Rumi: Maulānā Jalāl-uddīn Rūmī (1207–73), greatest Sufi poet of Persia.

St. Theresa: St. Theresa of Avila (1515–82), Spanish Carmelite nun, famous for her mystical writing and visions.

Agathias Sholasticus: A Greek poet and historian in the age of Justinian (5th century A.D.), of whose reign he wrote a history in five books.

Filippino's / Weary lady: Filippino Lippi (c. 1457–1504), Florentine painter and son of Fra Lippo Lippi. His painting *Apparition of the Virgin to St. Bernard* (1486) is in the Badia in Florence.

"Too many nakeds for a chapel,"/Said Evelyn: John Evelyn (1620–1706), principally remembered by his *Diary*, which describes his travels on the Continent. Quotation probably a reference to Evelyn's comments on the Sistine Chapel: "Now we came into the Popes Chapell, so much celebrated for the Judgement painted by M: Angelo Buonarti . . . of vast designe and miraculous fantasy, considering the multitude of Nakeds, & variety of posture." (January 18, 1645)

Benjamin West: (1730–1820), American painter.

Says Evelyn, "Turning to the right . . .": See Evelyn's *Diary*, February 23–24, 1645.

Cineasti and Milioni: Italian, "film makers and the millions."

"La mauvaise conscience . . . 'denature.' " / So Bakunin says: Mikhail Aleksandrovich Bakunin (1814–76), chief proponent of nineteenth-century anarchism, prominent Russian revolutionary, and antagonist of Marx. Bakunin believed in the virtues of violence and the value of terrorism. Quotation translates from the French as, "The bad faith of the bourgeois, I have said, paralyzed the entire intellectual and moral movement of the bourgeoisie. I correct myself and replace the word 'paralyzed' by another: 'falsified.' "

"The bourgeoisie, wherever . . .": See Marx and Engels, "Bourgeois and Proletarians," *Manifesto to the Communist Party*.

For Dante / Usury was . . . its heirs: See *Inferno*, Cantos XV, XVII, and XVIII.

The Taoist uncut block: The uncut block represents the concept of man's original nature, free of all hostility and aggressiveness, inherent in newborn infants.

"A, E, I, O, U—the spheres . . .": See Arthur Rimbaud's (1854–91) Symbolist poem, "Voyelles" ("Vowels"), in which the vowels are given colors: A black, E white, I red, O blue, U green.

Japan, the goddess / Of the sun: The sun goddess, Amaterasu Ōmikama, holds the highest place in the Shintō pantheon and is the progenitor of the imperial line in mythology.

The doctrine of Signatures: The philosophical system of the German mystic Jacob Boehme (1575–1624).

The Smaragdine Tablet: The *Smaragdine Table* is a medieval Latin work on alchemy (published 1541), attributed to the Egyptian Hermes Trismegistus.

"The children have put purple . . .": A dedicatory epigram by Anyte from *The Greek Anthology*.

pronaos: Greek, "church vestibule."

naos: Greek, "church."

Bashō's frog: Matsuo Bashō (1644–94), Japanese haiku poet. A well-known and often translated haiku of his is:
> An old pond—
> The sound
> Of a diving frog.

Shiva: In Hindu mythology, Shiva represents the destructive principle in life and also the power of reproduction.

from THE LIGHTS IN THE SKY ARE STARS

A *Living Pearl*
"It is as though . . . itself uncleft.": Dante, *Paradiso*, Canto II.

from MARY AND THE SEASONS

Mei Yao Chen's poems: (1002–60), Chinese poet under the Sung dynasty. Mei's wife died in 1044 at the age of thirty-six, and two of his children died as infants. Their deaths moved him to write some of the finest poems of personal emotion in Chinese literature.

Thou Shalt Not Kill

I

Lawrence: St. Lawrence, martyr, charged with the care of the poor, was summoned by the Roman governor to deliver up the church's treasures, and he delivered his poor. Lawrence was roasted on a gridiron.

II

Leonard: William Ellery Leonard (1876–1944), American poet, essayist, and teacher, whose autobiography was entitled *The Locomotive-God* (1927).

Timor mortis conturbat me: Refrain to the poem "Lament of the Makaris," by William Dunbar, a Scottish Chaucerian poet (*c.* 1460–*c.* 1520), which translates from the Latin as "The fear of death troubles me." The "Lament" records a litany of dead poets ("makaris"), beginning with Chaucer.

Jim Oppenheim: James Oppenheim (1882–1932), American poet and novelist, who lived in Greenwich Village. He died of tuberculosis.

Lola Ridge: (1871–1941), Irish-born poet, came to the United States from Australia in 1907. Editor of *Broom*, she was active in the defense of Sacco and Vanzetti.

bird of Rhiannon: In Welsh mythology, Rhiannon had three birds who, singing, could bring the dead to life or likewise kill.

mains etendues: French; "outstretched hands."

Ignacio the bullfighter: The subject of Federico García Lorca's poem "Lament for Ignacio Sanchez Mejias."

Bran: The dog of Fingal in James Macpherson's (1735–96) Ossianic poem "Temora."

Taliesin: Welsh poet, a semimythical figure, who reputedly was the leading bard of the 6th century.

from THE HEART'S GARDEN, THE GARDEN'S HEART (1967)

II

Kant on Euler's bridges / Of dilemma in Koenigsberg: Immanuel Kant (1724–1804), German philosopher, born and died in Königsberg. Leonhard Euler (1707–83), Swiss mathematician, whose greatest discovery, the law of quadratic reciprocity, is an essential part of modern number theory.

uguisu: Japanese bush warbler, known for its beautiful song. The bird frequently appears in Japanese poetry and art as a motif paired with bamboo, willows, cherry trees, or pine.

Nishikigi: In Japanese "nishiki" is a profusely decorated silk brocade cloth, used as a costume in Noh plays. Furthermore, "nishikigoi" is a highly prized carp.

The Three Jewels: The Buddha, the Dharma, and the Sangha.

St. John of the Cross said it, / The desire for vision . . . : St. John (1549–91), Spanish mystical writer and Carmelite friar.

VI

The Eve of Ch'ing Ming: "Clear Bright," the Chinese festival of the dead.

pachinko balls: Japanese pinballs.

Chidori: Japanese plovers.

Kannon: Popular bodhisattva in Japan, the personification of infinite compassion. When the name Kannon, meaning "the one who hears their cries," is invoked, one is supposed to be delivered from danger.

from NEW POEMS (1974)

La Vie en Rose
La Vie en Rose: French song from the fifties with lyrics by Edith Piaf (1915–63) and sung by her. The title translates as "Life Through Rose-colored Glasses."

from THE SILVER SWAN (1978)

XIV
Hototogisu—horobirete: "The Japanese cuckoo—perishing."

from THE HOMESTEAD CALLED DAMASCUS (1920–25)

I
"ineluctable modality": ["of the visible"], from James Joyce's
Ulysses.

Tammuz: Sumerian god who died each year and rose again in the
spring. Identified with Adonis in Greek mythology.

II The Autumn of Many Years
Enoch: Sixth in descent from Adam and father of Methuselah.
Two apocryphal works are ascribed to him, *The Book of Enoch*
and *The Book of the Secrets of Enoch.*

Didymus: Greek word meaning "twin," which was applied to St.
Thomas, as the name Thomas derives from the Aramaic word for
"twin."

Baldur: Norse god of light, son of Odin and Frigg.

Modred: nephew of King Arthur, who turned traitor to Arthur
and was killed by him in battle.

Loki: Norse god of strife and spirit of evil. Loki contrived the
death of Baldur.

III The Double Hellas
Chloris: A girl to whom Horace addresses one of his odes.

Bactrian Kings: Bactria was a kingdom, centered in present-day
Afghanistan, which flourished from 600 B.C.–A.D. 600 and was the
crossroads for East and West.

Pisanello: Antonio Pisanello (*c.* 1395–1455), early Renaissance
Italian painter and medalist.

from A PROLEGOMENON TO A THEODICY (1925–1927)

Scala: Latin; "steps" or "ladder."

scholia: Latin; "academy."

Lux lucis: Latin; "light of light."

Et fons luminis: Latin; "and the fountain of light."

Tris agios: Greek; "thrice holy."

INDEX OF TITLES AND FIRST LINES

Poem titles are printed in *italic* type.

"Aardvark," 102
A Bestiary, 102
". . . about the cool water, 25
A Dialogue of Watching, 83
A fervor parches you sometimes, 41
A Lesson in Geography, 11
A Letter to William Carlos Williams, 50
A Living Pearl, 87
All night I lay awake beside you, 82
Always for thirty years now, 107
An aging pilgrim on a, 119
Andrée Rexroth, 34
Andrée Rexroth, 47
"And what is love?" said Pilate, 53
Another Spring, 30
A Prolegomenon to a Theodicy, 132
"*A Sword in a Cloud of Light*," 85
At sixteen I came West, riding, 87
August 22, 1939, 4
Autumn in California, 3
Autumn in California is a mild, 3
Between Myself and Death, 41
Between Two Wars, 33
California rolls into, 46
"Cat," 102
Dear Bill, 50
Delia Rexroth, 33
Delia Rexroth, 46
"*Fall, Sierra Nevada*," 9
Fish Peddler and Cobbler, 107
Floating, 29
Fog fills the little square, 118
For Eli Jacobson, 89
"Fox," 103
"Goat," 103
G stands for goat and also, 103
"*Halley's Comet*," 84
Heaven is full of definite stars, 124
"Herring," 103
How short a time for life to last, 126
"I," 103

I am a man with no ambitions, 31
I didn't want it, you wanted it, 109
I Dream of Leslie, 117
In my childhood when I first, 81
In the theosophy of light, 118
Inversely, As the Square of Their Distance Apart, 31
It is impossible to see anything, 31
"*Kings River Canyon*," 48
Later when the gloated water, 35
La Vie en Rose, 118
Let me celebrate you. I, 83
Like the unicorn, Uncle, 104
"Lion," 104
Lute Music, 28
Lyell's Hypothesis Again, 45
Making love with you, 122
"Man," 104
Married Blues, 109
Martha Away (She is Away), 82
Mary and the Seasons, 92
Morphology repeats ontology, 129
"*Mt. Tamalpais*," 47
My head and shoulders, and my book, 42
My sorrow is so wide, 48
Never believe all you hear, 106
Now once more gray mottled buckeye branches, 34
Now the starlit moonless Spring, 117
Now the starlit moonless Spring, 117
Once more golden Scorpio glows over the col, 8
On Flower Wreath Hill, 119
On What Planet, 1
Our canoe idles in the idling current, 29
Pausing in my sixth decade, 110
"Raccoon," 104
Remember that breakfast one November—, 33
Requiem for the Spanish Dead, 2
Someday, if you are lucky, 104
"*Spring, Coast Range*," 7

"Spring Rain," 93
"Spring, Sierra Nevada," 8
St. Thomas Aquinas thought, 105
Suchness, 118
Take care of this. It's all there is, 103
The Advantages of Learning, 31
"The Autumn of Many Tears," 126
The Bad Old Days, 91
"The Double Hellas," 127
The Dragon and the Unicorn, 53
The earth will be going on a long time, 28
The fox is very clever, 103
The glow of my campfire is dark red and flameless, 7
The great geometrical winter constellations, 2
"The Great Nebula of Andromeda," 84
The Heart's Garden, The Garden's Heart, 110
The herring is prolific, 103
The Homestead Called Damascus, 124
The Lights in the Sky Are Stars, 84
The lion is called the king, 104
The Love Poems of Marichiko, 122
The man who found the aardvark, 102
The mountain road ends here, 45
The Phoenix and the Tortoise, 15
The raccoon wears a black mask, 104
There are few of us now, soon, 89
There are too many poems, 102
The Reflecting Trees of Being and Not Being, 81
The seasons revolve and the years change, 30

The Signature of All Things, 42
The Silver Swan, 121
The smoke of our campfire lowers, 93
The stars of the Great Bear drift apart, 11
"The Stigmata of Fact," 129
The summer of nineteen eighteen, 91
The Thin Edge of your Pride, 35
The unicorn is supposed, 105
The world is composed of a pair of, 127
They are murdering all the young men, 94
The years have gone. It is spring, 47
This morning the hermit thrush was absent at breakfast, 9
Thou Shalt Not Kill, 94
Toward an Organic Philosophy, 7
"Uncle Sam," 104
Under the half moon, 121
Under your illkempt yellow roses, 33
"Unicorn," 105
Uniformly over the whole countryside, 1
"Vulture," 105
Webs of misery spread in the brain, 15
We get into camp after, 84
We were interested in ways of being, 132
What is it all for, this poetry, 5
When in your middle years, 84
When We with Sappho, 25
"Wolf," 106
Written to Music, 109
You entered my sleep, 117
Your hand in mine, we walk out, 85

New Directions Paperbooks—A Partial Listing

Walter Abish, *In the Future Perfect.* NDP440.
　How German Is It. NDP508.
Ilango Adigal, *Shilapa-dikaram.* NDP162.
Alain, *The Gods.* NDP382.
Wayne Andrews. *Voltaire.* NDP519.
David Antin, *Talking at the Boundaries.* NDP388.
　Tuning. NDP570.
G. Apollinaire, *Selected Writings.*† NDP310.
C. J. Bangs, *The Bones of the Earth.* NDP563.
Djuna Barnes, *Nightwood.* NDP98.
Charles Baudelaire, *Flowers of Evil.*† NDP71,
　Paris Spleen. NDP294.
R. P. Blackmur, *Studies in Henry James,* NDP552.
Wolfgang Borchert, *The Man Outside.* NDP319.
Johan Borgen. *Lillelord.* NDP531.
Jorge Luis Borges, *Labyrinths.* NDP186.
E. Brock, *Here. Now. Always.* NDP429.
　The River and the Train. NDP478.
Buddha, *The Dhammapada.* NDP188.
Frederick Busch, *Domestic Particulars.* NDP413.
　Manual Labor. NDP376.
Ernesto Cardenal, *In Cuba* NDP377.
Hayden Carruth, *For You.* NDP298.
　From Snow and Rock, from Chaos. NDP349.
Louis-Ferdinand Céline,
　Death on the Installment Plan NDP330.
　Journey to the End of the Night. NDP84.
Jean Cocteau, *The Holy Terrors.* NDP212.
Robert Coles, *Irony in the Mind's Life.* NDP459.
Cid Corman, *Livingdying.* NDP289.
　Sun Rock Man. NDP318.
Gregory Corso, *Elegiac Feelings.* NDP299.
　Herald of the Autochthonic Spirit. NDP522.
　Long Live Man. NDP127.
Robert Creeley, *Hello.* NDP451.
　Later. NDP488.
　Mirrors, NDP559.
Edward Dahlberg, *Reader.* NDP246.
　Because I Was Flesh. NDP227.
René Daumal. *Rasa.* NDP530.
Osamu Dazai, *The Setting Sun.* NDP258.
　No Longer Human. NDP357.
Coleman Dowell, *Mrs. October . . .* NDP368.
Robert Duncan, *Bending the Bow.* NDP255.
　Ground Work. NDP571, The Opening of the
　　Field. NDP356, *Roots and Branches.* NDP275.
Richard Eberhart, *The Long Reach.* NDP565.
　Selected Poems. NDP198.
E. F. Edinger, *Melville's Moby-Dick.* NDP460.
Wm. Empson, *7 Types of Ambiguity.* NDP204.
　Some Versions of Pastoral. NDP92.
Wm. Everson, *The Residual Years.* NDP263.
Lawrence Ferlinghetti, *Her.* NDP88.
　A Coney Island of the Mind. NDP74.
　Endless Life. NDP516.
　The Mexican Night. NDP300.
　The Secret Meaning of Things. NDP268.
　Starting from San Francisco. NDP220.
Ronald Firbank. *Five Novels.* NDP518.
F. Scott Fitzgerald, *The Crack-up.* NDP54.
Robert Fitzgerald, *Spring Shade.* NDP311.
Gustave Flaubert, *Dictionary.* NDP230.
C. Froula, *Guide to Ezra Pound's Selected Poems.*
　NDP548.
Gandhi, *Gandhi on Non-Violence.* NDP197.
Goethe, *Faust,* Part I. NDP70.
Henry Green. *Back.* NDP517.
Allen Grossman, *The Woman on the Bridge*
　Over the Chicago River. NDP473.
　Of The Great House. NDP535.
Lars Gustafsson, *The Death of a Beekeeper.*
　NDP523.
　The Tennis Players. NDP551.
John Hawkes, *The Beetle Leg.* NDP239.
　The Blood Oranges. NDP338.
　The Cannibal. NDP123.
　Death Sleep & The Traveler. NDP391.
　Second Skin. NDP146.
　Travesty. NDP430.

Samuel Hazo. *To Paris.* NDP512.
　Thank a Bored Angel. NDP555.
H. D., *End to Torment.* NDP476.
　The Gift. NDP546.
　Hermetic Definition. NDP343.
　HERmione. NDP526.
　Tribute to Freud. NDP572.
　Trilogy. NDP362.
Robert E. Helbling, *Heinrich von Kleist,* NDP390.
William Herrick. *Love and Terror.* NDP538.
　Kill Memory. NDP558.
Hermann Hesse, *Siddhartha.* NDP65.
Vicente Huidobro. *Selected Poetry.* NDP520.
C. Isherwood, *All the Conspirators.* NDP480.
　The Berlin Stories. NDP134.
Ledo Ivo, *Snake's Nest.* NDP521.
Alfred Jarry, *Ubu Roi.* NDP105.
Robinson Jeffers, *Cawdor and Media.* NDP293.
James Joyce, *Stephen Hero.* NDP133.
　James Joyce/Finnegans Wake. NDP331.
Franz Kafka, *Amerika.* NDP117.
Bob Kaufman,
　The Ancient Rain. NDP514.
　Solitudes Crowded with Loneliness. NDP199.
Kenyon Critics, *G. M. Hopkins.* NDP355.
H. von Kleist, *Prince Friedrich.* NDP462.
Elaine Kraf, *The Princess of 72nd St.* NDP494.
Shimpei Kusano, *Asking Myself, Answering Myself.*
　NDP566.
P. Lal, *Great Sanskrit Plays.* NDP142.
Davide Lajolo, *An Absurd Vice.* NDP545.
Lautréamont, *Maldoror.* NDP207.
Irving Layton, *Selected Poems.* NDP431.
Christine Lehner. *Expecting.* NDP544.
Denise Levertov, *Candles in Babylon.* NDP533.
　Collected Earlier. NDP475.
　Footprints. NDP344.
　The Freeing of the Dust. NDP401.
　Light Up The Cave. NDP525.
　Life in the Forest. NDP461.
　Poems 1960–1967. NDP549.
　The Poet in the World. NDP363.
　Relearning the Alphabet. NDP290.
　To Stay Alive. NDP325.
Harry Levin, *James Joyce.* NDP87.
　Memories of The Moderns. NDP539.
Li Ch'ing-chao, *Complete Poems.* NDP492.
Enrique Lihn, *The Dark Room.*† NDP452.
Garciá Lorca, *Deep Song.* NDP503.
　Five Plays. NDP232.
　The Public & Play Without a Title. NDP561.
　Selected Letters. NDP557.
　Selected Poems.† NDP114.
　Three Tragedies. NDP52.
Michael McClure, *Antechamber.* NDP455.
　Fragments of Perseus. NDP554.
　Jaguar Skies. NDP400.
　Josephine: The Mouse Singer. NDP496.
Carson McCullers, *The Member of the*
　Wedding. (Playscript) NDP153.
Stephen Mallarmé.† *Selected Poetry and*
　Prose. NDP529.
Thomas Merton, *Asian Journal.* NDP394.
　Collected Poems. NDP504.
　Gandhi on Non-Violence. NDP197.
　News Seeds of Contemplation. NDP337.
　Selected Poems. NDP85.
　The Way of Chuang Tzu. NDP276.
　The Wisdom of the Desert. NDP295.
　Zen and the Birds of Appetite. NDP261.
Henry Miller, *The Air-Conditioned Nightmare.*
　NDP302.
　Big Sur & The Oranges. NDP161.
　The Books in My Life. NDP280.
　The Colossus of Maroussi. NDP75.
　The Cosmological Eye. NDP109.
　From Your Capricorn Friend. NDP568.
　The Smile at the Foot of the Ladder. NDP386.
　Stand Still Like the Hummingbird. NDP236.

The Time of the Assassins. NDP115.
Y. Mishima, *Confessions of a Mask.* NDP253.
   Death in Midsummer. NDP215.
Eugenio Montale, *It Depends.†* NDP507.
   New Poems. NDP410.
   Selected Poems.† NDP193.
Paul Morand, *Fancy Goods/Open All Night.*
   NDP567.
Vladimir Nabokov, *Nikolai Gogol.* NDP78.
   Laughter in the Dark. NDP470.
   The Real Life of Sebastian Knight. NDP432.
P. Neruda, *The Captain's Verses.†* NDP345.
   Residence on Earth.† NDP340.
New Directions in Prose & Poetry (Anthology).
   Available from #17 forward. #48, Fall 1984.
Robert Nichols, *Arrival.* NDP437.
   Exile. NDP485. *Garh City.* NDP450.
   Harditts in Sawna. NDP470.
Charles Olson, *Selected Writings.* NDP231.
Toby Olson, *The Life of Jesus.* NDP417.
   Seaview. NDP532.
George Oppen, *Collected Poems.* NDP418.
István Örkeny. *The Flower Show/*
   The Toth Family. NDP536
Wilfred Owen, *Collected Poems.* NDP210.
Nicanor Parra, *Poems and Antipoems.†* NDP242.
Boris Pasternak, *Safe Conduct.* NDP77.
Kenneth Patchen, *Aflame and Afun.* NDP292.
   Because It Is. NDP83.
   But Even So. NDP265.
   Collected Poems. NDP284.
   Hallelujah Anyway. NDP219.
   In Quest of Candlelighters. NDP334.
   Selected Poems. NDP160.
Octavio Paz, *Configurations.†* NDP303.
   A Draft of Shadows.† NDP489.
   Eagle or Sun?† NDP422.
   Selected Poems. NDP574.
St. John Perse.† *Selected Poems.* NDP545.
Plays for a New Theater. (Anth.) NDP216.
J. A. Porter, *Eelgrass.* NDP438.
Ezra Pound, *ABC of Reading.* NDP89.
   Collected Early Poems. NDP540.
   Confucius. NDP285.
   Confucius to Cummings. (Anth.) NDP126.
   Gaudier Brzeska. NDP372.
   Guide to Kulchur. NDP257.
   Literary Essays. NDP250.
   Selected Cantos. NDP304.
   Selected Letters 1907-1941. NDP317.
   Selected Poems. NDP66.
   The Spirit of Romance. NDP266.
   Translations.† (Enlarged Edition) NDP145.
Raymond Queneau, *The Bark Tree.* NDP314.
   Exercises in Style. NDP513.
   The Sunday of Life. NDP433.
   We Always Treat Women Too Well. NDP515.
Mary de Rachewiltz, *Ezra Pound.* NDP405.
John Crowe Ransom, *Beating the Bushes.*
   NDP324.
Raja Rao, *Kanthapura.* NDP224.
Herbert Read, *The Green Child.* NDP208.
P. Reverdy, *Selected Poems.†* NDP346.
Kenneth Rexroth, *Collected Longer Poems.*
   NDP309. *Collected Shorter.* NDP243.
   The Morning Star. NDP490.
   New Poems. NDP383.
   100 More Poems from the Chinese. NDP308.
   100 More Poems from the Japanese. NDP420.
   100 Poems from the Chinese. NDP192.
   100 Poems from the Japanese.† NDP147.
   Women Poets of China. NDP528.
   Women Poets of Japan. NDP527
Rainer Maria Rilke, *Poems from*
   The Book of Hours. NDP408.
   Possibility of Being. (Poems). NDP436.
   Where Silence Reigns. (Prose). NDP464.
Arthur Rimbaud, *Illuminations.†* NDP56.
   Season in Hell & Drunken Boat.† NDP97.

Edouard Roditi, *Delights of Turkey.* NDP445.
Jerome Rothenberg, *That Dada Strain.* NDP550.
   Poland/1931. NDP379.
   Vienna Blood. NDP498.
Saigyo,† *Mirror for the Moon.* NDP465.
Saikaku Ihara. *The Life of an Amorous*
   Woman. NDP270.
St. John of the Cross, *Poems.†* NDP341.
Jean-Paul Sartre, *Nausea.* NDP82.
   The Wall (Intimacy). NDP272.
Delmore Schwartz, *Selected Poems.* NDP241.
   In Dreams Begin Responsibilities. NDP454.
K. Shiraishi, *Seasons of Sacred Lust.* NDP453.
Stevie Smith, *Collected Poems.* NDP562.
   Selected Poems, NDP159.
Gary Snyder, *The Back Country.* NDP249.
   Earth House Hold. NDP267.
   The Real Work. NDP499.
   Regarding Wave. NDP306.
   Turtle Island. NDP381.
Gustaf Sobin, *The Earth as Air.* NDP569.
Enid Starkie, *Rimbaud.* NDP254.
Robert Steiner, *Bathers.* NDP495
Stendhal, *The Telegraph.* NDP108.
Jules Supervielle, *Selected Writings.†* NDP209.
Nathaniel Tarn, *Lyrics . . . Bride of God.* NDP391.
Dylan Thomas, *Adventures in the Skin Trade.*
   NDP183.
   A Child's Christmas in Wales. NDP181.
   Collected Poems 1934-1952. NDP316.
   Portrait of the Artist as a Young Dog.
   NDP51.
   Quite Early One Morning. NDP90.
   Rebecca's Daughters. NDP543.
   Under Milk Wood. NDP73.
Lionel Trilling. *E. M. Forster.* NDP189.
Martin Turnell. *Baudelaire.* NDP336.
   Rise of the French Novel. NDP474.
Paul Valéry, *Selected Writings.†* NDP184.
Elio Vittorini, *Women of Messina.* NDP365.
Vernon Watkins, *Selected Poems.* NDP221.
Nathanael West, *Miss Lonelyhearts &*
   Day of the Locust. NDP125.
J. Wheelwright, *Collected Poems.* NDP544.
J. Williams, *An Ear in Bartram's Tree.* NDP335.
Tennessee Williams, *Camino Real,* NDP301.
   Cat on a Hot Tin Roof. NDP398.
   Clothes for a Summer Hotel. NDP556.
   Dragon Country. NDP287.
   The Glass Menagerie. NDP218.
   Hard Candy. NDP225.
   In the Winter of Cities. NDP154.
   A Lovely Sunday for Creve Coeur. NDP497.
   One Arm & Other Stories. NDP237.
   Stopped Rocking. NDP575.
   A Streetcar Named Desire. NDP501.
   Sweet Bird of Youth. NDP409.
   Twenty-Seven Wagons Full of Cotton. NDP217.
   Vieux Carré. NDP482.
William Carlos Williams.
   The Autobiography. NDP223.
   The Buildup. NDP259.
   The Farmers' Daughters. NDP106.
   I Wanted to Write a Poem. NDP469.
   Imaginations. NDP329.
   In the American Grain. NDP53.
   In the Money. NDP240.
   Paterson. Complete. NDP152.
   Pictures form Brueghel. NDP118.
   Selected Poems. NDP131.
   White Mule. NDP226.
   Yes, Mrs. Williams. NDP534.
Yvor Winters, *E. A. Robinson.* NDP326.
Wisdom Books: *Ancient Egyptians,* NDP467.
   Early Buddhists, NDP444; *English Mystics,*
   NDP466; *Forest* (Hindu), NDP414; *Spanish*
   Mystics, NDP442; *St. Francis,* NDP477;
   Sufi, NDP424; *Taoists,* NDP509; *Wisdom of*
   the Desert, NDP295; *Zen Masters,* NDP415.

For complete listing request complete catalog from
New Directions, 80 Eighth Avenue, New York 10011   † Bilingual

BO WHALEY'S
FIELD GUIDE
TO SOUTHERN WOMEN

BO WHALEY'S FIELD GUIDE TO SOUTHERN WOMEN

Bo Whaley

RUTLEDGE HILL PRESS
Nashville, Tennessee

Published in Nashville, Tennessee, by Rutledge Hill Press, Inc., 513 Third Avenue South, Nashville, Tennessee 37210.

Typography by Bailey Typography, Inc., Nashville, Tennessee.

Library of Congress Cataloging-in-Publication Data

Whaley, Bo, 1926-
    [Field guide to southern women]
    Bo Whaley's field guide to southern women / Bo Whaley.
      p. cm.
    ISBN 1-55853-088-6
    1. Women—Southern States. I. Title. II. Title: Field guide to southern women.
    HQ1438.A13W43   1990
    305.4'0975—dc20   90-45185
                                               CIP

Printed in the United States of America
2 3 4 5 6 7 8 — 96 95 94 93 92

Contents

Make Mine a Mint Julep,   9

Part One: Vive la Différence 21

What Is America's Number One Spectator Sport?   23
Observations on Women by Literary Legends,   25
Never Pry into Women's Affairs,   27
The Woman Shopper's Slogan: Watch and Wait,   29
Perpetual Dieters,   32
The .45 Caliber Shoulder Bag,   36
Challenge of the Sexes,   38
Pssssst! Did You Hear About . . . ?   41
The Belles of Saint Mary's,   43

Part Two: A Southern Accent 47

Traits of a True Southern Belle,   49
More Traits of a True Southern Belle,   51
Oops! Wrong Zip Code!   53
Southern Women Never Walk Alone,   55
Aerobics with a Twist,   57
Who Wears Short Shorts?   59
Where There's a "Will" There's a Way,   61
Would You Please Say That Again?   62
We've Got Snobs in Dixie, Too!   65

Part Three: Love, Romance, and Memories 67

To Every Boy Comes That Moment of Awareness,   71
How to Start a Conversation with a Good-looking
    Stranger,   73
Without Women Around, Men Strike Out,   75
Bridal Fishing Is Big in the South,   77
Single vs. Married,   80
Blessed Are the Matchmakers,   82
All Singles Aren't Sad and Lonely,   84
My Romance Was Dunked,   86
"Dear John" Fire May Never Go Out,   89

Part Four: Husbands and Other Accouterments 93

Why Not a Prenuptial Agreement for Everybody?   96
Warning! Watch Out for Women in the Spring,   98
In Defense of Women's Rights,   101
The ERA Goes Both Ways,   103
A Husband's Nightmare,   106
Learning a Lesson of Life—The Hard Way,   109
They Let the Flame Die along the Way,   111

Part Five: On the Wild Side 115

Anytime Is Cocktail Party Time in Dixie,   117
Sometimes It's Better to "Just Say No,"   120
Beware of Cheri Bombs on New Year's Eve,   124
Topless Art: A Touch of Genius,   127

Part Six: In the Market Place **129**

Women Perform Lunch Hour Magic, 130
A Job Makes a "Heap o' Difference," 131
Secretaries: Cream of the Corporate Wine List, 135
Waitresses Must Live with Don Juans, 138
Never Interfere with a Woman's Soap Opera
 Schedule, 140
A Marriage Counselor's Nightmare, 142
Redneck Roosters Welcome Women with Open
 Arms, 144

Part Seven: Mothers Are Special **147**

The Joys of Becoming a Mother, 149
Why Mothers Get Gray Early, 153
Mothers Are Very Special People, 155

Conclusion, 159

Dedication

To Cindy, the wife of my son, the mother of my grandsons, Jeremy and Brett, and the sweetest and greatest daughter-in-law a man could ever hope for. I picked her from a cast of thousands at Georgia Southern College and conspired with her until the day she walked down the aisle to become my son Joe's wife.

Cindy is in all probability the best choice I ever made. I love her.

Make Mine a Mint Julep

I guess it must have been shortly after 5:00 P.M. when they walked in, each carrying a portfolio and wearing a shoulder bag, both standard items for today's young businesswoman. From my vantage point at the end of the bar in the Birmingham, Alabama, hotel lounge, I saw them choose a table and take their seats. I momentarily lost interest in the television newscast I had been watching with Frank, the bartender.

I wasn't really eavesdropping, but I couldn't help but overhear the conversation between the three and Cindy, the cocktail waitress. It was obvious that the four of them were not strangers; strangers don't refer to each other by first names. During the next twenty minutes or so I jotted down their names on the back of a cocktail napkin: Jeri, Mona, and Robin. I knew Cindy from previous visits to Birmingham and the lounge.

There was a good mixture of locals and transients partaking of the happy hour finger food and drink, engaging in small talk and casting aspiring glances in the general direction of the table where Jeri, Mona, and Robin were seated.

Jeri was drinking a vodka and tonic, Mona a margarita, and Robin a glass of white wine. I had momentarily turned my attention back to the television set behind the bar to see how the Braves had fared against the Dodgers, as if I couldn't have guessed, and almost missed the entrance of the fourth member of their group.

9

The finger food immediately went on hold, the tinkling of glasses ceased, and the small talk suddenly became mere whispers. All eyes, including mine, were on her as she walked to the table to join Jeri, Mona, and Robin. I still have no idea what the final score of the Braves-Dodgers game was or whether the Dow Jones went up, down, sideways, or in a circle.

I listened closely as Cindy greeted the newcomer. "Hi, Marie! I was about to think you wouldn't make it today."

"I almost didn't," she said in the sweetest southern voice this side of Guy Lombardo. "I thought the meeting would never end."

I already had withdrawn the napkin from my pocket and jotted down "Marie" on it before she finished her explanation to Cindy.

"What'll you have?" Cindy asked.

"Oh . . . make mine a mint julep," she said.

Frank could have turned off the television set as far as I was concerned. I tried to be discreet with my glances, frequently sneaking a peek at Marie and her three friends whose names I had completely forgotten.

What was so different about Marie? Her appearance, certainly. She was beautiful. Probably thirty-two to thirty-five years old with shoulder-length honey blonde hair, flawless peaches-and-cream complexion, impeccable makeup, television toothpaste commercial teeth, and medium suntan. She was neatly attired with a bright red blazer, white blouse topped with an antique cameo on a dainty sixteen-inch gold link chain, white pleated medium-length skirt, and black-and-white patent leather pumps with medium heels.

On the left lapel of her blazer was an attractive, but conservative, gold pin, probably a professional sorority pin or a service award. On her left wrist she wore a neat, feminine gold watch, while on her right was an almost-invisible-to-the-naked-eye gold serpentine bracelet. Rings? A dainty solitaire pearl in a gold mounting on her right ring finger and an emerald surrounded by apparent diamond chips on a raised mounting on her left. Her nails were polished in a red that matched her blazer.

Marie was special, and it was obvious to everyone.

I watched for the better part of an hour as the four women sat in the lounge, but my eyes repeatedly focused on Marie. She knew how to sit, when to laugh (but not too loud), when to talk, when to listen, how to greet and be greeted, and where to draw the line (softly but firmly). She gave and received respect. And her voice! A melody mingling with the music the wind makes when whistling through the trees. And southern. Distinctly southern.

When the four women left—the gin and tonic, the margarita, the white wine, and Marie—there was a void, even though the lounge was filled near capacity. Even Vanna White, who had replaced the newscaster, couldn't fill it. Marie had left.

I fiddled with a glass partially filled with ice, swirling it round and round for no apparent reason, lost in my thoughts. Then I reached in my coat pocket and withdrew my napkin. I was scribbling when Frank broke my train of thought.

"Like another drink?" he asked.

"Oh . . . no. No, thanks, Frank," I answered.

He eyed the napkin and my ballpoint, then asked, "Whatcha' doin', writin' another book on that napkin?"

"Not hardly, Frank," I answered. "Just the title."

"The title?"

"Right. I just decided what the title of my next one will be," I confided. I had known Frank for a while.

"Oh, yeah? What's it about?"

"Southern women, Frank," I said seriously. "*Real* southern women like the pretty lady who just left with her three friends."

"You must mean Marie," he said. "Now there, my friend, *is* a *real* southern lady!"

"I assumed as much from watching her," I agreed.

"And what's the title gonna' be?" he asked with apparent renewed interest.

I handed the little napkin to him and said, "Read it for yourself, Frank."

He unfolded it and was reading aloud as I walked away: "Make Mine a Mint Julep."

"Hey! I know what you mean!" he called out. "She always has just one, and she says I make the best."

What you have just read is true. It happened on an August afternoon in Birmingham, Alabama, in 1989. I haven't seen Marie since that day, don't know her last name, or where she works or lives. I just know that she is a credit to femininity.

By the time the book was done, however, the title had to be changed. My publisher decided that it made a better name for an introduction than it did for a book. How do you argue with the guy who decides whether or not your book is going to get published? But Marie and her friends were the inspiration for this book, and they deserve their credit. Without them, I probably would not have written it.

Southern women are a special breed of femininity, and I love 'em for it. I know of no other women who can tell a fellow to drop dead and actually make him look forward to the trip. I guess it's the southern drawl that does it. I call it the "Melody of the Southland" and will be the first to admit that a southern belle can make a vowel last longer than the NBA playoffs, a filibuster, or a root canal.

It was my misfortune to have been away from my beloved Dixie for fourteen years—an eternity—when I lived and labored in Washington, D. C., Michigan, New York, and New Jersey from 1954 to 1967. The sweetest song I heard upon my unheralded return came from the lipstick-caked lips of a waitress in an all-night coffee shop just north of Macon, Georgia, on a hot August night in 1967 when she greeted me with "How y'all? Kin I hep ya'?" while Merle Haggard accompanied her on the corner jukebox with his rendition of "The Fightin' Side of Me."

As I listened and sipped coffee, I thought to myself, "Hotamightyknows! This is it! I'm back in the Promised Land to stay—forever!" I dropped a quarter in the jukebox and made two selections, "Is It True What They Say About Dixie?" by Pete Fountain and "Oh, It's Good to Be Back Home Again," by John Denver.

I searched the jukebox listings diligently, and in vain, for

"Dixie" by Elvis. With appropriate apologies to the Memphis legend, wherever he is, I mumbled the words to myself accompanied by frying bacon on the grill, "Then I wish I was in Dixie . . . Hooray! Hooray! [And I was!] In Dixie Land I'll take my stand, to live and die in Dixie. Away, away, away down South in Dixie! Away, away, away down South in Dixie!"

That was twenty-three years ago, and I have devoted untold hours to the subject of women, especially southern women. There really is nothing like them.

I can't for the life of me recall when it became obvious to me that girls were different. Maybe it was when I entered first grade and those of us under the guidance and tutelage of Mrs. Bertha McQuirter held hands everywhere we went: to the lunchroom, to recess, to assembly. Everywhere. I learned right off that girls had softer hands than boys. I also learned that as a general rule they smelled better, and at the end of the school day their clothes were cleaner.

As I progressed through primary and elementary school, it was obvious that girls were lacking in certain fundamental skills that, to me, were very important. Girls, as a rule, ran like an ostrich with a sprained ankle and threw a baseball like a wounded octopus. But they made better grades, had better handwriting, and had much better posture. No girl in her right mind would slouch down in her desk, extend both feet all the way across the aisle, and wiggle her toes to scare flies away so they could be caught and put in inkwells. Maybe, just maybe, that's why they usually made better grades than fidgety boys.

A landmark revelation for me came when I was in the third grade and saw a classmate, Willie Kate Jernigan, fall off her bicycle as I was walking home from school. Willie Kate went head over heels down an embankment in her neat little blue and white polka-dot pinafore, and at that precise moment in history I realized that there was something decidedly different about Willie Kate that I had never noticed before. We were opposites, male and female. She smelled good, like a fresh gardenia, when I helped her to her feet. She felt nice and soft when I brushed her off and wiped her eyes with my shirttail. I learned then and there the power of female tears and walked her home, pushing a girl's bicycle with crooked handlebars. From that day forward—in 1936—Willie Kate was no longer an outfielder in pickup baseball games after school and on Saturdays in Gordon Cato's cow pasture, but rather a neat and pretty cheerleader who always cheered for my team.

At the tender age of nine, I had a girlfriend. Someone to fight over. Someone to send Valentines to and receive Valentines from. Someone to fantasize about on rainy nights. Someone's name to write over and over on fences, trees, sidewalks, abandoned buildings and draw make-believe tattoos of on my arms and hands—BW + WK—in a crudely drawn heart, complete with arrow. Someone to glance at repeatedly in church on Sunday mornings. Someone to show off for at recess and lunch. Someone to write classified notes to in study hall. Had study hall notes required postage stamps in 1936, I would have been bankrupt at the age of nine.

That was fifty-four years ago, and I've often wondered what happened to Willie Kate. We parted company in 1939 when my family moved to another town, and the last I heard some thirty years ago she had never married. Poor girl. I never should have left her. She cheered long and loud for me on Saturdays in Gordon Cato's cow pasture, and down through the years I could have used a few cheers to drown out the boos.

Willie Kate was a good little girl, and hopefully she will one day get over the heartbreak I caused her by leaving her at the age of twelve. I've fallen many times since that fateful afternoon in 1936, and had she been around I know she would have picked me up and brushed me off. And she would have walked me home and rolled my bicycle. Willie Kate was like that: loyal.

Much water has gone under the bridge in the past fifty years since I said goodbye to my first love, and I have watched with abiding interest the transition that has taken place among women—north, south, east, and west. There are those who say that beginning in the early forties America embarked on a sexual revolution and that women have come into their own. That could well be, as the term sexual revolution is tossed about freely these days.

My friend Ludlow Porch, Atlanta radio station WSB-AM's premier talk-show host, has said repeatedly that in his teenage years there were a few skirmishes, no battles, and certainly no revolution.

"I can state for a fact that in some junkyard in Georgia is a long abandoned 1940 Ford with three condoms taped to the underside of the dash," Ludlow says. "There was, of course, no prestige to having them there if no one knew about them. So I told everyone who would listen about my hidden prophylactics. If there was indeed a sexual revolution, it passed me right on by, and I never fired a shot."

Barefoot and Pregnant No More

I have devoted a considerable amount of time to researching the sexual revolution, especially when it first became evident that women were abandoning the dark environs of the basement and moving into the living room to be seen and heard, especially to be seen.

For far too long the women of the South were characterized by carpetbagging writers as barefoot and pregnant, marrying at thirteen, and having three children before they could legally drive an automobile. No more. Women now stand toe to toe with their male counterparts and take a back seat to no one.

When did the great escape begin? I really don't know, but I have studied about it and have reached certain conclusions.

The whole movement could have started with Adam and Eve in the Garden of Eden. Surely Adam became instantly aware of the differences in the anatomy of male and female when he first laid eyes on his female companion who was decked out in her mini fig leaf. On the other hand, it could have started with Lady Godiva who may have been the first female protester.

For me, the reality came in a series of revelations that date back to the early 1940s, the first being the release of a movie by Howard Hughes that shocked America, *The Outlaw,* staring Jane Russell. Remember the movie? I was fifteen years old when it hit the movie screens and saw it the first of many times with Lawrence Mashburn on a Friday night at the theater in Lumpkin, Georgia.

We sat as silent as King Tut, wide-eyed and amazed at what we were seeing on the screen. The overriding obsession of Hughes, as director of the movie, was to show Jane Russell's breasts, and did he ever!

The movie was based on the story of Billy the Kid, played by Jack Butel, and a buxom half-breed girl, played by Jane Russell. Infamous billboards pictured the voluptuous and seductive Miss Russell reclining in a haystack, revolver in hand, her skirt rising to the regions of her upper thighs where no movie camera had dared to focus before. Her blouse, which rested at half-mast and falling, drew hundreds of thousands, including two fifteen-year-old boys in Lumpkin, Georgia, into America's theaters for the anxiously awaited premiere of *The Outlaw.*

One scene in which Jane, tied between two trees by leather thongs, writhes sensuously in a futile effort to free herself, prompted old man Claude Morven who was seated down front to break the silence in the theater when he spoke out to no one in particular but loud enough for everyone to hear, "Lord, have mercy, that youngun's got a shirt full of goodies!"

I'm now convinced that *The Outlaw* and Jane Russell had an enormous impact on the sexual revolution in its early stages and prompted America to focus on the upper portion of the female anatomy with great interest. It may also have marked the beginning of the now accepted practice of women never buttoning the top two buttons on their blouses that gave real meaning to cleavage.

Just prior to the release of *The Outlaw,* another phenomenon swept the world wherever America's servicemen were stationed that contributed heavily to the sexual revolution. It spread all over Europe, the South Pacific, Africa, China, Burma, India, and anywhere else where a soldier or sailor's locker was located. It became universally known as the pinup girl. Betty Grable and Lana Turner led the pinup parade and millions of boys lay for hours at night watching and dreaming.

Two other females who made outstanding contributions were the creation of Al Capp in his popular comic strip, "Li'l Abner." Surely you will remember them as Daisy Mae Scraggs and Moonbeam McSwine. To this day, no female can approach the enticing manner in which Daisy Mae wore her miniskirt. By his own admission, old man Claude Morven was in love with Daisy Mae, and although he couldn't read a word, he subscribed to the newspaper to glance at her every day. He absolutely despised Li'l Abner who, according to old man Claude, "had to be the dumbest man in the world for ignoring the obvious advances of Daisy Mae to garner his attention."

Magazines played a major role in the sexual revolution and the liberation of women. *Esquire* had the Vargas girl long before *Playboy, Penthouse, Hustler,* and many others featured the lovely creatures in centerfolds. The Vargas girl had the longest and shapeliest legs of any girl in captivity, and her expression plainly said, "I'm yours." I'd have willingly given up my bicycle and pet goat to have been able to take the Vargas girl to a cane grinding or on a hayride.

And there was *National Geographic,* the magazine that convinced my parents that their little boy would grow up to be a geologist because of his obvious interest in the publication.

Also, the lingerie section of the Sears, Roebuck catalog educated many a country boy regarding women's apparel, although the models wearing it wouldn't look their viewers in the eye but gazed off into infinity gazing at the horizon or something.

The next major step came with the burning of bras, hippies, flower children, and free love. Television raised its risqué head and eased formerly forbidden words into its dialogue. Who among us today can believe that Jack Parr, host of *The Tonight Show,* was booted off the air for having the audacity to mouth the phrase "water closet" during the show?

Bathing suits (bikinis) became all but invisible to the naked (no pun intended) eye, and it seemed that the challenge was to see just how little a girl could wear (or not wear) without being arrested. We have now reached the point, thanks to *Sports Illustrated,* where bikinis are really nothing more than rumors.

Next, in the early eighties, came the split skirt, and women began showing their petticoats. This seemed a strange practice to me since I grew up watching my mother and grandmother tugging repeatedly at their hemlines to keep theirs from showing.

The women of the South are indeed no longer barefoot and pregnant. Instead, they wear spiked heels, display a few inches of petticoat, wear unbuttoned blouses, carry designer briefcases to fashionable offices, and maybe get pregnant with one and no more than two children between business trips and seminars. Women have reached the point where they now occupy jobs and positions formerly reserved for males only, and rightly so. Do the job; earn the position. That's what I say.

This book is intended to take a look at the women I know best, the women of the South, with occasional glances north of the Mason/Dixon Line where I spent fourteen years. While women seem strange to us men, they are delightful and fun, and I ask you, is there anything in the world more challenging than a beautiful woman? I think not.

Welcome to the wild, wacky, and wonderful world of women as seen through the eyes of a southern boy who has studied them for years—all over America—with great interest.

For those men contemplating matrimony, remember these words:

"Before marriage the three little words are 'I love you.' After marriage they are, 'Let's eat out.'"—*Unknown.*

BO WHALEY'S
FIELD GUIDE
TO SOUTHERN WOMEN

Part 1

Vive la Différence

God, in all his wisdom, chose to make woman different. Did He ever! And man has been indebted to Him since day one for that.

We all learned at an early age, either at our Mother's knee or in Sunday school, the story of Adam and Eve and how they came to be, Adam from dust and Eve from one of Adam's ribs.

God was the first surgeon and also the first anesthesiologist. This we learned from reading Genesis 2:21–22 that reads as follows: "And the LORD caused a deep sleep to fall upon Adam, and he slept. And He took one of his ribs, and closed up the flesh instead thereof. And of the rib, which the LORD God had taken from Adam, made He a woman, and brought her unto the man."

From these two verses come two great revelations. First, it marks the earliest known instance where an anesthesiologist put an individual to sleep at no charge. Second, it also marks the first time in the history of the world where surgery was performed for free.

No forms to fill out. No preoperative consultation. No deductible. No extended hospital stay. Just same-day surgery by the greatest physician the world has ever known. No ridiculous hospital gowns because both were naked for a short spell, until Eve became the world's first fashion designer by sewing fig leaves together and making aprons for the two of them.

Don't laugh. There are more ridiculous fashions on the market today, and there's no telling how popular Eve's designs would be today were she still in business.

In today's world women are more to be pitied than ridiculed, and as John Conrad has written, "Being a woman is a terribly difficult trade, since it consists of dealing primarily with men."

In this section my prime purpose is to underscore the fact that women are indeed different. We'll take a look at the wonderful world of girl-watching, the uncanny manner in which women shop, their dieting habits, and an innovative method of doing aerobics that Jane Fonda and Richard Simmons never dreamed of.

Also, we'll take a look at the work of fashion designers that send women scampering to the stores in an effort to "keep up with the trends." Hemlines are like a yo-yo, up and down. When a fashion designer is stymied he resorts to hemlines, lowering them one year and raising them the next. I mean, he can't go sideways, can he? What's left? Up and down.

Standard equipment for women is the traditional shoulderbag. The things can be lethal, and you'll find out why. A permit should be required to carry one, the same as a revolver or an AK-47.

There are certain areas in this world that men should fear to tread and have no business treading, like afternoon teas, a woman's checking account, her kitchen, her telephone conversations, shopping trips, and her family tree. I'm telling you never to pry into women's affairs.

Love 'em and pamper 'em, but never give them the advantage by making stupid statements that they can, and will, rebut. For example, take the case of the husband and wife who were involved in a deep discussion of money affairs and the family budget:

"Helen, I absolutely refuse to discuss this with you any further because it is a proven fact that men have better judgment than women," the husband said.

"I agree wholeheartedly, George," Helen said.

"You do?" George asked, surprised.

"Yes. I married you, and you married me."
('Nuff said).
Yes, the women, God bless 'em, are decidedly different.
Thank God there are enough to go around.

What Is America's Number One Spectator Sport?

Movies? Television? Baseball? Basketball? Football?
Wrong! The Number One spectator sport—way ahead of all
the rest—is girl watching.

Girl watching has been with us for a long, long time. How
long? I'm convinced it was going on before Lady Godiva
took her famous horseback ride through Coventry wearing
nothing more than her long blonde tresses and dogged de-
termination to demonstrate against heavy taxes on the
town.

I've often wondered what would have happened had Paul
Revere met Lady Godiva on his midnight ride. You can bet
your short shorts he would have executed an immediate
about face in his stirrups and followed the naked lady. Hun-
dreds of unsuspecting sleepers would never have received
the warning "The British are coming!"

In addition to her famous ride in the buff, Lady Godiva is
also famous for another reason, according to Georgia
Southern College head football coach Erskine Russell.
Here's how he explains it.

Lady Godiva is credited with prompting the very first
cheerleader squad. She rode sidesaddle, of course, as ladies
did in the eleventh century, and during her ride she passed a
group of Coventry boys on the side of the street she was
facing. As she rode by them they yelled at the top of their
voices, directing their cheer to another group of Coventry
boys on the other side of the street who saw nothing but her
backside.

"Hooray for our side!" they yelled as she passed.

Even Adam, of Garden of Eden fame, would attest to the
fact that girl watching can be dangerous. Remember what
happened? His eyes were opened, and he saw Eve. She was

clothed in similar fashion to Lady Godiva, and when he saw her he was in trouble immediately. He ate the forbidden fruit and did what any self-respecting girl watcher would do—he ran and tried to hide after getting caught!

Girl watching knows no season. In winter it's tight jeans. In summer it's bikinis and short shorts. Some of the bikinis are a sight to behold, if you can see them. The string bikini is the ultimate in beachwear, and I recall having seen a girl wearing one that would knock a fellow's hat in the creek. There wasn't enough string to tie a reminder around your forefinger, and the girl wearing it should have been ashamed of herself as she sunbathed by her pool. And the things can be dangerous to a girl watcher's health. I know this for a fact because I almost fell off the hood of my car when I climbed up on it to look over her backyard fence!

Down through the years I have known some All-American girl watchers, and age is no factor. There are inside girl watchers and outside girl watchers. Having spent a lot of time in various offices around the country, I've noticed that desk position is vitally important to an inside girl watcher. For instance, the choice desk is the one that is located by a window with an outside view and overlooks the pool—the steno pool. This is known as a "double-barrel" position in that it affords a fellow the opportunity to watch both inside and outside.

The next best position for an inside watcher is somewhere along the route from the steno pool to the ladies' restroom, near the water cooler if at all possible. This is because the women know you are watching and at every opportunity swish by and blast you with Youth Dew, Halston, Opium, Giorgio, Obsession, Chanel No. 5, White Shoulders, or some other fragrance. An inside girl watcher wouldn't trade his seat for one on the New York Stock Exchange.

It is a known fact that in the South there is an abundance of beautiful women, and any true southern gentleman loves to watch them. It is also a known fact that the women love for men to look at them. If they didn't, would they spend their Saturdays going from store to store in search of "just the right thing" to make men look?

One other thing regarding girl watching: it's always open

season. And there is no admission charge for this favorite spectator sport.

Observations on Women by Literary Legends

Men have been trying to solve the mystery of woman for centuries. While not one has succeeded in doing so completely, here are some thoughts by some of the world's greatest thinkers and writers:

• "Women's minds are cleaner than men's—they change them more often" *(Oliver Hereford)*.

• "It always puzzles me to hear of professional women. Are there no amateurs?" *(Arthur Godfrey)*.

• "Women have a much better time than men because there are so many things forbidden to them" *(Oscar Wilde)*.

• "Woman learns how to hate in proportion as she forgets how to charm" *(Friedrich Nietzsche)*.

• "To find out a girl's faults, praise her to her girlfriends" *(Benjamin Franklin)*.

• "Woman was God's *second* mistake" *(Friedrich Nietzsche)*.

• "Beauty that doesn't make a woman vain makes her very beautiful" *(Josh Billings)*.

• "There is no such thing as a dangerous woman; there are only susceptible men" *(Joseph Wood Krutch)*.

• "Women without principle draw considerable interest" *(Unknown)*.

• "A woman is someone who reaches for a chair when answering the telephone" *(Detroit News)*.

• "A woman is a person who will look in a mirror any time, except when she's pulling out of a parking space" *(Atchinson* [Kansas], *Globe)*.

And these gems of wit and wisdom on women from Will Rogers, legendary American humorist:

• "Money and women are the most sought after and the least known of any two things we have."

• "There are two types of men in the world that I feel

sincerely sorry for: one is the fellow that is always saying, 'I know the Mississippi River,' and the other one is the fellow that thinks he knows women."

• "Another American woman just swam the English Channel. Her husband was carried from the boat, suffering from cold and exposure. I offer this, for a revised edition of the dictionary, explaining which is the weaker sex."

• "Although the gamest woman can keep back tears in sorrow, they can't keep them back in happiness."

• "The Nineteenth Amendment, I think, is the one that made women humans, by act of Congress."

• "Everybody is always asking: 'Has women voting made any real change in our political system?' It has! It has doubled the number of candidates."

• "The whole country has gone 'legs!' Every imaginable shape, size, and contour was on exhibition. You see, short dresses were made for certain figures, but fashion decrees that everybody be fashionable, so that meant there were women trying to keep up with fashions who were financially able but physically unfit. So now, with longer skirts that will all be remedied. Every woman gets an even break—until she hits the beach."

• "Do you think women are buying 'Glorious Tradition' at the polls? No, sir. They want to know what kind of break they are going to get in Commerce and Industry. If they are going to make the living for the family, they want to know what kind of inducement the government is going to make to them for doing it. They are no smarter than their mothers were, but they think they are. So what we got to do, is to make 'em think we think they are."

＊   ＊   ＊

And some parting shots on women's fashion:

• When the Bishop of London was taken to a fashionable ball at which the ladies' dresses were cut extremely low, he was asked if he had ever before seen such a sight.

The Bishop looked around, surveyed the scene, and replied, "No, not since I was weaned."

• The carefully protected young lady, looking for the first time at a fig tree, said: "Good gracious! I surely thought the leaves would be larger than that."

• A fashion editor was interviewing a Hollywood star on television who said: "I think women's clothes are very interesting. I've been very successful with them, on and off, for the past ten years."

• "The worst way to torture a woman is to put her in a room with a hundred new dresses and no mirror" *(John P. Medbury)*.

• "As soon as Eve ate the apple of wisdom, she reached for the fig leaf and in so doing initiated the practice that when a woman begins to think, her first thought is of a new dress" *(Heinrich Heine)*.

Never Pry into Women's Affairs

There are many subjects about which I'm not knowledgeable, but then we all have our limitations. Even Einstein and Edison didn't know everything.

I'm not knowledgeable about computers, atomic energy, mechanics, carpentry, masonry, aeronautics, art, music, farming, gardening, flowers, and many other things. I probably know just enough about each to participate in a conversation at a cocktail party, but that's as far as it goes.

The thing men are least knowledgeable about, however, is women. But we're learning.

So far I've learned that there are certain things peculiar to females that you just don't mess with. Things like age, weight, and surgery are good examples.

Here's a little advice on these three subjects:

Age: If you ever attend a birthday honoring a woman, it's a big no-no to open your big mouth and ask, "How old are you?" That's like asking a burglar where he keeps his burglary tools.

Weight: Never mess with a woman's weight. If she looks you straight in the eye and says she weighs 118, accept it as fact, even if it is obvious to the naked eye that one hip weighs that much.

Bear in mind that every female twelve and over is on a diet and they are very weight-conscious. I know a fourteen-year-old girl who could hide behind a drinking straw and whom three Band-Aids would cover completely, but she still diets.

Surgery: Never, but never, probe into a woman's surgery. I learned the hard way that she might tell you about it. If a woman says she's been in the hospital for a few days and had surgery, your best comment would be "Oh?"

There are times when it's best for a man to just go ahead and act dumb where a woman is concerned. Believe me, it's not difficult. Here's an example of what I mean. It took place in a restaurant in my hometown:

I was having lunch when a pretty young lady strolled in with a look on her face like somebody had stolen her Green Stamps. She's a good friend, and seeing that I was alone in the booth, she joined me but said nothing. She just sat there looking very sad.

I was really concerned and asked the obvious question: "My goodness! What's wrong? You look like you've lost your last friend."

She didn't answer right away, but just lowered her eyes. I thought the sweet little thing was going to cry right there in my banana pudding.

"Are you all right?" I pressed.

Slowly, she lifted her eyes and tightened her lips before speaking.

"Well, I might as well tell you. I've got to tell somebody and . . ."

"Go ahead, and if there's anything I can do . . ." I interrupted.

"It's just that . . . well . . . oh, it's just awful!" she whimpered.

My mind was in a tizzy. What could have happened? Overdrawn at the bank? Diet on the blink? Jilted by her boyfriend? Lost half of her bikini?

"Trust me," I said.

She regained control of herself and came right to the point.

"I've just learned this morning that I have spider mites in my juniper!" she said.

"Good Lord!" I blurted out. "How terrible!"

Then I became concerned, really concerned. I mean, there I was sitting in broad open daylight in a restaurant full of people with a female who had spider mites in her juniper.

I didn't pursue the matter. I simply shifted my peas from one side of my plate to the other, buttered a roll that I had already buttered, and put some salt in my coffee.

She wouldn't drop the subject, and I had no way out.

"Isn't that just terrible?" she asked.

"Well . . . uh . . . yeah," I stammered. "Sure sounds terrible to me. But are you sure?"

"Positive," she said. "The symptoms are there as plain as day—brown spots. I consulted a juniper specialist, and he verified it. I've definitely got spider mites in my juniper."

I looked around to see if anyone might have heard. I'm sure the fellow in the next booth did, but he was nice enough not to let on. But he did shake his head in sympathy.

I tried to finish my lunch but couldn't. She was so pretty and neat, the last person in the world I would ever have suspected of having them . . . spider mites in her juniper.

It could have been worse, I guess, like lice in her lilies, bugs in her begonia, ticks in her tulips, ants in her asters, germs in her geraniums, or worms in her wisteria.

If it happens, she'll have to tell me. I doggone sure ain't gonna' ask her.

The Woman Shopper's Slogan: Watch and Wait

I have never even so much as hinted that I understand the way women think, or shop. Like most men, if I need a shirt or two, I just hop down to the men's store and buy a couple. In less than ten minutes, it's done. I don't say that's the way to shop. I just say that's the way I do it, and I might add that a lack of patience probably has a lot to do with my shopping habits. Colors don't really matter because I'm color blind.

Shopping with women, however, is a happening, like going to a concert or furnishing a house. There's nothing wrong with that. It's just that to most men shopping isn't really that big a deal. If you want proof of this, just look around the next time you're in the shopping mall in your city and see who's in the stores and who's sitting on the benches reading the newspaper or watching the passing parade.

Women, of course, shop in different ways. Some, like my daughter, can check out a dress shop before I can turn to the sports page. Others can wear out a credit card in one shopping trip. Still others employ the unique strategy of watching and waiting. Watching and waiting? Yes, watching and waiting. I learned firsthand how it works on a shopping (watching) tour with a friend.

I was having dinner with a lady and her nephew. We had almost finished eating when she asked a perfectly sane question: "What time is it?"

"It's 9:15," I replied. "Why do you ask?"

"Oh, I just wanted to run by K-Mart before it closes, that's all," she said matter-of-factly.

"Why? Do you need to buy something tonight?" I asked innocently.

"Oh, no. I don't want to buy anything. I'm watching a cooler there," she said, maintaining an "everybody does it" expression.

I expected more. It didn't come.

"You say you're 'watching' a cooler?" I asked ignorantly.

"Yes, I've been watching it for a couple of weeks now," she said dryly.

"Watching it for what?" I asked.

"To see when it's reduced," she said. "Then, I'm gonna' buy it. I watch a lot of things."

The plot was beginning to thicken. Even the nephew became interested. The waitress, obviously a watcher herself, understood and smiled knowingly.

"Like what?" I prodded. "What else are you watching?"

"Well, there's a pair of black slacks at Belk's. I've been watching them for about two weeks. There's a T-shirt there, too. It would go well with the black slacks. I've got a good one going at The Vogue, a dress. Been watching it for a few weeks. Been reduced twice. Down to $29.95 yesterday. One more reduction and it's mine!"

"But what if someone else beats you to it?" I asked.

"Simple. I just start over on another one. It happens lots of times," she said, and the waitress nodded and smiled.

I concluded that if you are going to be a watcher, you need lots of patience. I doubt there are many male watchers unless, of course, they watch the women watchers.

I decided to try the watching and waiting game myself, convinced that if a woman could do it, I could, too. I went strictly by the rules.

The next afternoon I cruised into a men's shop, put on my best "Just looking, thanks" face, and casually leaned against a rack of beautiful sport coats. My right elbow was flirting with the sale sign: "All Coats on This Rack 20 Percent Off."

Twenty percent? Hah! They weren't about to get this boy with that. I mean, I've been around the barn a couple of times, under the house once, and all the way to Daytona Beach by myself. I wasn't about to fall for that 20 percent jazz.

Two days later I returned. It was working! By George, it was working! "All Coats on This Rack 40 Percent Off," the sale sign said. That did it. I was a confirmed sport coat watcher. I even made my selection, a blue blazer size 42-Long.

I couldn't believe what I saw the next afternoon: 50 percent off!

I had to go out of town on business, and when I returned four days later, I strolled by "my" store again. There was "my" blazer and right above it was a sign: "All Coats on This Rack 60 Percent Off."

The clerk caught me eying the blazer. That's a no-no for a watcher.

"May I help you, sir?" he asked.

"No, uh . . . no thanks. I'm just watching . . . er . . . uh . . . looking," I told him.

I couldn't wait to tell my lady friend what had happened. She listened with wide-eyed enthusiasm.

"And I'm going to go back down there and buy the coat,"
I concluded.

"No, wait one more week," she insisted. "Be patient."

I promised, and I did. When I returned the blazer was still
on the rack, at 70 percent off! I couldn't get my American
Express card out fast enough. The price? $28.50 for a $95
blazer! I had won the watching game, or had I?

I hurried to "her" house to show my prize to a profes-
sional. Her nephew stood by as I tried it on.

"It really is a beauty," she said. "See? It really does pay to
watch and wait, right?"

"You better believe it!" I said as I fingered the gold but-
tons with the little coat-of-arms on them.

She walked with me to my car and true watcher that she
is, she glanced into the back seat.

"What are all those packages?" she asked.

"Oh, just a few accessories the salesman said would go
well with the blazer," I said, shrugging.

She was already in the back seat and opening bags.

"Did you say a *few* accessories? Pants, $59.75. Shirt,
$28.50. Tie, $12. Socks, $3.95. Belt, $17.95. Shoes, $87.50."

She climbed out of the back seat and shook her head in
disappointment.

"You violated the cardinal rule of watching. *Never* buy
anything extra! You pick out an item, stake it out for
months, buy it when the price hits rock bottom, and leave,"
she said.

I've learned that in addition to a lot of patience, you need
a lot of willpower to qualify as a professional watcher. I'm
working on it.

You see, I've got this little Mercedes sports coupe that
I'm watching and . . .

Perpetual Dieters

The whole country has gone diet crazy! The way women
talk nowadays about food, calories, and cholesterol one
would think sugar had been added to the Drug Enforcement

Agency's list of controlled drugs along with marijuana, cocaine, hashish, heroin, and LSD.

I know a twenty-year-old "no-cal" string bean who's on a diet. But then, she's always on a diet. Her latest is called the banana, egg, and hot dog diet:

First Day—Four bananas, three times a day.

Second Day—Four boiled eggs, three times a day.

Third Day—Four hot dogs, without buns, three times a day.

Fourth Day—One banana, one egg, one hot dog, three times a day.

She says this diet guarantees that she will lose ten pounds in four days.

Her parents took her on a cruise to the Bahamas and somehow became separated from her in midafternoon. Her daddy says he found her about midnight high up in a coconut tree, cackling and barking at the moon. He says it took two diet Cokes, a diet Pepsi, and three no-cal wafers to coax her down.

Whether she lost any weight or not, she sure learned to climb a coconut tree in a hurry.

I'm not quite sure how the banana-egg-hot dog diet originated, but I have a sneaking suspicion that Chiquita, the Little Red Hen, and Hormel started it.

Remember the days of Juicy Fruit, Spearmint, Beech-Nut, and Doublemint? Gone, taking the same route as cloth diapers and real ink pens. Trident Sugarless moved in like a hurricane. Sadly, we now have an entire generation that will never know the taste of a real stick of chewing gum.

The dieting thing has also seriously affected the bathing suit market, like the two women who waddled into a store in May in search of one.

"I'll take this one," Bertha said without even trying it on.

"Bertha! You can't get in that! It's at least three sizes too small for you," her neighbor and fellow shopper, Gertrude, said.

"I know that, Gertrude. But we're going to the beach in July, and I'll get in it by then if I have to eat grass for six weeks!" Bertha countered.

Have you taken your dieting wife or girlfriend out to dinner lately? If so, then you can probably relate to this:

You order prime rib, baked potato, green beans, tossed salad dripping with thousand island dressing, rolls, butter, and cheesecake.

The little woman? "Just cottage cheese and a peach half for me, please," she announces with a triumphant flair.

Then you sit back and watch her "just taste" half your prime rib and all your cheesecake. "Oh, goodness no! Nothing else for me. The cottage cheese and peach half will suffice. I'm on a diet," she declares to the waitress as she busies herself straightening her halo and wiping cheesecake from her chin.

Then your turn comes, Harry.

"I would like another piece of cheesecake, please."

"Harry! That's ridiculous! You simply must watch your calories," she scolds.

You did, Harry. You just watched them disappear, right down your fair lady's gullet!

Then there's the little miss who's bent on losing five pounds, not because she needs to (she weighing in at a hefty ninety-three pounds), but because dieting is the "in" thing. All the girls are doing it. You've probably seen a girl like her in your favorite restaurant, or seated across the dinner table from you at home. She's fifteen and a Sweet N' Low addict. She puts it in her tea, on her grits, under her arms and behind her ears, and even brushes her teeth with it occasionally.

Lose five pounds? Why? You could cover her posterior with a Band-Aid. Should she get lost, don't sweat it. Just check the nearest coconut tree. She may have heard about the banana-egg-hot dog diet.

Stretch your imagination and see if you can possibly imagine a telephone conversation like this. But don't laugh too soon because it could come to pass if the diet mania continues.

"Hi, Gail! Watcha' doin'?"

"Oh, hi Gloria. Nothin' much. Just cookin' dinner."

"Watcha' cookin'?"

"Hmmmm . . . let me see. Ravioli, barbecued ribs, meat

loaf, baked potatoes, cornbread dressing, okra and tomatoes, creamed corn, cauliflower with cheese sauce, asparagus, boiled cabbage, butterbeans, turnip greens, cornbread, biscuits, and banana pudding. I think that's all."

"All!? Who in the world are you feeding tonight? Death row or the Pittsburgh Steelers?"

"Nope. Nobody here but me. Jim and the kids have gone on a ten-day cruise to the Bahamas. Spring holidays, you know."

"And you're gonna' eat all that food, Gail?"

"Heavens no! Are you out of your mind, Gloria? I'm not gonna' eat any of it."

"Well then, what are you cookin' it for?"

"Because I'm on a new diet, that's why. It's called the Sniffing Diet, and it works."

"Never heard of it. How does it work, and where did you get it?"

"It's in Bo Whaley's new book, *Everything You Always Wanted to Know about Dieting, but Were Afraid to Fast.*

"Did you say 'Sniffing Diet,' Gail?"

"Right. You just cook all your favorite foods every night for ten nights, put them on the table, and sniff them. It's great! You don't eat any of them, you just sniff them."

"But what in the world do you do with all that food, Gail?"

"Oh, I give it to my toy poodle when I finish sniffing it."

"Does it work? Have you lost any weight?"

"Yeah, I've lost four pounds in three days. But it has its drawbacks."

"How's that?"

"Well, like I said, I've lost four pounds, but my poodle has gained thirty-two! Plus my nose is as big as a large cucumber!"

"Wow! Must be the biggest poodle in town. Well, let me go and . . . oh, I almost forgot. How are Jim and kids doing in the Bahamas? Havin' a ball, I'll bet."

"Not really, Gloria. Jim is on that banana-egg-hot dog diet, you know."

"I know. What about it?"

"Well, he called last night. He's in the hospital in Nassau with—."

"In the hospital! What in the world happened?"

"Oh, he fell out of a coconut tree about midnight last night and broke his leg."

The .45 Caliber Shoulder Bag

More and more women are taking advantage of firearms training in the safe use of handguns offered by various law enforcement agencies. This is good. I can imagine the shock and surprise of some burglar, robber, or would-be rapist who suddenly finds himself in the sights of a .38 revolver held with a viselike grip by his intended victim, who is barking, "Freeze!"

Most communities offer courses for women in the safe handling and firing of handguns. Forty-two women attended one held on a Saturday morning in the Superior Courtroom in my town, along with their "Saturday Morning Specials."

The women received instruction from local law enforcement officers in the art of loading, unloading, and safe handling of handguns. They then boarded a bus and went to the firing range to test their skills.

Women have long utilized such weapons as hatpins, umbrellas, handbags, and high-heeled shoes in the art of self-defense. Now, they are adding revolvers to their arsenal and learning how to shoot them, accurately.

I found it somewhat coincidental that on the Saturday morning when forty-two of the women in my town were learning to load, reload, and handle their weapons safely in the courtroom, yet another was packing an equally dangerous weapon, one owned by all females, less than a block away in a downtown restaurant. It caused quite a stir among the breakfast regulars, to say the least.

Have you by chance ever had the opportunity to watch a woman operate with a shoulder bag in such settings as restaurants, elevators, crowded supermarkets, and department stores? The things can be lethal. Any woman sporting a shoulder bag, and most do, is definitely armed and dangerous.

The woman armed with the .45 caliber shoulder bag that Saturday morning was destined for difficulty from the moment she entered the restaurant, what with the narrow aisles between the tables and booths and all. A tightrope walker, hopscotch champion, or ballet dancer would have experienced difficulty negotiating the narrow passageways. It didn't make her task any easier that she was built like a small elephant or that her shoulder-bag weapon approached the dimensions of a duffel bag. And it was loaded.

I watched her. Everybody in the restaurant watched her. She could have made an abrupt about-face and cleared out the restaurant, or at least cleaned off the tables!

What happened was this:

She finished eating at a back table and made her way to the cash register, shoulder bag hanging, loaded and ready. She suddenly realized that she had left some of her ammunition—cigarettes and lighter—on the table and whirled around to go back and get them, flattening a young boy with a smash to the head in the process. She also scored a bullseye on an unsuspecting coffee drinker reading a newspaper.

After retrieving her cigarettes and lighter, she whirled around again and ruptured an unsuspecting man who was exiting the men's room. When she turned to apologize to him, she demolished a tray of dishes held by a waitress.

En route back to the cash register, she slammed a senior citizen who was seated at the counter, in the back of the head, and an alert lawyer ducked just in time to avoid a sure concussion.

"Dern woman's dangerous with that thing," remarked the senior citizen.

"She sure is," said the lawyer. "It just don't pay to turn your back on a woman with a shoulder bag."

"No, or your front either," said the stooped over, agonizing rupture victim in his newly acquired high-pitched voice. "She must have a slot machine, two or three bricks, and half-a-dozen or so of my wife's biscuits in that bag."

We watched her pay up, walk out of the restaurant, sling

her weapon in the cab of her pickup, burn a little rubber, and drive away, but not before lighting up a cigarette.

I glanced around the restaurant, surveying the casualties and the walking wounded. There were many.

A waitress limped to the cash register and spoke to the owner. "The lady with the shoulder bag left this package in a chair at the back table," she said.

With that announcement, all seated at my table stood up in unison, reached for their checks, and made haste to leave.

"Where's everybody going in such a hurry?" the owner asked.

"I'm gettin' the heck outa' here 'fore she comes back," said one. "I survived World War II and the South Pacific, but I ain't stickin' aroun' for this 'un."

Well, like they say about war: "When the going gets rough, some men get brave. Others get exercise."

Me? I ran.

Challenge of the Sexes

I've heard them all, and so have you: Put up or shut up. Put your money where your mouth is. Lay it on the line. Fish or cut bait.

There comes a time in our lives when someone calls our bluff. I now know the feeling, thanks to my secretary, Lillie, who shot me down after I made the mistake of commenting on the outrageous size of women's handbags and added fuel to the fire by saying that women load the modern-day cotton sacks with every unnecessary item they own.

My tongue-in-cheek comment was made in jest, but Lillie didn't take it that way and challenged me immediately to a showdown—the contents of her shoulder bag versus the contents of my billfold (and pockets), which was only fair, inasmuch as women's dresses and pant suits don't, as a rule, have pockets.

What could I do? She had backed me into a corner and had witnesses. I reluctantly agreed to the showdown, and she made the rules.

"Whoever produces the most items has to buy lunch at the restaurant of the winner's choice," she said.

We flipped a coin to determine who would go first. I lost and proceeded to place everything from my billfold and pockets on her desk. I might add that the inventory was quite revealing to me. Here it is:

Billfold: An expired library card; an out-of-date insurance card; Social Security card; motorcycle warranty card; driver's license; business card from Morgan Builders; automobile registration; telephone credit card; American Express card; a three-year-old calendar; Regency Club card; four photographs (grandsons, son, and daughter); insurance identification card; six personal business cards; twelve dollars; two tickets to political fund-raiser barbecue (held two years previously); parking ticket; note regarding Industry Appreciation Week (three years before); business card of the God Notes; two gasoline receipts; four cigarette lighter flints; three blank checks; two deposit receipts; a button; a bank identification card (account closed twelve years previously); three raffle tickets on .12 gauge shotgun (drawing held eighteen months previously); golf handicap card; press card; health insurance card; Mastercard; Visa card; Macy's card; Atlanta telephone number 404-526-1187(?); and Atlanta Braves ticket stub.

Pockets: Two ballpoint pens; book of thirteen-cent stamps; comb; key case; handkerchief; knife; nail clipper; ninety-six cents in change; rubber band; four paper clips; car keys; cigarette lighter; package of Winston cigarettes; six blank three-by-five cards; Certs; appointment book; two toothpicks; book matches; two golf tees; and car keys.

Total: Ninety-three items, and I wasn't even wearing a coat. Lillie then stepped to the line, unloaded her shoulder-bag, and the inventory began. This is what she removed and placed on her desk:

Billfold: A good luck charm; $6.12 in cash; checkbook; five charge cards; Social Security card; expired charge card; driver's license; two snips of baby hair—fourteen years old—from granddaughters; sunglasses; ring; grocery list; a Canadian penny; and a memo pad.

Shoulder bag: Pump and Pantry gas receipt (three years

old); JC Penney mail order form; weekly calendar; two political campaign brochures; paid drug statement; patient information form; cigarette lighter; package of Salem cigarettes; one eight-track tape; paid JC Penney bill; twelve keys; nail clipper; lipstick; paid bill from Smiths Jewelers; paid bill from Rowe's Flower Shop; Pilot Club meeting agenda; paid bill from hospital emergency room; purchase order; twenty-three Green Stamps; medicine bottle (empty, last refilled nine years previously); two Asbron medicine bottles; three antihistamine bottles; paid C&S Bank bill; map with directions to Fox Hollow; two free passes to Village Theatre; book of matches (empty); letter from California friend (three years old); newspaper clipping; watch with broken crystal; brochure on Rogers silverware; IRS tax information; two letters to be mailed for daughter (written eight months previously); stick of gum, and two empty wrappers; car keys.

Also . . . two Kleenex; two packets of sugar; one packet of Coffee-Mate; three packets of Sweet N' Low; two safety pins; two rubber bands; one box of aspirin; three hairpins; one belt; C&S payment book; eight supermarket check-out receipts; paid receipt for TV repair; receipt for Pilot Club dues; $1.00 coupon for Vantage cigarettes; receipt from Diana Shop; chamber of commerce questionnaire; Herman Talmadge report on Panama Canal; insurance policy; receipt from Shamrock Photography; two 1975 achievement test scores; insurance identification card; C&S receipt; voided check; prescription (five years old); letter from orthodontist; receipt from Duncan Tire Company; sweepstakes ticket (drawing held six years previously); insect repellent; broken watch; watch stem from broken watch; nineteen paper clips; wrapper from drinking straw; three pencils.

Also a note on lined sheet of paper as follows: "Mom: Please get me a watch band today if you can. Try to get a big wide one. I love you." (The noted is signed "The Watch Band Wanter," and dated fourteen months previously. The note is from her son, who still has no big wide watch band.)

The final score was 93–219, in my favor. I have in my files this affidavit from Lillie:

I, Lillie Harkins, being of sound mind (although I'm not so sure about Bo), do hereby swear and affirm that the 219 items listed and described above as having been in my shoulder bag at the time of the showdown are true and correct.

(Signed) Lillie Harkins

The lunch? Ribeye and baked potato at the country club. Delicious!

Pssssst! Did You Hear About . . . ?

It would be impossible to write a book about women without including a segment on gossip, even though I am convinced that since Day One women have been unfairly tried and convicted as the prime conveyors of gossip.

Stories abound about gossipy women whispering taboo secrets at beauty shops and bridge club gatherings. But what about the men?

It is unfortunate that when we think of gossip, we automatically think of women. You can forget that. I have a thirty-minute tape recording of barber shop conversations that I recorded with a hidden microphone, and the men make the women look like kindergarten gossipers by comparison. I also have another tape recorded at a morning coffee table gathering and one made at a weekly poker game. No doubt about it, the men win the gossip contest hands down.

The art of gossip, regrettably, is almost a profession with many, male and female. The bigger the scandal, the better. Truth has nothing whatsoever to do with it. There are those, male and female, who would rather spread news than win the Irish Sweepstakes, get a hole-in-one, or lose forty pounds.

Some people would wade through briar-infested swamps in their best clothes to be the first to deliver bad news. And there are others who, had they been in Massachusetts the night of April 18, 1775, would have been at least three furlongs ahead of Paul Revere.

Down through the years, women have been stuck with the reputation as gossipers, and these thoughts on the subject, sent to me by an unidentified reader, seem to bear this out:

A gossip is a person who

- Always gets caught in her own mouth-trap.
- Always gives the benefit of the dirt.
- Believes much more than she hears.
- Can give you *all* of the details without knowing *any* of the facts.
- Gets her best news from somebody who promised to keep it a secret.
- Can keep the secret going.
- Has a terrific sense of rumor.
- Has a small vocabulary but a large turnover.
- Is always the knife of the party.
- Is a newscaster without a sponsor.
- Listens in haste and repeats in leisure.
- Tells everything she can get her ears on.
- Tells things before you get a chance to tell them.
- Turns an earful into a mouthful.
- Would rather listen to dirt than sweep it.

More thoughts on gossip picked up at random:

- More people are run down by gossip than automobiles.
- She says she doesn't like to repeat gossip, but what else can you do with it?
- The most useless thing in the world is gossip that isn't worth repeating.
- Talk about others and you're a gossip; talk about yourself and you're a bore.
- Children would get less dirt in their ears if adults wouldn't gossip in front of them.
- Everyone needs two friends, one to talk to and one to talk about.
- The difference between gossip and news depends on whether you hear it or tell it.
- Some people will never repeat gossip, but they will start it.

• Gossip comes in three varieties: The vest-button type, always popping off; the vacuum-cleaner type, always picking up dirt; the liniment type, always rubbing it in.

• A woman's word is never done.

• If you really want your wife to listen to what you have to say, talk to another woman.

• She who thinks by the inch and talks by the yard needs to be kicked by the foot.

• She's not really a liar; she merely arranges the truth in her favor.

And here's a thought to remember: Women don't really talk more than men, they just use more words.

The Belles of Saint Mary's

I have been to goat buttings, calf ropings, frog giggings, candy pullings, cane grindings, and peanut boilings. I even went to a cock fight in the Philippines, the Miss America pageant and the Democratic National Convention in Atlantic City, and the Republican National Convention in New Orleans.

I finally completed the cycle recently, however, when I was invited to be a judge in a local beauty contest. The invitation came by telephone.

"Bo, I'd like to ask a favor. Will you be a judge in a make-up show? There'll be about a hundred ladies in it and . . ."

"You bet your mascara, Make-Up Lady! How much do I have to pay?"

"Not a cent. All you have to do is look at the girls and vote," she said.

"Hot dang! You got a deal! Let me at 'em! When and where is all I need to know," I yelled.

"Good. April third, 7:30 P.M. at the Holiday Inn."

I hung up the phone, wrote all the information down, and leaned back in my chair, grinning. Man! A hundred ladies and ole Bo! Just like turning a hog loose in a watermelon patch!

*   *   *

I thought April 3 would never come. Around the end of March I even wondered if the whole shebang might be an April Fool prank.

If it is, I'll kill her! I vowed. How? I'll strangle her with eye shadow, that's how. And to add insult to injury, I'll smear her mascara!

Finally, the big day arrived. I arose early, put a mud pack on my face, and promptly forgot about it. I showed up at my breakfast table downtown and nobody noticed. That should have been a clue.

About midmorning I bought a four-pack of Bic shavers and played Dr. Pepper with them all day. Shaved three times: at 10, 2, and 4. At 6:30 I used the fourth and followed with some foo-foo stuff I won at the Laurens County Fair last October knocking milk bottles down with baseballs. Had to be good stuff because it cost me $16.50, but I still didn't win one of those pandas that tear open before you get home with it. The foo-foo stuff? A consolation prize. Looked like burnt motor oil and smelled something like diesel fuel. The name on the label read "Sic 'Em," and right underneath was this: "Warning: Please do not use this if you're bluffing!"

So, oiled and ready, I finally found my hair and combed it. I would have put some slickum on it, but I ran out of quarters trying to win the panda.

I was on my way to a make-up show! Top drawer. Top of the heap. Blue ribbon and all that jazz.

I arrived for my judging duties early, something like 6:15, I reckon. What the heck, if I was going to judge I wanted to get on with it. I was the first to arrive, and I placed a chair near the entrance. I hadn't been seated there long when the contestants began arriving. Two, then eight, and, shortly, nearly a hundred!

Oooohhhh, they looked pretty! Complexions like ice cream, all flavors. I was as busy as a nervous hornet giving each the once-over as she walked in. I had a pretty good score sheet going until a lady tapped me on the shoulder and cautioned me:

"Excuse me. The judging doesn't begin until 7:30. If you'll just have a seat at the judge's table . . ."

Well, I did like she said, and pretty soon the parade started. All those pretty ladies came and stood right in front of my table, and I was really getting with it when a judge on my right whispered, "We're only judging their faces!"

Well, maybe, but ole Bo was being most thorough. A once-in-a-lifetime chance, and I wasn't going to look? No way. I may have been the only person in the room that could verify that the contestants had on shoes.

Somebody did a good job of preparation. The show was well organized, the ladies were stunning, and the whole affair went as smoothly as if it had been oiled with a few drops of my Sic 'Em.

And I learned something. I learned that when a group of dedicated ladies in the cosmetics field have a get-together, you have to really watch what you say. Like, for instance:

It's *okay* to mention to one that her slip is fourteen inches too long, there's a run in her right stocking that looks like a Seaboard Coastline Railroad track, her bra is on backwards, or the zipper in back is only half-fastened. No sweat with any of these.

But, you just tell her that her right eyebrow is crooked or that her eyeshadow doesn't complement her lipstick, and you've got a fight on your hands. They know what they're doing when it comes to make-up and cosmetics.

I listened to satisfied customers for an hour, and I'll tell you they convinced this ole boy. I thought they just rubbed all that stuff on. Not so!

Like the stuff around the eyes? It's put on with Morse code! Dot, dot, dash, dash, dot, dot . . . and *then* they rub it!

Yep, I had a ball at the show. There I was all scrubbed and oily rubbing elbows with "The Belles of Saint Mary's" (Kay, that is).

Like I told 'em before we broke up, I'm sure that Eve wasn't wearing their product in the Garden of Eden. Why?

"If she had been, Adam would never have seen that apple!"

Part 2

A Southern Accent

I guess chauvinism has never enjoyed greater popularity than it does today, female chauvinism, that is. Not a day passes but what some women's organization is lambasting their male counterparts regarding sexual discrimination, sexual harassment, job discrimination, or equal rights. And the list goes on.

Down where I live, chauvinism is not really a bad word. In fact, there are many places where it is virtually an unknown adjective.

Not long ago I was traveling with my secretary and right-hand woman, Robbie Nell Bell, from Alma (Robbie Nail Bail, fum Almer). Robbie Nell is the chief waitress and keeper of the jukebox at Mel's Juke, about a six-pack north of Broxton, Georgia. Somewhere along the way, the subject of male chauvinism came up, and I asked her about it.

"What do you think of chauvinism, Robbie Nell?" I asked.

"I guess it's awright, but to tail ya' th' truth I'd druther have a Ford," she allowed between sips of a long-neck Bud.

As you can see, Robbie Nell isn't bothered by having to attend too many Phi Beta Kappa meetings. Her time is occupied more with what to play on the jukebox, whether the hamburger is to be all the way, and where to go dancing when Mel's closes.

Northern women seem to be more into causes and who

has what rights. They live defensively and will argue at the drop of a controversial subject. Southern women seem to roll more with the flow. Just give 'em a Coke, a pool, a radio, a bikini, a couple of credit cards, and a date for the Saturday night dance at the club, and they're happy.

In my years spent "up nawth," it seemed that women were more suspicious than "down here." Status meant a lot more, like what kind of car, clothing labels, anything original or one-of-a-kind, ethnic background, job title, and a weekend hideaway someplace in the mountains or at the shore. Atlanta has become the same since the migration south began; the ratio of native-born Atlantans now stands at only one in seven. I'm old enough to remember when Atlanta was a southern city. Now you can go for weeks and never hear a southern accent, see a boiled peanut, or find anybody barefoot.

There was a time, too, when Atlanta was famous for its well-dressed women, some said the best-dressed in America. That distinction now goes to Birmingham, Alabama. New York City, of course, has the worst. I saw women there dressed in outfits that a southern girl wouldn't go possum hunting in, and they paid big bucks for 'em, just to be different. Of course, there is an advantage to wearing scary outfits like that. They'll make a possum come out of a tree before you can say "Scat!"

The bottom line is attitude. Southern women have a tendency to take things slow and easy while their northern sisters tend to want to get it done because the whole world might cave in tomorrow.

A legendary story has been making the rounds for years down my way. It has to do with a southern belle who paid a visit to her aunt in New York. She visited for three weeks and came to dislike the city very much.

Shortly after she arrived back home, she was invited to have dinner with a young New York executive who, during dinner, repeatedly praised New York City and ran down the South in general.

"Well, I can tell you one thing," the girl said. "When my time comes, I am going to New York to die."

"That's a wonderful compliment!" said the young ex-
ecutive. "I'm pleased that you like New York so much."

"Oh, it's not that," replied the girl. "It's just that I can
leave it with less regret than any other place on the face of
the earth."

Traits of a True Southern Belle

The true southern belle is as identifiable as magnolia trees
and kudzu. In addition to her soft and warm southern ac-
cent, she is recognizable by scores of traits and traditions
handed down to her by her mama and daddy, their mama
and daddy, and their mama and daddy, and so on. . . .

Here are some to watch and listen for.

A true southern belle:

• Must know who all her *real* cousins are, even if her
mama and daddy won't allow her to discuss them outside
the confines of the house or when company comes.

• Must know what turnip greens are. She may hate them
and become nauseated by their smell, but she needs to
know just in case her northern cousins visit and ask about
them. She would never want to appear ignorant regarding
southern delicacies.

• Must know that the things [turnip greens] are actually
green.

• Must know the difference between turnip greens, mus-
tard greens, and collard greens.

• Keeps a dictionary close at hand for spelling and look-
ing up words that her northern cousins use.

• Always wears a dress to church and never sneaks out
during the closing hymn or opens her eyes during the prayer.

• Always appears to have an IQ larger than her waist size.
It's nice to have a small Scarlett O'Hara waist, but she must
never let on that her IQ is smaller.

• Never wears a corset or a girdle. She attains the desired
waist measurement through dieting, aerobics, or prolonged
breath holding.

• Doesn't waste hours engrossed in soap operas. She much prefers living out her own fantasies, which have more excitement and intrigue than is ever shown on television.

• Knows that a Blue Plate Special does not mean that mayonnaise is on sale.

• Would never ride a horse sidesaddle.

• If talented, can take a bubble bath and read *Cosmopolitan* at the same time.

• Always takes her cordless telephone with her to the bathtub when the time comes for a long bubble bath.

• Can shoot a hook-shot and dribble with both hands.

• Always prays that the IRS agent who does her audit is single.

• Loves to shag.

• Knows where the old home place is and where all her ancestors for generations are buried, and what they died from.

• Can say "No!" while smiling sweetly.

• Knows how to pump her own gas, but usually doesn't have to.

• Thinks silicone is Baskin-Robbins' thirty-second flavor.

• Displays the correct technique when kicking her tires so everyone watching will conclude that she knows mechanics and can change her own oil, install new spark plugs, and set the idle on her carburetor.

• Stands nearby and watches every move when a mechanic is repairing her car.

• Does not call her brother Bubba or her cousins Cuz.

• Makes no effort to keep up with the Joneses but gloats at their efforts to keep up with her, not necessarily with regard to material things.

• Does not wear black bobby pins with blonde hair.

• Knows that blondes are supposed to have more fun but scoffs at the idea, realizing that down in Dixieland all shades of hair color have a ball.

• Will go to a wrestling match, hide underneath a scarf, and forever deny having been there.

• Knows the difference between a wide receiver and a cornerback, a safety and a field goal, and can explain a two-minute drill or a down-and-out in detail.

• Never goes to bed in rollers, or any place outside of the house with her hair in rollers.

• Never drives the kids to school while wearing her robe and bedroom shoes.

• Can drive a car, drink a Coke, smoke a cigarette, adjust the radio, and watch the baby all at the same time.

• Can parallel park.

• Loves to eat out.

• Is always looking for a new low-calorie salad to go with her Shoney's hot fudge cake.

• Believes that to go "all the way" really does mean with mustard, catsup, and onions.

• Knows that stoned ground crackers are not good ole Georgia boys that have smoked too much marijuana.

• Always has a quarter in her pocket or purse to make a telephone call if necessary.

• Never pops chewing gum in public.

• Keeps in touch with her mama regularly, even though at times she would just as soon not.

More Traits of a True Southern Belle . . .

A true southern belle:

• Speaks to everyone she passes, whether she knows them or not.

• Attends the family reunion every year and knows and kisses everyone there.

• Expects a man to remove his hat (or cap) indoors and won't hesitate to tell him.

• Doesn't expect people to call before dropping by. Friends are always welcome.

• Never returns a pie plate or a casserole dish to a friend empty.

• Says "ma'am" and "sir" to her elders no matter how old *she* gets.

• Starts cooking the minute she hears there's been a death in town.

• Fits in as well at a formal dinner party as she does at an outdoor barbecue and can be ready for either in less than an hour.

• Never says "No" to just one more for dinner, especially when it's one of her children's playmates.

• Talks as sweet as sugar until you mess with one of her young'uns. Then she'll let you have it with both barrels so quick you won't know what hit you.

• Won't live anywhere but in the South and can't understand for the life of her why anyone else would.

• Can bait a hook, load a gun, catch a fish, and kill a bird, but lets her husband clean the fish.

• Never has to measure anything when preparing one of her favorite recipes.

• Knows what pot likker is and that overindulgence in it won't put her over the .10 mark on the intoximeter.

• Knows how to make redeye gravy.

• Never shaves her legs above the knees, except in summer.

• Always goes to Daddy for money, married or not.

• Never notices cobwebs in her own house but can spot even the smallest in yours.

• Knows everyone's ancestors for at least three generations back and holds you responsible for your grandfather's wild ways.

• Would never allow her daughter to date your son.

• While shopping, will tell her best friend that the dress she's trying on is "really you" and "simply gawgeus" because it makes her look ten pounds heavier and five years older.

• Only gossips in the name of sympathy. "Poor Violet. I'm so concerned for her sanity. You know how bad Vernon is to drink an' all."

• Travels to the city to buy her expensive clothes with designer labels—at the Junior League's annual yard sale.

• Never admits her ineligibility for membership in the Daughters of the American Revolution or the United Daughters of the Confederacy. She just "doesn't have the time" for either, she says.

• Always leaves one important ingredient out of a recipe

before she shares it and adds one visible ingredient to any recipe she borrows.

• Sheds genuine tears in private, preferably in a locked bathroom; public tears have an ulterior motive.

• Smiles sweetly but says nothing when she visits her Yankee in-laws with her husband and they make fun of her southern drawl.

• Hides the Visa bill from her husband. If she really becomes desperate, Daddy always comes to her rescue; and she accepts both his check and the lecture.

• Has a family story for each piece of furniture, bric-a-brac, table linen, and wall hanging—all true in her mind.

• Keeps sheets draped over the best furniture until company comes. Local drop-ins get to view the sheets but sit elsewhere.

• Will serve a drop-in guest the last drop of soup or spoonful of grits and with her eyes dare the children to say they're hungry.

• Cleans out the accumulated gook in the bottom of the sink with her bare hands, but wouldn't touch a mousetrap on a dare—or a double-dare—or a double-dog-dare.

• Has her own monogrammed cue stick and carrying case that one would best not touch.

• Never sweats, even if the temperature is 105 degrees in the shade.

Oops! Wrong Zip Code!

Never underestimate the fury of a woman, especially a southern woman. She doesn't get mad; she gets even, as depicted in this story told to me by a good friend.

He says that a husband and wife down in Albany, Georgia, had a violent and prolonged argument, and both were still fuming when they went to bed, she in the bedroom and he on the sofa, the Siberia for errant husbands.

The next morning, they didn't speak. Both worked and were getting dressed when she put on her favorite dress but couldn't reach the zipper. Without saying a word, she backed up to her husband and pointed to the zipper.

He proceeded to zip it up. Then he zipped it down. Then up. Then down. He thought how funny that was, so he just stood there zipping it up and down until he broke the zipper—at half-mast. He then had to cut her out of her favorite dress, and you can imagine what that did for her disposition, which already was at the boiling point.

She was livid with rage and ran off to her bedroom crying, slipped on another dress, and left for work without saying a word.

All day she thought about two things: her favorite dress with the broken zipper . . . and *revenge!*

She arrived home late in the afternoon. Pulling into the driveway, she parked behind her husband's car. She saw two legs sticking out from underneath his car and knew then and there what her course of action would be.

She walked over to his car. Saying nothing, she reached underneath the car and got a firm hold on the zipper she found there. Zip! Zip! Zip! She ran it up and down repeatedly until it broke.

"There! That'll take care of him!" she thought to herself.

She then went on in the house, where, to her amazement, sitting at the kitchen table drinking coffee and reading the newspaper was her husband!

And this one was told to me by another good friend, a Georgia state patrolman who swore it was a true story. I'm in no position to refute it, so I'll just tell you what he told me and let you draw your own conclusions.

He said he was patrolling on a state road in a rural area of South Georgia on a cold and rainy night when he came upon a two-car accident about 1:30 A.M.

He then said he would have to go back a little ways, before the accident, for background purposes and explain that a girl named Sarah Taylor lived in the area not far from the accident scene. Sarah lived with her sister Irene, the driver of one of the cars involved in the accident.

Irene worked nights, and Sarah worked days. Sarah had been to the beauty parlor that afternoon and had her hair fixed. When she got ready to go to bed, she couldn't find her hair net. Not wanting to mess up her new hairdo, she had to improvise.

Sarah searched the house over from top to bottom, including all closets and boxes in the attic, but found no hair net. The closest she could come to duplicating one was a pair of nylon underpants. So she pulled them down over her hair. It felt just fine, so she turned out the light and went to sleep.

At two o'clock in the morning, the patrolman radioed the state patrol post and had the night man call Sarah to tell her that her sister had been in an automobile accident and needed her automobile insurance policy. Sarah immediately hung up the telephone without waiting to learn that Irene was not seriously injured. Not knowing if her sister was half dead, badly injured, or what, she was scared to death.

Sarah jumped out of bed, jerked on a housecoat, removed the insurance policy from a chest of drawers, and drove the short distance to the scene of the accident.

Then, the trooper paused and chuckled.

"I'll tell you, that was the toughest job I ever had," he said, "standing there in the rain at two o'clock in the morning, looking poor Sarah in the eye, and trying to keep a straight face while relating to her what had happened to her sister . . . wondering to myself why she had her underpants on the wrong end!"

Southern Women Never Walk Alone

I have no idea at what stage in life little girls are cautioned to never go to the ladies' room alone. Maybe it starts in kindergarten or first grade when children are paired up to go everywhere, holding hands: to the lunchroom, to the gymnasium, on field trips, to the library.

Then again, maybe it all started in the Girl Scouts where the buddy system is employed for safety reasons when the girls go swimming or hiking.

I guess it could have started, too, at home in the country

years ago when the ladies' room was way out behind the house in the dark, vulnerable to boogers and ghosts in the form of older brothers who would scare the daylights out of a little girl making her way after dark to the little outhouse with the half-moon cut in the door.

Wherever and whenever the tradition got its start, it has been sustained to this day. Women absolutely will not make the trip to the ladies' room alone.

I am convinced that deep, dark secrets are transmitted in ladies' rooms all over the South. Danger surely lurks behind those closed doors.

Does every mother caution her little girl at a very early age to "Never accept gifts from strangers, and *never* go to the ladies' room alone"? No doubt in my mind they do, because they don't. They go together, in coveys, like quail.

Here is a typical scene: Harriet, Lois, Marlene, Grace, Ramona, Virginia, and Margaret are at the club for dinner with their husbands. Less than three minutes after they arrive, Grace pops the question, "Would anybody like to go with me to the ladies' room?" And like quail, off they march—Harriet, Lois, Marlene, Ramona, Virginia, Margaret, and Grace—with Grace leading the march.

Once they enter the secret chamber, they stay longer than the NBA playoffs. Finally, they return to the table only to learn that John and Jane have arrived.

After greetings are exchanged all around, the girls take their seats. They're seated for no more than thirty seconds when Jane pops the welcomed question, "Would anybody like to go with me to the ladies' room?"

Right on cue, up stand Harriet, Lois, Marlene, Ramona, Virginia, Margaret, and Grace to join Jane for the trip. Do any of them really have to go to the ladies' room? Is nature calling? Certainly not! Each is afraid, but not of boogers, ghosts, or big brothers scaring the daylights out of them. Each is afraid of what might be said that she would miss if she stayed behind to sip the white wine and nibble on mixed nuts and didn't go.

A southern woman never passes up an opportunity to go to a ladies' room, and if she's alone in any establishment she'll approach a complete stranger and extend an invitation to join her. When they exit after an extended stay, they will be chatting like long-lost sisters.

No, a southern woman would no more pass up an opportunity to go to a ladies' room than an alcoholic would pass up a bar if it meant missing his plane.

Those of us who escort ladies to restaurants, clubs, and lounges can only guess as to what deep secrets are shared in ladies' rooms, because only the ladies know for sure.

And they never walk alone . . . At least not to the ladies' room.

Aerobics with a Twist

Aerobics have taken over mornings as far as women are concerned. Nearly every female from kindergartens to nursing homes is deep into aerobics of some sort, either at a fitness center or on the floor of the den in front of a television set.

I even read recently that thirty women have organized an early morning Christian aerobics class at Eastside Baptist Church in Marietta, Georgia (called Mayretta by the natives) just outside of Atlanta (called Atlanter by the few natives left).

"We enjoy a beat with a message," said Sheila Hunt, one of Eastside Baptist's aerobics instructors. "It's a welcome alternative to commercial health club aerobics with the suggestive moves and lewd music. We exercise to contemporary Christian music at Eastside Baptist. We jump for Jesus!"

No matter whether the grunt and groaners jump for Jesus or dance for the devil, they're still huffing and puffing their way along the sweaty road to losing pounds and inches. It also makes for good conversations at club meetings, afternoon teas, and the Elk's Club Hawaiian luau where it would be embarrassing to wear a grass skirt that doesn't quite cover the whole lawn.

For those women who belong to the television aerobics cult, the routine is pretty much the same every morning in every household. It goes like this:

A pretty fella' with a bunch of muscles, a bunch of hair, a bunch of teeth, a tank top, and a Jimmy Carter smile who looks like the sort of guy who would kick sand in the face of a ninety-seven-pound weakling on the beach, is flanked by two scantily clad (almost naked) girls who never sweat. The three of them are on the tube before daylight going through multiple gyrations to the beat of foreign music.

The setting has an ocean in the background and the two nymphs make every effort to emulate the hulk's every move. If he jumps in the ocean, in they go, too. In all probability, the home television exercisers would jump in the bathtub inasmuch as their ultimate goal is eventually to look as much like the two nymphs as possible.

I ask you, have you ever seen a fat girl doing aerobics on television? Never! They all weigh in at ninety-four pounds and look like Twiggy. Aerobics didn't do it for them. They were born that way.

There is one exception to this morning routine, a pretty Middle Georgia housewife and mother of four beautiful daughters more beautiful than the two nymphs on the television screen she watches every morning. I'll just call her Ruth.

Ruth has her own morning aerobics routine, and it makes a lot of sense to me. Here's what she does:

Ruth climbs out of her warm bed, even on cold winter mornings, turns on the television set, and switches the channel selector knob to "her" aerobics program. After adjusting the set to get the picture and the volume just right, Ruth the aerobics buff crawls back in bed, pulls up the covers . . . *and watches!*

"She never misses," her husband, Joe, assured me. "She's as regular with her morning home aerobics as Hayley's MO."

It must work, because Ruth looks great despite the fact that the only exercise she derives from her morning aerobics sessions is throwing back the covers and pulling them back up again. She could eliminate those routines if she could ever talk her husband into buying her a television set equipped with remote control. While she deserves it, she ain't gonna' get it in the near future. I know ole Joe pretty well. Of course, she may well have one stashed out in the garage underneath all her yard sale loot. If so, she'll find it when she makes good on her promise to Joe to "go through it all one of these days."

"I'm not holding my breath," says Joe. "We've got the only house in town with $50,000 worth of automobiles parked in the driveway and $7.45 worth of junk parked in the garage."

There's a sequel to this story. Ruth has a good friend in Macon, Georgia, who, thanks to Ruth, is also into morning television aerobics. After hearing Ruth explain her morning routine, the young lady (I'll just call her Lisa) subscribed to it and now does it regularly.

She adds her own twist to Ruth's regimen. She eats Hershey bars while she watches!

I think maybe Robert M. Hutchins must have had Ruth and Lisa in mind when he said, "Whenever I feel like engaging in vigorous exercise, I lie down until the feeling passes."

Who Wears Short Shorts?

The coming of summer in the South ushers in many things: watermelon, swimming, sunbathing, 100-plus temperatures, hand-held cardboard funeral home fans, camp meetings, dinner on the grounds, gnats, and . . . short shorts.

With appropriate apologies to the rest of the United States and California, nobody wears shorts as well as the girls of the South. What is more eye-catching than a pretty southern girl with a golden tan decked out in a pair of white shorts and a pink blouse? I doubt there is anything, and they do attract attention.

Short shorts are so popular that I recall a song having been written about them several years ago: "Who wears short shorts? We wear short shorts . . ." Remember?

Girl watching has been an art form for as long as there have been males and females, and most males put in a lot of overtime in summer at such places as swimming pools, beaches, and shopping malls. I mention shopping malls simply because they seem to attract pretty girls in short shorts.

Saturday mornings are good for girl watching, and it's amazing how long a cup of coffee or a Coke will last while sitting at a table in an open-air mall cafe while the passing parade strolls by, and back, and by again. On and on.

I was sitting in a shopping mall one Saturday morning with my newspaper and coffee when I witnessed an unusual occurrence. A boat show was in progress, and lots of men were on hand to look them over.

Now then, bear in mind that admirers of pretty girls in short shorts are by no means limited as to age. I hope I never reach the age where I fail to admire a pretty girl, one of God's greatest creations. And I do know something about pretty girls because I've had one of my own, Lisa, for thirty years. Bragging? Yes. Proud? Yes. Lisa is my idea of a true southern belle.

Those of you who are familiar with malls in summer know that pretty girls parade there in droves. It's known as "walking the mall," repeatedly, from one end to the other.

As I sat and watched, spilling coffee in my lap several times, I saw a man stroll by. He was nonchalantly admiring the boats on display and probably mentally picturing himself on his favorite lake in one of them. He was also munching on a candy bar. I would put his age at probably in the early sixties.

As he walked past a beauty salon, three short shorts parade beauties wearing rumors approached him. They passed and, predictably, he turned to watch them move on through the mall. And he turned and looked again . . . and again. Then it happened.

The candy muncher decided to take one last look before the trio of lovelies disappeared into Belk's. While doing so, he ran head-on into a 220 horsepower outboard motor mounted on the back of a beautiful blue and white boat and broke his glasses!

The man wasn't injured, but you can bet he got more than he bargained for: an eyeful of three pretty girls and an outboard motor.

As I saw him walk away, broken glasses in hand, I wondered exactly how he would explain to his wife what had happened!

Where There's a "Will" There's a Way

The ingenuity and determination of a southern woman should never be underestimated. Many men have, only to shake their heads in disbelief in the end.

Take the case of the South Alabama housewife and her no-good and inconsiderate husband:

Legend has it that the husband came home one afternoon to pick up his fishing tackle. His wife met him at the door and said, "Honey, I'm so glad you're home. I need your help. My car won't start, and I have to take little Jenny to the dentist in half an hour."

The husband stared at her briefly, then said, pointing to the area just above the pocket, "Woman, take a good look at my shirt. Do you see 'Mr. Goodwrench' there?" And with that he went on his way, fishing tackle in hand, leaving his wife to manage as best she could.

A few days later, he was again greeted by his wife when he arrived home from work to grab a bite to eat before going to his weekly poker game with the boys. "Herman, before you leave would you please take a look at the washing machine? I have a load of clothes in it, and it just stopped while in the middle of the wash cycle," she told him.

"Woman, take a good look at my shirt," he said, again pointing to the area above the pocket. "Do you by any chance see 'Maytag' there?" And with that he went on to the poker game, leaving her to manage as best she could.

The very next week, after arriving home, the wife approached ole Herman as he was changing clothes before heading to the golf course on a Wednesday afternoon. "Herman, I hate to bother you but the electricity is off in the kitchen and I can't cook supper. Could you please . . ."

"Woman, take a good look at this shirt," he said, again pointing to the area above the pocket. "Do you see 'Electrician' there?" And he left to go to the golf course, leaving her to manage as best she could.

The next afternoon, upon arriving home, Herman noticed that his wife's car was humming like a sewing machine in the driveway. Once inside the house, he heard the washing machine purring like a kitten. The lights were on in the kitchen, with supper cooking on the stove.

"Well, I see you managed to get the car, the washing machine, and the kitchen lights fixed," he said. "How'd you do that?"

"Oh, no problem, Herman. You know that nice new neighbor, Will, who moved in across the street last week?" she asked.

"You mean the ski instructor?"

"Right."

"Yeah, I know him. Why?"

"Well, he had the day off today, and he fixed them all this morning," she said.

"Oh? What'd he charge you?"

"Nothing," she said, smiling. "He just gave me a choice."

"A choice? What kind of choice?"

"Well, he told me that I could either go to bed with him or bake him a cake so . . ."

"Well? What kind of cake did you bake him?"

"Cake? What cake? Herman, take a good look at my blouse," she said, pointing to the area just below her left shoulder. "Now then, I ask you, do you see 'Betty Crocker' there?"

Would You Please Say That Again?

I thought I had heard all the descriptive phrases that flow from those who pour coffee, make toast, and feed quarters to the jukeboxes in fast food coffee shops that dot the Southland.

I didn't think I would ever hear what I heard as I ate breakfast on a rainy morning in a Huddle House in my hometown. A waitress arrived late for work and explained to the manager, "I jus' couldn' get here no quicker. Man, them roads is slicky out where I live!"

But my eyes and ears were opened one Sunday when I was in a favorite South Georgia town and stopped in a Huddle House to ask directions.

I directed my inquiry at Carol after waiting, and watching, as she served a customer. I concluded right off that Carol and her uniform were at odds with each other. Where her uniform was too big, Carol was too little; where her uniform was too little, Carol was too big. And her cap was on crooked. So was her lipstick, all three pounds of it. But her nametag was straight.

"Excuse me," I said, "can you direct me to the country club?"

"Naw, 'fraid not," she said. "Only club I know 'bout roun' heah is Maybelle's out on th' road to th' dump."

"Maybelle's?"

"Right, but it ain't open on Sunday, at least th' front door ain't. But if Maybelle knows ya', she'll let ya' in the back."

"Thanks," I said. "I think I'll pass on Maybelle's for now. I'm supposed to meet a friend at the country club to play golf and . . ."

"Oh! Ya' lookin' f'r th' place where they play golf at?"

"Right."

"I know where tha's at," Carol said. "My ex-husband took me there to his Junior–Senior Prom an' he showed me th' field where they play golf at 'tween daintzes, if ya' know what I mean."

"Yeah. I get the picture."

"I'll never f'rget that thing they call th' fifth tee," she said. "Boy!"

"Good. Can you tell me how to get there?"

"Sure. No problem," she assured me. "Jus' take 441 North out there in front o' th' res'runt, go 'bout a mile to Walker Street, turn right an' go til' ya' see a big curve. Well, it rilly ain't no curve. Th' road jus' kindly goes crookedy off to th' right and . . ."

"You say it just kindly goes crookedy?"

"Right."

"I see. You mean it veers to the right?"

"Well, naw, it don't. Like I said, it jus' kindly goes crookedy. Ya' can't miss it," she said.

"Thanks, Carol," I said. "I just go to Walker Street, turn right, and look for the first road that kindly goes crookedy off to the right."

"Yeah. Ya' got it."

"One more thing, Carol," I said.

"Yeah? Wha's that?"

"The road ain't slicky, is it?"

"Naw. It's a hard road, mister."

I arrived at the country club with twelve minutes to spare. My friend was waiting.

"Any trouble finding the place?" he asked.

"No, not a bit," I said.

We played holes one, two, and three without incident or serious injury. He had two pars and a tap-in for a birdie. I had two bogies and a struggling par.

On four, he hit his tee shot out of bounds on the left. I managed to stay in the fairway and bogied the hole. He took a double and a shot of Jack Daniel's.

On five, he cautioned me as I stepped up on the tee. "Better be careful on this one. Straight away for 200 yards and then . . ."

"I've heard about Number Five," I said.

"You have? When?"

"About an hour ago, in the Huddle House," I said. "It kindly goes crookedy off to the right, correct?"

"Huh? Kindly goes crookedy?"

"You got it."

"No, man! It *doglegs* right!"

"Yeah. That, too."

"What are you smiling about? Because you won the last hole?"

"No, I was just thinking about this tee, a Junior–Senior Prom, and a girl named Carol," I said.

"What the heck does that have to do with golf?"

"It's a long story, Ed," I assured him. "I'll tell it to you one day when we get rained out . . . and the golf course is slicky."

"Slicky? Have you been in my Jack Daniel's?" he asked. "Hit the ball before the cheese slips all the way off your cracker."

I teed my ball up, swung, and watched it take its usual path, It went about 180 yards, sliced, and went kindly crookedy to the right. A perfect shot on Number Five. And that makes two that I know of.

We've Got Snobs in Dixie, Too!

It always pleases me to hear an individual from another section of the country comment on the friendly welcome he received in my beloved Southland. But I have to be realistic. We have our snobs, too.

I went to a cookout in a small southern town. The invitation said "Dress Casual." To the crowd I run with, that usually means "Clothes Optional."

It was a nice party in a spiffy neighborhood where the streets wind around but go nowhere and have sexy names like Way, Vista, Drive, Circle, Court, and Place—but no streets like Oak, Maple, or Third.

There was BYOB beer, liquor, wine, and white stuff on the kitchen bar, along with personalized bottle holders from brown bag days, and printed napkins saying, "Sonny and Sherri."

Most wore jeans, windbreakers, and athletic shoes sporting a price tag that would take care of the down payment on a Mercedes or a Jaguar.

The men huddled four or five to a group talking golf and fishing, depending on the group. The women likewise talked children and clothes, depending on the group.

In the kitchen, two women were standing at the bar talking cars and cruises. One had a Mercedes, the other a Jaguar. The Mercedes had just been on a Caribbean cruise, the Jaguar to the Mediterranean. I had just returned from Savannah. They didn't know I was alive. To them I was on the same social level as the paper towel holder and the used Brillo pad on the sink. But I listened briefly.

Neither would have spoken to me had I parked a bulldozer on her big toe, even the one with the ingrown toenail. And my ten-year-old car didn't fit in.

The Mercedes was decked out in a pale pink linen designer jumpsuit from Jamaica and a wide gold belt from Barbados. The Jaguar sported a black velvet toreador outfit and silver slippers from Barcelona

They had two concerns: which had the best car and whether the Mediterranean or the Caribbean had the clearest water. I heard them voice another major concern: how would they survive without Perrier water, which had just been taken off the market?

"I'm glad we have a large supply on hand," said the Mercedes. "We're having four parties next month, and what's a party without Perrier?"

"You lucky girl! We only have a little more than four cases. Bruce and I will go through that in two weeks," the Jaguar stated. "He said last week that he might fake a business trip to Paris to get some."

I went back to golf and fishing. A man can listen to only so many problems, and the pros and cons of Mercedes and Jaguars, Mediterranean and Caribbean, and the absence of Perrier on the shelves of America's liquor stores weren't three of them.

I've known both girls for years. The Mercedes is married to a doctor who makes more money than a pitcher with a ninety-eight miles-per-hour fastball and a 1.21 ERA; a six-foot, eight-inch wide receiver who runs the 40 in 3.9 and has hands like Paul Bunyan; a seven-foot, eight-inch center with a per game point average of 45, 38 rebounds, 29 assists, and a free throw average of .97; a PGA touring pro with a per round average of 62 and average yearly tour earnings of $5,866,322; a heavyweight boxer contending for the world championship; or a major college basketball coach with a Nike shoe contract.

The Jaguar? Nobody knows, but it is generally believed that her old man is either a sports agent or a counterfeiter.

I knew both before they could afford to be snobs, when the Mercedes was an Edsel and the Jaguar a Henry J.

Perrier? Both toted water from a backyard well.

On my way home I heard on the news that a house had burned and two children, ages four and seven, had perished. Somehow the snobs' Perrier problem didn't seem important to me anymore.

Part 3

Love, Romance, and Memories

The language of love and romance is universal. It's just done with a different slant in various locales. In the South sharing is a common denominator, like the good ole boy from South Georgia who promised to be faithful and loving after proposing to his girlfriend of long standing. He made the ultimate commitment when he looked her straight in the eye, took her hand, and said, "Mary Sue, you jus' 'member one thing. Long's I got a biscuit, you got half."

Then there was the fellow from North Florida who, while discussing his recent divorce, said to his beer buddy over long-neck Buds, "They won't nothin' to it, Gator. No fussin', no fightin', ever'thing went real smooth. We jus' split ever'thing fifty-fifty, includin' th' house and—"

"Huh? Come on, Billy Bob. How in th' heck can ya' split a house fifty-fifty?" questioned Gator.

"Easy," Billy Bob replied. "She got th' inside, an' I got th' outside."

Southern girls have a way of taking care of themselves when the split comes. It's a little like a tetanus shot in that it takes a while for a fella to realize what hit him.

Southern men (good ole boys) have set ideas on romance and marriage. Love 'em, marry 'em, get 'em pregnant a few times, and then start hanging out again with the boys at the pool room or the gas station and hunting and fishing on weekends.

A prime example is good ole C. L., who lived in South Alabama with his wife, Ida Mae. They had been married for six years and had four kids, ages three months, eighteen months, three years, and four-and-a-half—and another on the way. Understandably, Ida Mae was a young-looking woman with old-looking eyes, tired eyes filled with disillusionment.

C. L. and Ida Mae lived in a ramshackle tenant house some eight miles from the nearest town. Only a wood stove and a lone fireplace provided heat in winter. A crippled circulating fan stirred a little air in summer.

It was a cold and dreary January day, and along about dusk Ida Mae stood in the front doorway surrounded by young'uns and called to C. L. as he shuffled out to the road to wait for the school bus to go to a high school basketball game.

"C. L., you ain't a' goin' to th' basketball game are ya'?" she asked.

"I'm a-plannin' to. Why?"

"Well, it's cold an' they ain't no stovewood in th' house, C. L.," she moaned.

"Well now, Sugarbritches, I ain't a-takin' th' axe," C. L. called back as he kept walking.

Things are a little different in the North. The girls up there are much more progressive and urbane. Dining out is as big as eating at home is in the South. Of course, southern women are better cooks, and maybe that explains why.

Status is also a priority with northern women, whereas southern girls are content to dine in any establishment that features an all-you-can-eat buffet for $3.99 and high chairs for the younguns. The women of the North have a tendency to want to be seen in spiffy restaurants that provide Monday morning conversation at the club or office, whereas the women of the South want to eat and status be damned.

Northern girls have a strong desire to be wooed and won by young executives in three-piece suits who wear Rolex watches and drive a BMW or a Mercedes and work at the art of wooing and winning. Southern girls are content with backyard barbecues, a quick trip to the river or the beach, or just being with their men doing whatever comes naturally.

The men of the South don't usually major in wooing and winning, just dancing and doing. They are also not exceptionally knowledgeable in the areas of sweet talk and sugar phrases, but I know of one good ole boy who's learning.

Bobby Joe, a dedicated boy of the soil who lives on his spread in the South Carolina Low Country, won a trip to Paris for raising the best hogs in South Carolina. It was his first trip out of the United States. Heck, it was his first trip outside South Carolina. Big trips to Bobby Joe were weekend jaunts to his alma mater, Clemson.

On his fourth day in Paris, he encountered three suave Frenchmen in his hotel lobby, and they became engaged in deep conversation regarding the subject of lovers and such. Bobby Joe was all ears and asked probing questions regarding the ways of the French with women.

"Well, looka' here, Hoss," Bobby Joe said. "Since I've been here, I've been a-hearin' about somethin' called savvy fur. Whut's that?"

"Ah, monsieur! You are no doubt referring to savoir-faire," said the first Frenchman. "Savoir-faire is when a man comes home, finds his wife in bed with another man, and says, 'Pardon me, monsieur. I apologize for the intrusion,' tips his hat, and leaves. That, my friend, is savoir-faire."

"No! No! No!" said the second Frenchman. "Savoir-faire is when a man comes home, finds his wife in bed with another man, and says, 'Pardon me, monsieur. I apologize for the intrusion. Please continue,' tips his hat, and leaves."

"Absolutely incorrect!" said the third Frenchman. "That is not savoir-faire. When a man comes home, finds his wife in bed with another man, and says, "Pardon me, monsieur. I apologize for the intrusion,' tips his hat and leaves, and the man *can* continue—that, monsieur, is savoir-faire!"

Northern women tend to be overly inquisitive and often evasive when questioned about a given situation. Not southern women. They ask little, accept the status quo, and give straight answers, as this little story shows.

On her way to Florida on vacation, a social worker from

Chicago stopped at a dilapidated shack in the mountains of Tennessee and inquired of the bedraggled young girl who came to the door about her family, not believing that humans could survive in such drab surroundings.

"Could I please speak to your mother?" she asked.

"Maw ain't heah. She's in the County Home," the girl told her.

"How about your father? Is he home?"

"No, ma'am, he's in the penitentiary for making moonshine whiskey," the girl said without a blink.

"Is anyone home but you? Don't you have brothers and sisters?"

"Ain't nobody heah 'cept me," the girl replied. "My sister, Louise, is in a home f'r bad girls, an' Gran'ma is keeping her young'un. I got a li'l brother, Jack, but they got him in reform school. And my other brother, Hank, he's been up at Harvard Medical School f'r two years."

"Your brother is studying at Harvard Medical School?" the social worker asked in disbelief. "He must be real smart."

"No, ma'am, he ain't smart, an' he ain't studyin' up there. They're a-studyin' him."

I have many memories of women, North and South, mostly good. I am proud to number among my friends several women who are married—happily married.

There is Mariet, from Holland, who has lived in America with her husband, Pieter, since 1985. I love her very much, and Pieter knows it. She is young, beautiful, talented, courageous, and very much a lady. Would I marry Mariet if I had the opportunity? Try me. But that ain't gonna' happen because Pieter is much too intelligent to ever let her go, and the guy is in excellent health.

There is Sue. She has identical attributes as Mariet and is a southern belle to the core. I love her, too, but marriage is out. Her big old mean husband, a good friend, would kill me. He might even moon me.

There was Marlene, who lives in Michigan. I had my chance and blew it. I lost my nerve somewhere between her front porch overlooking Lake Superior on a moonlit Friday night designed specifically for marriage proposals and the

center aisle of a Methodist church in Sault Sainte Marie.
She was an excellent cook, a fantastic dresser, and went to
church and Sunday school every Sunday. I went with her
and failed to show up only once. That was the Sunday after-
noon when I blew it. Regrets? I have to be honest, a few. But
she did better.

And Deborah. I have to mention sweet Deborah. Why, I
don't know, but she told me on more than one occasion that
she adored me. I think it was my hands. She's an artist and
said often that I had the kind of hands she'd like to paint.

Deborah said "Yes" during dinner in Macon, Georgia. I
was thrilled beyond belief and had to tell somebody quick. I
told the waitress, who cried. Frankly, I've shed a few tears
myself since. But Deborah did better, too. Fine husband
and three lovely daughters that I love. I'm fortunate. They
love me, too.

When asked about women and marriage over the past
eighteen years, I have said so many times, "I have no time
for women, but I have all the time in the world for ladies."

Believe me when I tell you, there is a big difference,
North and South.

To Every Boy Comes That Moment of Awareness

At what age does a boy become acutely aware that girls are
different and are something other than objects at which to
hurl insults, make faces, ridicule, and generally ignore?
While I really can't pinpoint it, I know that the time comes
when he realizes that girls ain't really all that bad, that they
smell better than he smells, and possess a magnetism that
mystifies him no end.

The time also comes when he leafs through the Sears,
Roebuck catalog at a much slower pace and isn't in as big a
hurry to get to the bicycles and toys as he once was. Sud-
denly, the lingerie section fascinates him, and there are days
when he never gets to the bicycles and toys.

I recall vividly just when the moment of truth came for
me, and I was reminded of it a few years back while driving

on Interstate Highway 16, near Macon, Georgia, as I pulled up behind a caravan of vans, motor homes, and tractor trailers. It didn't take me long to figure out where they were going; they were carnival vehicles headed for the Macon Fairgrounds to set up for the upcoming Middle Georgia Fair.

I laughed to myself as I followed the caravan for a few miles, purposely not passing it. I laughed because I thought of two stories, one fictional and one factual. I'll go with the fictional one first.

A young Tennessee lad of fourteen was getting ready to go to the Tennessee State Fair in Nashville many years ago and was being addressed by his mama.

"Now, Rodney, you go an' have a good time on them rides an' everthing. But I'm warnin' ya', don't you go in that ole girlie show they got out at th' fairgrounds 'cause I hear tell they's things a-goin' on in there whut you don't need to see," his mama told him.

"Like whut, Mama?" the boy asked.

"Never you mind 'bout that," she said. "You jus' don't go in there, ya' heah?"

"Yes'um."

The boy went to the fair, rode the rides, ate the cotton candy, and strolled along the midway. Shortly, he came to the tent that housed the girlie show and heard the band music issuing from inside. He also heard the sound of loud male voices yelling and urging, "Take it off! Go ahead, take it all off!"

Curiosity got the best of the youngster, and he eased up to the ticket seller, stood on his toes to appear as tall as possible, bought a ticket, and slipped inside where he took a back row seat. It was dark with the exception of the small stage on which a scantily clad girl was going through her routine, divesting herself of flimsy, transparent articles of clothing until there was nothing left to divest. She ended her act as naked as a hammer handle while the assembled men cheered and whistled, hooted and hollered.

The boy eased outside and walked home, his mind boggled by what he had seen inside the tent. His mama greeted him upon his return.

"Well, didja' hav' a good time at th' fair?"

"Yes'um, it wuz rail good."

"Ya' didn' go in that ole girlie show, didja'?"

He studied his hands and feet, then confessed. "Yes'um, I did. I know I done wrong, but I went."

"Whut! Ya' did!" his mama bellowed. "Ya' orta' be 'shamed o' y'sef, ya' know that? An' atter I tol' ya' plain as day you'd see things in there ya' won't sposed ta' see. Well, didja'?"

"Yes'um, I did," the boy confessed. "When they turned the lights on at th' end o' th' show I seen—"

"Whut? Ya' seen whut, boy?"

"I seen Daddy standin' in a chair right down on th' front row jus' a-yellin' his head off!"

Now, for the factual.

I guess it was along about 1939 or 1940 when I went to the local fair in my hometown in South Georgia with several buddies one Saturday night. We were all about fourteen or fifteen, and, like the young boy from Tennessee, we were strolling along the midway when all of a sudden, out of no-where, a girl sprang from a tent, stood on a small platform about the size of a medium pizza right in front of us, slung her flimsy dance dress up over her head, and yelled, "Yaaaaahhhhh-hoooooo! It's showtime, boys!"

It was, too! It was *really* showtime. So we bought tickets and went inside to see our first girlie show. I can tell you this: we didn't ride another ride the rest of the time the fair was in town because at the precise moment that gal threw her dress over her head and yelled, we became acutely aware that there's something definitely different about girls.

We said goodbye to the ferris wheel and the merry-go-round forever!

How to Start a Conversation with a Good-looking Stranger

I've never really been one to shy away from initiating a conversation, although I'll admit that there are times when it's difficult to arrive at a starting point. In other words, what, if anything, does a fellow say in situations that dictate words should be exchanged?

For instance, when in a men's rest room with one other individual, what does a guy say? Or should he say anything? I'm never quite sure, but, at any rate, here are a few for starters.

"How's it going?" is usually a safe bet.

"How 'bout them Braves?" is a loser. So are them Braves.

"Sure is a hot day, ain't it?" is a safe bet.

"Boy! They sure build these rest rooms a long way from the bleachers, don't they?" will usually draw an affirmative reply.

So much for rest rooms. What about the checkout line at the supermarket? This can be a little ticklish. I found that out a few weeks ago. It happened this way:

I stood there at register number three in the Piggly Wiggly, my little buggy filled with goodies, scanning the periodicals that grace every checkout line. I was engrossed in the covers of *People, Woman's Day, Redbook,* and the *National Enquirer,* particularly the cover of *People,* where Dolly Parton graced the cover.

My concentration was broken with the arrival of a buggy-pushing woman and her husband, boyfriend, or whatever. She was (almost) wearing a halter top and was constructed (in certain areas) much like the woman gracing the cover of *People.* The man, dressed out in faded jeans, a western shirt, and cowboy boots, was constructed much like Paul Bunyan, only bigger.

The man puffed on a cigarette while the woman munched on a pear. I sensed that I should greet them, and that's when the "hoof-in-mouth" attack hit me as I said to the cover-girl look-alike, "Hi! Sure is a nice pear you have there."

I knew how it sounded the moment the words escaped my big mouth, and I braced, fully expecting Bunyan to send me flying in the general direction of the tomato paste, vinegar, and mustard—three aisles away. It didn't happen. Luckily, for me, he was busily engrossed in viewing *People* magazine, too.

The woman either overlooked or excused my dumb comment and responded, "Sure is. Would you like one?"

I stammered something else dumb, paid for my goodies, and gave her my Green Stamps. A woman, you know, will forgive any indiscretion if you offer her Green Stamps. Flowers and candy won't always get the job done; but Green Stamps will do it every time. I wouldn't leave home without them.

Should you find yourself in a situation where an opening line is called for—especially if the person is of the opposite gender—you might try one of these. They've always worked for me:

- "Excuse me, but can you change a $100 bill?"
- "Do you have the correct time?"
- "Which contestant do you think posed for the nude photographs?"
- "What do you think the Democrats' chances are of winning the White House?"
- "Do you miss Howard Cosell?"
- "Do you think Michael Jackson *really* has a tattooed photograph of Vanessa Williams on the back of his hand?"
- "Which team are you picking in this year's Georgia-Georgia Tech (or whatever) game?"
- "Did you hear that Brooke Shields is engaged to George Burns?"

These are all acceptable, and will probably initiate an interesting conversation—or a fist fight. But if not, there *is* one that never fails: "Where 'bouts y'all from?"

Without Women Around, Men Strike Out

Now hear this: most men are helpless at home when the woman of the house is absent. Here are two examples told to me by one of the principals involved in each:

Jack and Mary have been married for more than forty years. They lived all over the United States until Jack retired and they settled in a small town in Middle Georgia where their daughter, who is married to a doctor, lives. Just plain good folks.

Jack is a personable, easy-going, hail-fellow-well-met individual with a good word for everybody, especially his golfing friends, whom he sees every day. It was in the pro shop at the country club that Jack told me this story. His wife, Mary, was out of town and had been for several days.

The night before, Jack had suddenly become quite domestic and decided to do his laundry at home. Sounds simple, right? It is, with one exception: Jack. During his long, happy marriage, he had never done his own laundry. Mary always took care of that.

Jack knows about shanks, sand traps, handicaps, chili-dipping, slicing, and hooking—and he'd heard rumors that there is a thing called a birdie—but the man doesn't know diddley about fabric settings, delicate permanent press, wash, spin, final rinse cycles, detergents, bleaches, and dryer settings. Mary knows about all these, but she was a thousand miles away when Jack had his late-night Maytag attack.

So what did Jack do? He did what any all-thumbs, male chauvinist would do. He called Mary long distance, not once but *six* times between the wash and final rinse cycles.

"Bo, I was as lost as a second shot in the lake on Number 12," Jack confessed. "Lights kept coming on, buzzers buzzed, suds gushed from the washer. It looked like a rabid elephant. How was I to know that half a box of Tide was too much? I figured the more the better. Then, drying time came. Heck, I didn't dry my clothes. I parched 'em! Just look at this shirt and pair of pants. More wrinkles than a case of prunes."

You can bet that the next time Mary flies the coop, her rooster will head for a commercial laundry with his dirty shirts and britches. After all, a fella can't hang around a country club pro shop wearing wrinkled clothes.

Gerald and Janet are good friends of mine. Gerald's story was passed on to me by another good friend of theirs and mine, Deborah.

Janet was out of town visiting relatives, and Gerald was batching it. Although he's big enough to go bear hunting with a switch, he doesn't know diddley about cooking.

According to Deborah, this is what happened the first morning after Janet left:

Deborah's telephone rang about 7:00 A.M. It was Gerald calling.

"Hey, Deb! How the heck do you cook grits?" he asked.

"Just look on the box, Gerald," Deborah told him. "The directions are right there and—"

"I can't do that," he growled.

"Why not?"

"Because Janet poured the grits out of the box into one of them dang cannister things and then threw the box away," he explained. "Now I don't know how many grits, how much water, how long to cook 'em, or nothing," Gerald moaned.

Sweet Deborah then proceeded to go through the entire procedure of grits cooking, and Gerald wrote it down. When she finished, he made one request.

"Do me one favor, Deb," he pleaded.

"What's that?"

"Please don't tell Janet about this phone call!"

As far as I know, Deborah has remained mute, so I guess I'm spilling the beans now!

Bridal Fishing Is Big in the South

Fishing has always been big with men in the South, and there are few den walls south of Richmond, Virginia, that don't have prize catches mounted on them.

I am not a good fisherman. What I know about fishing could be tattooed on the belly of a Louisiana pink, but I know enough about the sport to talk with some degree of intelligence about pole fishing, casting with rod and reel, and the use of a spinner and a fly rod, all popular with men who fish. But none of these is the most popular with the women. The use of the trotline is their choice, engaged women especially.

A trotline, for the benefit of the uninformed, is a strong fishing line suspended over the water with short, baited lines hung from it usually at two- to three-foot intervals.

I used to go with my daddy to fish his trotlines many years ago, but I hadn't really given much thought to them until I visited a jewelry store to purchase a wedding gift for a friend's daughter. The visit jarred my memory.

I browsed around the jewelry store for a few minutes before I saw them, the matrimonial trotlines. There were six of them, and they work like this:

The bride-to-be begins casting for the big fish at about age seventeen, using such bait as blinking eyes, a big smile, all sorts of good-smelling stuff, tight jeans, enough hair rollers to curl Vassar, and the cunning of Scarlett O'Hara. Shampoo? By the gallon.

She fishes various streams for about two years until she hooks one and verifies her catch with a third finger, left hand trophy. Then she runs to the newspaper engagements page with a picture of her and her fish to tell the world, "I hooked him!"

This done, her next move is to set out the matrimonial trotlines in jewelry and department stores. The bait is a little card with her name on it, along with the type of fish she's fishing for—called bridal selections. Some of the more popular species are:

Dresden Rose, Strasbourg, Candlelight, Old Master, Castle Garden, Solitaire, Elypse, Moonspun, Cherrywood, King Edward, Cottonwood, Harvest Garland, Heritage Fostoria, Colonial Shell, and Williamsburg.

I left the jewelry store and moved on to another lake, a department store, where I saw an unbelievable eighteen matrimonial trotlines! The fish were biting, too. Although I was only there for a few minutes, one trotline caught two pieces of informal dinnerware and another a piece of informal flatware. The weather must not have been right for the good stuff.

It is useless to set out the trotlines unless they are checked regularly. Here's the way that's done:

There's a card accompanying each trotline to record the catch. A couple of times a week the bride-to-be, or her authorized trotline checker, drops by to check the line and pick up the catch, take it to the bride-to-be's home, and display it on the dining room table or on a bed in the guest room. Should both overflow, borrowed folding tables from the church are brought in.

All kinds of fish are caught on a matrimonial trotline. Some of the more popular ones caught during the prewedding fishing season are:

Three ironing boards; sixty-three assorted pots and pans; three electric coffee pots and a Mr. Coffee; a microwave oven; 756 potholders; seventy-seven napkin rings; twelve dozen napkins; six cookbooks; two grills; four toasters; five blenders; two electric mixers; trailer loads of everyday dishes and stainless; three unidentified contraptions with electric cords made in Korea, Hong Kong, and Taiwan; enough sheets, towels, and pillowcases to supply a Holiday Inn for two months; coasters and more coasters; glasses by the case; wooden bowls; plastic bowls; glass bowls; twelve what-the-heck-is-that's?; commode seat covers with matching bathmats; long-handled forks; short-handled forks; thirteen spatulas; six cannister sets; nine brooms and an equal number of mops; a hamburger cooker; five popcorn poppers; and the all-important electric can opener.

Most of these items, but not the can opener, will remain at Mama's for an eternity inasmuch as Florence, the bride-to-be, and Fred, the groom, will be moving into an apartment so small that there will barely be room for the coasters.

So much for Florence. But what about ole Fred? I walked down to the sporting goods store after leaving the department store confident that there would be a trotline for him.

Was there a little card to identify the groom's selections? There was not! But why not a matrimonial trotline for Fred identifying his choices such as a Zebco 33 reel, Speed Stick fly rod, and fishing lures such as Rapala, Hawaiian Wiggler, Super R, Big O, and Rooster Tail? Or Titleist golf balls, .12 gauge Western X-Pert shotgun shells, a Remington 1100, a Winchester 30-06 with a Weaver scope, a Coleman stove, wading boots, a pair of Keds, or a dip net?

There you have it, twenty-one matrimonial trotlines for Florence but not one for Fred. Not even a lousy minnow hook. What other evidence is needed to substantiate the fact that there is absolutely no justice when it comes to matrimonial trotlines?

There is no closed season. The matrimonial trotlines are set twelve months a year, and some brides-to-be set them out more than once in a lifetime.

Single vs. Married

It started off as just another routine Wednesday. You know how it goes. Check the mail, do a little typing before having lunch and heading for the first tee, followed by the woods, water holes, and sand traps for the better part of three hours—at the country club. (Do you know why the game of golf was named golf? Omega Rodgers told me it was "because that was the only four-letter word they had left!")

After drowning four balls on Number three, hooking one in a cornfield on five, another in the river on fourteen, my game fell apart. I hooked one over Jack Caldwell's house and into Sessions Lake, turned in my scorecard (92), and drove downtown for my usual afternoon coffee and conversation, joining my good friend, the Rev. Bill Jordan.

It was when the waitress, Lucy Mae, brought my coffee that this Wednesday made a 180-degree turn for the worse. Not the coffee. It was great! My conversation with Lucy Mae was the kicker.

I enjoy a good give-and-take with waitresses. I should, considering that I eat some 1,200 meals a year in restaurants, with about 1,000 of them in the restaurant where Lucy Mae works. She's a nice girl, eighteen, pretty, a good waitress, a great sense of humor, a definite asset when dealing with me and the crowd I hang out with for coffee.

Lucy Mae was beaming as she brought my coffee and lost no time revealing what had put the glow on her face. An engagement ring adorned her left hand.

"Yep," she confirmed. "I'm gettin' married August nineteenth."

I congratulated her and let it slide, but she didn't. After some thought she commented when she brought me a refill. "You need to get married, too!" she fired at me without warning.

"Me? No, thank you!" I told her. "I've been down that road and bogged down."

"Why not?"

"Because I'm happy as I can be single," I assured her.

"But you could be just as happy married," she said in rebuttal.

It was at this point that an elected county official, seated at a nearby table and privy to the cross-examination Lucy Mae was giving me, came to my defense.

"But Lucy Mae," he argued, "if he's only going to be *just* as happy, why should he get married?"

"Well, he just needs to get married and have somebody to cook for him and do his laundry," she said with an air of finality.

"But," I injected, "the cooks here cook for me, and I send my laundry out."

She wouldn't surrender.

"Well then, you need somebody to go home to at night," she said. "You know, somebody to talk to and be with. Companionship."

"But I have companionship, somebody to talk to and be with."

"Who?"

"Me," I said. "I get along just fine with me. And no arguments! Plus, I'm too selfish to be married."

"You know what I mean. You wouldn't be lonesome," she said.

"Lucy Mae, I haven't been lonesome since my first (and only) 'snipe hunt' with Louie and Brady Williamson in Oglethorpe when I was fourteen," I countered. "Besides, I know more happy single people than I do happy married people."

That hit the bull's eye.

"Oh, yeah!" she fumed. "Well, my mama and daddy was happy! And they loved each other to death—right up to the day they got divorced!"

The elected county official fell out of his chair hooting with laughter. The other waitress, Corina, who had eased up to the front near the cash register to listen to the debate, dropped a handful of menus and howled.

"I'm sure they did, Lucy Mae," I told her. "And I hope you will be very happy. You'll be a good wife."

"Thank you, but I still think you need to be married," she persisted.

I didn't pursue the subject. I finished my coffee, helped the elected county official up off the floor, picked up a few menus for Corina, and went home to gather up my dirty clothes and make my semiannual trip to the laundry.

Need to be married? Lucy Mae, nobody *needs* to be married. Like nobody *needs* to eat liver.

Best wishes.

Blessed Are the Matchmakers

"Blessed are the matchmakers; for they shall endure forever." Surely, this must be the eleventh Beatitude.

Matchmakers are a determined group. There's no doubt in my mind that Romeo and Juliet would have married long before Juliet's fourteenth birthday if the matchmakers could have gotten to them.

I'm fully convinced that there exists—nationwide—a secret society whose sole purpose is to seek out, identify, match, and march perfectly happy and contented people to the altar. The organization is the Loyal Order of Matronly Matchmakers (LOMM), with national headquarters in Atlanta and branches in every other city and town. They even have a slogan: "Match 'Em and Marry 'Em!"

They meet every third Monday underneath a magnolia tree, sip mint juleps, review the latest divorce news and obituaries gleaned from local newspapers, and pair names.

The only criterion necessary to fall under the matrimonial eyes of LOMM is that you be single. Male or female is of no consequence, and you don't have to be beautiful, handsome, wealthy, or intelligent. Just single. I am ample evidence of that.

My first encounter with LOMM came in 1972, shortly after I made the LOMM hit list on December 8, 1972, at 10:38 A.M. when I walked out of Superior Court and began again my journey in the single lane after twenty-two years in the double. It happened this way:

A charter member of the Savannah chapter of LOMM approached me that first Sunday morning before I had had time to do my first load of laundry, burn the toast, or oversleep and be late for work. She had known my family for many years.

"My sister and I would love for you to join us for dinner at Morrison's if you have no plans," she said, smiling. It should be noted here that LOMM members wear perpetual smiles.

I had no plans. The dinner was delightful, and I was well into pecan pie and vanilla ice cream, surely a creation of God, when she made her pitch. "I have this friend that you simply must meet. She's absolutely delightful."

"Oh?" was my award-winning reply.

"She has a lovely home at the beach and a charming home in the mountains of North Carolina," she said, "and she's a member of the yacht club where she berths her cabin cruiser. Her third husband died eight months ago. She's really well-fixed, and I just know you two would hit it off just great. Don't you think so, Martha?"

"No doubt about it," Martha agreed.

I continued eating, but at a much slower pace. Have you ever seen a tiger when cornered? He stalls, looking for a way out.

"I know her real well and have for a long time," the matchmaker went on. "Is there anything in particular you'd like to know about her?"

I didn't answer right away. But after devouring the remnants of the pie and ice cream, I took a final sip of coffee and said, "Well, I would like to ask one question, if you don't mind."

"Go right ahead. Anything you like," she agreed, savoring my apparent interest.

"Well, tell me this. Just exactly what did her three husbands die from?"

Like I said, the dinner was delicious.

All Singles Aren't Sad and Lonely

Contrary to what the bylaws of the Loyal Order of Matronly Matchmakers (LOMM) say, all singles aren't sad and lonely, searching night and day for companionship or a lifetime mate.

"Not so!" counters the LOMM. "They just say that while putting up a brave front."

Not long after re-entering the delightful world of bachelorhood, I attended a singles club meeting at the insistence of a (male) friend. I would have had more fun at a hockey game.

The subject of the LOMM came up, probably by me, and we all laughed and talked about it. Everyone in attendance agreed that such an organization did indeed exist.

The first thing LOMM teaches new members is how to make a mint julep, then how to approach a suspect. Much like opening lines at singles bars, they all begin with, "I know someone you simply must meet!"

Experience has taught me that the best response to that is, "Why?"

"Because she's such a lovely person, and you two have so much in common," is the usual counterreply.

That's when you fire the other barrel and reload, with magnum shells.

"What?"

Other than that we've both cut the dinghy loose, and both are looking on the shady side of fifty, she'll be unable to come up with a common denominator. As a last resort, she will use the standard LOMM standby: loneliness, which I explained earlier.

Now hear this. I'm going to tell you how to spot LOMM members. With practice, it's relatively easy to single (no pun intended) out the matchmakers.

First, they never work alone. They're almost always in pairs.

Second, they whisper and smile a lot.

Third, they wear crossed wedding bands on their collars.

Also, matchmakers are rewarded handsomely for their efforts: they get trading stamps. For every successful match-up that results in a walk down the aisle, the matchmaker responsible is rewarded with fifty books of trading stamps at the annual LOMM Awards Banquet in

Reno in January. Leap year is double-stamp year, and even an engagement is good for ten books.

If you have reason to suspect that you have been targeted by the LOMM, be ye male or female, don't make the mistake of underestimating them. They have the patience of Job, the chicanery of Eve, the fortitude of David, and the curiosity of Garfield.

They can be compromised, however. You can catch 'em red-handed if you work at it. I had a good friend who caught one a few years ago.

Her target was a very well-to-do widower. Her client? Her sister, a lovely lady who was happy and contented. Not lonely, just single.

The LOMM member was outraged when I refused to become a co-conspirator and demanded to know why.

I referred her to the Ritual of the Methodist Church, pages 546–547 and 548–558. I haven't seen her since, so I have to assume that she read both sections. What are they?

Pages 546–547 is "The Order for the Solemnization of Matrimony," followed immediately by pages 548–558, "The Order for the Burial of the Dead."

Then there is the classic story about the LOMM member who spotted the sad-faced male sitting alone on a park bench and staring empty-eyed across a lake. Naturally, she eased over and sat down beside him.

"You look so sad and lonely. Want to tell me what's wrong?" she asked.

"My wife ran off with my best friend last week," he said, sobbing.

"Oh, what a dreadful shame! And with your best friend, you say?" she whimpered, mentally contemplating her trading stamps.

"Yes, ma'am, and I sure do miss him."

My Romance Was Dunked

As the kids boarded a school bus not long ago for the late night ride home after a basketball game, I stopped to watch the in-fighting to determine who would sit by whom. If a referee had been there, three boys would have fouled out.

The incident made me think about Hazel Rigdon, a fine basketball player in the early forties at my high school.

Hazel was a senior my freshman year. She was seventeen and beautiful; I was thirteen and ugghhh! I'd have married Hazel Rigdon at center court, under the goal, on the bus, or in front of the concession stand. She was my first true love, although I never got around to telling her about it.

I had this one recurring problem in my torrid, but one-sided, romance with Hazel. His name was Jack Houston, also a senior and seventeen. Jack was ruggedly handsome, six feet, four inches, 195 pounds, and star of the boys' basketball and football teams. Nickname? Tarzan. And he rode a red Harley Davidson.

Me? A freshman and thirteen, unbelievably ugly, five feet, five inches, 125 pounds, and my main concern was getting a seat on the bench. I rode a decrepit, third-hand, faded green Rollfast bicycle. My nickname? Muscles. Lord how I hated Jack Houston!

It was usually my lot to sit next to Luther Quillian, head cheerleader and the only boy in school who ever took home ec. He made his own cheerleader outfit, complete with embroidered Wildcat. Luther's pleats were always pressed and straight, and he also wore clean socks. After home games, win or lose, Luther served pink punch and homemade cookies with little birds and flowers on them.

I would rather have sat by Hazel Rigdon than have my back scratched. She was that special. I tried it once near the end of the 1941 season. I just plopped down beside her. (Actually, I intended to pop the question on the way home that night but was interrupted.)

I'd hardly settled into my seat (well, Jack Houston's seat) when I glanced left and saw a giant kneecap. Jack's kneecap. Then I did a very wise thing. I got up from there, and fast!

"Why don't you sit down here, Tarzan, next to Hazel?" I stammered.

There was no response, but he gave me a look that would curdle milk. Naturally, I moved to another seat—the only other seat next to (who else) Luther Quillian who was busy embroidering a handkerchief for the home ec teacher. Luther hoarded those A's.

I fumed while Luther embroidered. Can you imagine my frustration? There I sat, my hands handcuffed with a ball of lavender yarn while not six feet away my future wife was holding hands with Tarzan and scratching his back! I jerked my hands and Luther dropped a stitch. He was furious, but who could blame him? Give your home ec teacher a hankie with a deformed daisy and the A drops to a B automatically, right? And Luther, the creep, never had a B in his life.

It was easy to tell when we played home games. The pool room closed early, poker games were rescheduled, and traveling salesmen lied to the home office, and others, in order to stay overnight.

Ours was the only school in Georgia selling season tickets the four years Hazel played. It wasn't uncommon to be sold out in May for the home opener in November. Hazel was a drawing card.

The men came early. Pregame warm-up consisted of cleaning their glasses, taking heart pills, and deep-breathing exercises. Once the game started, they became cheerleaders.

"Go Hazel! Go baby!" "Bounce, Hazel, bounce!" "Fall down, Hazel!" These were some of the more popular cheers chorused by the pool shooters, poker players, and salesmen. Homer Troutman, a yard-goods salesman from Columbus, said it was worth the price of admission to see Hazel fall down, and, another to watch her get up. Lord, she was lovely . . . an architect's dream.

Barney Holder may have said it best. "I'd give my cue stick just to guard Hazel for one quarter. That girl invented the double-dribble."

The annual awards banquet was nothing fancy, mind you. It was a war year. Refreshments were furnished by Gator Brogdon and Sonny Redmond, owners of the pool room. Gator's brother had been in the infantry in New Guinea and brought him a case of K-Rations after being dishonorably discharged for stealing. Sonny threw in a case of raspberry

Kool-Aid he'd won shooting eight-ball with a grocery sales-man from Americus.

The cheerleaders were in charge, and Luther Quillian did an outstanding job with the K-Rations au gratin and Kool-Aid punch. He made little ruffled plates and hand-painted swans on the paper cups. Nobody dug the swan bit seeing as how our mascot was a wildcat.

"That Luther could make sawdust taste like caviar," Mrs. Thompson, the home ec teacher, said proudly.

Coach Pleugh presented the awards, dropping several. He also forgot his speech. Jack Houston was voted Most Valu-able on the boys' team and was presented a big trophy. Hazel was just named *most,* and nobody laughed when Coach Pleugh handed her two trophies. "Facts are facts!" said Barney Holder after the presentation.

Mrs. Thompson presented the cheerleader awards. Lu-ther Quillian was named best cheerleader but refused the award sweater. He didn't care for the orange block L, de-manding that it be in script, hand-embroidered, and lav-ender.

The highlight of the evening came when Hazel's bus seat was retired with appropriate remarks by Clarence Coogle, the bus driver. He almost choked when he said, "Ain't no-body can do justice to this seat ever again." Clarence's over-sized rearview mirror should have been retired, too.

The banquet was nice, but it got nicer as the evening wore on and the punch bowl got lower. Coach Pleugh asked me to stay and help Luther clean up, and I must confess that once, when Luther went to the home ec room for a broom, I slipped over and sat in Hazel Rigdon's bus seat. Luther caught me.

"Luther Quillian, so help me, I'll break your embroidery needles if you ever tell Jack Houston," I threatened.

He joined me, sitting in Jack's seat, which was a definite insult. So there we sat, eating leftover K-rations and drink-ing raspberry Kool-Aid until well after midnight.

Jack Houston had left his trophy on the stage. If he'd returned for it that night, I know I'd have challenged him. That white stuff Buttercup Hill poured in the Kool-Aid would have made me do it.

"Dear John" Fire May Never Go Out

I guess about the four saddest words ever written are, "I've found somebody new." They just sorta gnaw a fellow's guts out, slowly.

This is about your average, everyday, run-of-the-mill "boy goes in service—boy comes home from basic training—boy meets and flips over girl—boy goes overseas—girl writes boy and tells him, 'I've found somebody new.'" Yes, this is about the "Dear John" letter. I received mine in September 1944 while in the Philippine Islands, the only wound I received during fifteen months overseas.

I guess the logical place to start is at the beginning and that would be March 3, 1944, the day I was inducted into the United States Army at Fort McPherson. From there, after shots for everything from typhoid fever to tetanus, I went to Camp Blanding, Florida, for basic training and weekend passes to such romantic retreats as Starke and Hampton. I think they figured if a recruit could survive Starke and Hampton on Saturday nights, the rest of World War II had to be a piece of cake.

I survived Camp Blanding, Starke, and Hampton somehow and returned home for the well-known "delay en route" before reporting to Fort Ord, California, and on to somewhere. Where I didn't know. But, when you're eighteen, you don't worry about such trivial things as where you'll be tomorrow, next week, or next year when the threat of the world being blown to bits is for real. There is only now, and you grab the brass ring at every opportunity.

I met her on my third day home, and the next seven came right out of Hollywood. A fuzzy-faced soldier boy home on leave before moving on to the big war.

Her name was Rhonda. She was beautiful and gave me days and nights to remember. Like swimming together in the river and swinging together on her front porch. And movies, Sunday night church services, late-night snacks in her mama's kitchen, songs on the car radio, memorable songs like "Near You," "Heartaches," "Elmer's Tune," "Moonlight Serenade," "Smoke Gets in Your Eyes," "That Old Black Magic," "Long Ago and Far Away," "Now Is the

Hour," and (our song) "The Shadow of Your Smile." And holding hands and making promises . . . many promises.

It was like I was gonna' run on "over there," win the war, and be back Sunday night in time for church with Rhonda.

My ten days ended, and I boarded a bus on a hot night in July in front of the drug store in Metter. Mama, Daddy, and Rhonda were there to see me off to where the war was. And that night my folks saw me kiss a girl for the very first time ever, and as far as I was concerned I was kissing their daughter-in-law to be. "Rhonda Whaley," I rolled the name over and over in my mind as the bus took me to Savannah so I could catch a train that would take me to California.

Thirty-three days later I landed in the Philippines. I wrote letters to Rhonda like there was no tomorrow, and she answered them faithfully. Her picture hung above my bunk in the tent just like in the movies, the first thing I saw in the morning and the last thing I saw at night. I was positive she was grieving her heart out, poor girl.

I lived for mail call and a letter from grieving Rhonda. But then, in September 1944 it happened. "Whaley, Walker W.!" the mail clerk called out.

"Here!" I yelled back.

I opened the letter from Rhonda while sitting under a coconut tree, read the opening, and started over. Surely my eyes were playing tricks on me. "Dear Bo: I've found somebody new . . ."

Bull's eye! From ten thousand miles away she had hit me right between the eyes with the war's most dreaded weapon: a "Dear John" mortar. I dang near died and drank my first beer ever. It didn't help. My guts were on fire and were being gnawed away . . . slowly.

The story made the rounds during World War II about a young soldier, Billy, who received a "Dear John" epistle from his girl back home, Debbie. It began in the usual manner: "Dear Billy: I've found somebody new. Please return my photograph . . ."

Poor Billy. He almost died from grief, was unable to eat or sleep, and threatened to kill himself. His commanding officer decided to do something about it and called a meeting of the entire outfit after sending Billy on a fictitious mission. He called on everyone in the outfit to bring him at least one photograph of a girl, any girl. They complied, coming up with 237 photographs of every type girl imaginable.

The commander then wrote this note to Debbie and enclosed the 237 photographs: "Dear Debbie: I received your letter in which you request that I return your photo. While your name sounds familiar I can't quite place your face. Please be kind enough to select your photo from the enclosed photographs and return the others to me. Thank you. Billy."

So why this chapter about "Dear John" letters? Because not long ago Rhonda stopped by to see me after forty-six years. And, do you know what? Her visit made my guts burn a little . . . slowly.

Who knows? Maybe the fire never goes out completely.

Part 4

Husbands and Other Accouterments

It has been said, and rightly so, that "The greatest miracle is birth; the greatest mystery is death." Surely, somewhere in between comes marriage.

I have often been asked how many times I've been married. My answer is always the same: "One too many." For what it's worth, I saw this bumper sticker while vacationing in Reno, Nevada, a few years ago: "Marriage Made Me What I Am Today . . . Happily Divorced." I waited for the owner of the vehicle to return, asked him where he bought the bumper sticker, and went forthwith and bought ten for $1.89 each. I have two left, and I think one will adorn the rear bumper of a good friend within weeks.

I know there are good marriages. I've seen a few in my lifetime. Like Wallace and Shirley, because they're best friends to each other; Derry and Frieda, because they've been sweethearts for fifty years; Fred and Mary, because of undying devotion and loyalty to each other; and Don and Ann, because they're Don and Ann. And Ed and Marthele . . . just because.

I know of but one thing more unsightly than a runny nose, and that's a henpecked husband. Were I a woman, I don't think I'd want a henpecked husband. I know quite a few.

It is beyond my comprehension how a 105-pound woman can wrap a 200-pound man around a two-ounce little finger.

I have about concluded that she couldn't if he wasn't a willing pawn.

I have been to a few weddings and funerals in my time, and I subscribe to the theory that there is no such thing as a sad wedding or a happy funeral. And in some cases there really isn't much difference.

The most unusual wedding I ever saw happened in Estes, a beer joint in my hometown, Dublin, Georgia, on a hot July afternoon. The reception, also held in Estes, was equally unusual. I swear to you on my long-neck Bud and beef jerky that it happened, and I have witnesses: Ronnie Estes, the owner of the wedding chapel, and Randy Shumny, a local roofer who was on a beer break from a downtown job.

The couple met at the bar. Howard was nineteen, and Molly was eighteen. Howard bought Molly a beer, and from there it was all downhill. They were married the following afternoon standing by the pool table. Howard was decked out in a dirty tank top and ragged jeans, and Molly chose an X-rated T-shirt and Z-Rat shorts for the solemn ceremony. Both were barefooted.

Being a firm believer in protocol, both Ronnie and Randy agreed that the young newlyweds should have a reception, and they took care of the arrangements.

They spread newspapers on the pool table and opened several cans of Vienna sausage and potted meat. They also spread a few beef jerkys, pickled eggs, and salted peanuts along with saltine crackers. A pair of Hostess Twinkies served as the wedding cake, and a case of long-neck Bud was opened. I dropped in a quarter and played Molly's favorite song on the jukebox: "You Ain't Woman Enough to Take My Man."

A guy named Robert was mad because he couldn't shoot pool, and another named Rex was upset because the beef jerky supply had been exhausted. A girl named Prissy kicked the jukebox because her song, "All My Rowdy Friends Are Coming Over Tonight," was cancelled, and she demanded a refund but settled for a long-neck Bud and a Vienna sausage or two.

Howard and Molly cut the Twinkies and kissed long and

hard. The kiss sounded like a suction cup on a clogged-up sink.

Ronnie broke out a beat-up Polaroid and took a few pictures. Whether they ever turned out is anybody's guess because he ended up throwing the camera at Edsel, the town drunk, shattering it to bits. "Don't sweat it," he said. "Some fella from Florida pawned it this mornin' for three dollars and a pint of Mad Dog 20/20."

As evening neared, Howard and Molly were both up to their rednecks in long-neck Buds. An argument ensued after Molly danced real close with the best man, Pigeye Whitfield, and Howard insisted vehemently that they leave and go on to Willacoochee for their honeymoon.

"Heck, Howard, they's a half of a case of Bud left," Molly said. "I ain't leavin' now."

"Awright! Be that a' way!" Howard yelled. "But I'll tell you one thing. If you don't leave with me now, I'm gonna' tell ever'body in town that I slept with ya' 'for'n we wuz married!"

"Oh, yeah?" said a snoockered Molly. "Well, you jus' go right ahead an' tell 'em smarty, an' I'll be right behin' ya' a-tellin' 'em that you won't th' onliest one!"

Mercy, have mercy. I think it must be true. The prime causes of squabbles between husband and wives are . . . husbands and wives.

On the pages that follow in this section I'm going to show you some prime examples of marriage in the raw, the matrimonial mountains that must be scaled, and the pitfalls to be avoided if at all possible.

Remember, nothing is forever, not even some marriages. Take the marriage of John and Marie Callahan, for instance.

Marie was John's seventh wife, and he divorced her after seven months. Within weeks, John took Doris for his eighth wife.

While sorting through the remains of her broken marriage less than a month after John married Doris, Marie found a box of calling cards, engraved "Mrs. John Callahan." She promptly mailed them to Doris, with a note reading, "Dear Doris. I hope these reach you in time."

Why Not a Prenuptial Agreement for Everybody?

While riding along the fourth fairway on my home golf course, a friend and fellow duffer (a lawyer of all people) pulled his golf cart alongside mine and asked out of a clear blue sky, "What do you consider to be the prime reason for divorce today?"

I pondered the question for maybe thirty yards, and said, "Money problems is number one. It happens because young people jump in over their head. Number two is marrying prematurely, not knowing enough about each other and having little in common. The third is unfaithfulness, for whatever reason."

He didn't comment, just moved to his ball and proceeded to hit it into a sand trap. I followed suit. We dug out with no further discussion of the reasons for divorce.

I considered his question as I drove home, realizing that today one in every two marriages ends in divorce within seven years. Here's my solution: a required prenuptial agreement that would be signed and notarized by both parties. If movie and television stars can have prenuptial agreements, why can't run-of-the-mill, try-and-make-it-till-payday, share-the-double-wide and get-me-another-beer folks have one?

A standardized prenuptial agreement would reduce anticipated difficulties to writing and clear at least some of the air in the event disagreements arise. And they will arise.

Here are a few anticipated obstacles on the matrimonial road that should be included in Whaley's Standardized Prenuptial Agreement.
• Who will provide the kid's lunch money?
• Who will wash, and who will dry?
• Who will mow, and who will rake?
• Whose parents will be visited at Christmas?
• Will there be joint or separate checking accounts?
• Credit cards? How many? In whose name? What spending limits?
• In the event of a tax refund, what will the split be, if any?
• Who will sign the report card?

- Sweetened or unsweetened tea?
- Grits or (heaven forbid) Cream of Wheat?
- Who will attend PTO meetings?
- Who will handle the two o'clock feeding?
- At what time of day do the hair rollers come down?
- Will the husband shave on weekends?
- Will the hanging of pantyhose on the shower curtain rod be permitted? (Probably the fourth most frequent cause of divorce.)
- Who takes out the garbage?
- If the wife works, what does she do with her paycheck?
- Who controls the television set following the six o'clock news?
- Who will wash the windows?
- Who pays for the quart of milk and loaf of bread when the wife calls the husband at work and tells him to pick them up on his way home?
- Vacation: mountain or beach?
- Candy or flowers on Valentine's Day?
- If candy, who gets the pieces with the nuts?
- In case of a fight, the eight-count is mandatory in the event of a knockdown. No crying by either party.
- There will be no comparisons to former girlfriends or boyfriends, ex-husbands or ex-wives.
- No unscheduled headaches in the absence of a twenty-four-hour written notice.
- No night fishing with the boys in the absence of a twenty-four-hour notice.
- No interrogation regarding winnings or losses at the weekly poker game.
- Who gets the white meat?

And . . . one more: an ironclad provision that the wife will have x-number of dollars provided by the husband to spend as she darn well sees fit, with no accounting. Blow it, save it, or whatever.

Good luck and best wishes.

Warning! Watch Out for Women in the Spring

For the man of the house the sunshine and gorgeous weather that come with spring usher in visions of long-awaited hours on the golf course or fishing in a favorite lake.

First, there are two major obstacles to overcome: the neighbor and the wife. How so? Let us take a look at the neighbor, and if any man has the misfortune of living next door to one like this, he's in big trouble.

It is a beautiful Saturday morning with bright sunshine beaming down, prompting the urge to take out the driver or two-iron, "really get into one" and hit the perfect shot that has been on hold all winter. Mentally, it soars some 260 yards "right down the middle," and the choice of the club for the second shot is a difficult one. He goes with a three-wood. Another perfect shot!

Then, you hear it! The sound is unmistakable. Handy Andy, who can do everything around the house, has cranked up his lawn mower! He's been up since dawn puttering around in the yard, and now he's going to mow the lawn.

Your wife snaps her eyes to the kitchen window with all the precision of the finest and most sophisticated radar detector, and her hair rollers almost unwind. She says nothing. She doesn't have to. Her silence is deafening, but her eyes speak loudly as they methodically snap to and fro, from the window to the golf glove you shift back and forth in your hands.

The look in her eyes causes instant guilt feelings as you steal a glance over the rim of your coffee cup and view your yard that strongly resembles the Okefenokee Swamp. Andy's lawn mower just whines away in the background.

You wonder why the guy couldn't have waited just ten more minutes to crank the darn thing up, and why his mower always starts on the first pull while you have to play tug-of-war with yours for half the morning to get it started—maybe.

You actually hate Andy, but all the neighborhood women love him. A regular Mr. Fixit. Besides, the guy couldn't hit a golf ball with a bulldozer!

No doubt about it, with the first sign of spring, the little lady wants her man out in the yard getting it done, like Handy Andy.

Remember when you moved into the neighborhood? You bought pesticides, insecticides, herbicides, phosphate, nitrate, peat moss, Vigoro—you name it. You also went to the Agriculture Extension Office and picked up every pamphlet ever printed about putting in lawns. In your yard you had sprigged, sodded, clumped, broadcast and sown, and sprinkled enough water to float the Empire State Building. But did you get a lawn? No! Only a barely visible trace of green here and there.

What about Andy? When he moved in, he just poked a few holes in his yard, dropped in the sprigs, kicked a little dirt, and turned on the sprinkler for a few afternoons. What happened? His yard now looks like an exact replica of the sixteenth fairway at the Masters, and yours like the giant sand trap that dominates the middle of it.

Try and explain to the little woman why your yard looks like the aftermath of the great drought as she stares at you with that look, a look that says, "Ours might look like Andy's if you would stay off the golf course long enough to 'repair the green' in our yard."

You say nothing because you know she's right. But you fantasize. "Boy! Would I like to get that troublemaker on the golf course at a dollar a hole! I'd have him going to the Christmas party in a straw hat, seersucker suit, and perforated shoes."

The spring sunshine also brings other danger signs, like the great painting escapade. Why is it that women are happiest when they have their men up on a ladder juggling a paint can when the temperature is a perfect 72 degrees? And how do they get them up there in the first place? Simple. They use looks, and their favorite is the neglected look. It works like this:

You are out in the storage house pulling your rod and reel from underneath all the leftover Christmas wrapping paper and tinsel. She suspects as much instantly and comes out with the gallon of "outside white" she bought on special two years earlier. Again she says nothing, but puts on her best neglected look as you walk toward the back door pulling tinsel from your reel. The moment you see the paint can, you know that the old spring paint-up fever has struck. So, back goes the reel and rod to rest another day with its Christmas companions, and you accept the fact that you must paint the carport.

Now it's time to play the annual game of "find the paint brushes." You must have bought a thousand since you moved in. After moving two boxes of old clothes, a broken vacuum cleaner, two shovels, a broken lawn chair, and a lawn sprinkler that doesn't work, you find the brushes. They are in the same paint can that you left them in twelve months earlier when you painted the kitchen. They are as stiff as a celluloid collar and will forever be stuck to the bottom of the can. They're as hard as jawbreakers, and it would take a blowtorch or three well-placed sticks of dynamite to remove them.

You just shake your head as you drive to the hardware store to buy two more brushes and wonder why the women always say, "I'll paint the trim." No woman ever lived who didn't picture herself as a great trim painter, wearing one of your old shirts, of course.

I once saw a great cartoon. It was in five panels. The first showed two men—neighbors—on ladders with paint and brush. The second showed them looking at each other. In the third, one is saying to the other, "How much vacation you got?" In the fourth, he answers. "Only two weeks." In the fifth, the other fellow says, "You lucky devil. I've got three!"

Then there is the story of the husband who promised his wife faithfully that he would mow the lawn while she was at the local laundrymat doing the family wash for nine. He headed for the golf course as soon as she left, and after completing his round he confided to his golfing buddies what he had done.

"Boy! I'll bet your wife hits the ceiling when you get home!" one said.

"Yeah, I guess she will. But she always does. She's a lousy shot," he said.

Finally, there was the woman who tried repeatedly to get her husband to work in the yard, to no avail, as he spent his days off fishing. So she tried a new tactic.

Before leaving the house, she stuck a shovel in the yard with this note attached to it: "Henry. Start digging and see what satisfaction you will find. Helen."

When she returned home, she immediately saw the shovel and walked to it only to find this note scribbled on the back of hers: "Started digging. Found worms. Gone fishing. Henry."

Remember, the wife who drives from the back seat is no worse than the husband who cooks from the dining room table.

In Defense of Women's Rights

It is well documented that I am not a women's libber, but right is right and I detest seeing anyone mistreated or being taken advantage of, no matter the gender.

I'm speaking out here in defense of a pretty housewife and mother of three whose husband just ain't done right by her in their three years of marriage.

Both Nanette and Richie have children by previous marriages. Both work. Their hobby is moving. It must be. In the three years since they married, they've moved seven times, and even as I write this they're moving again, at least Nanette is. That is what prompts me to write about them.

I talked to Nanette by telephone, and she was up to her pretty neck in curtains, drapes, and everything else that goes along with moving. I don't know why she bothers to unpack.

My concern centers around the way in which the move was scheduled by Richie, who is big enough to pick up the rear end of a bulldozer while petite Nanette would do well to raise a power window or a nickel's worth of cotton candy. That is precisely what prompts me to speak out in support of women's rights.

Richie began setting the stage for the move several weeks

before it actually took place when he casually mentioned to Nanette, "How would you like to go with me to New Orleans for the weekend?"

Nanette responded with a resounding, "Yes!"

Visions of a leisurely automobile ride to exotic, romantic New Orleans danced through her pretty head as she packed and planned. She was thrilled when she told me about it.

"I can hardly wait!" she said. "All that great food, the French Quarter, the little shops on Bourbon Street, Pete Fountain and Al Hirt, dinner at Arnaud's, the Superdome . . ."

It didn't exactly turn out that way. What Richie purposely neglected to tell Nanette was that they would be making the trip in a rented two-and-a-half-ton truck to pick up some equipment for the radio station he manages, and that they would leave Friday, make the 1,200-mile round trip, and be back for work on Monday morning.

I greeted Nanette on Monday morning when she arrived at her office.

"How was New Orleans?" I asked.

"Shut up! Just shut up! I don't want to talk about it!" she yelled as she marched to her desk.

"Why? Something go wrong?"

"No, *something* didn't go wrong! *Everything* went wrong! And I'm so sore all over right now that I can't sit still. Even my ear lobes hurt," she groaned. "Have you ever ridden 1,200 miles in two days in the cab of a two-and-a-half-ton truck cooped up with a conniving gorilla?"

"A truck?"

"Right, a truck," she fumed. "I told Richie repeatedly on the way back that he'd better not stop because if he did I was gettin' out."

"Where's Richie now?"

"I don't know, and I don't care. I ain't speaking to him," she said with an air of finality.

So much for the leisurely ride to New Orleans.

Are you familiar with the old saying, "You get me once, it's your fault; you get me again, it's my fault"?

Well, he got her again.

Shortly before the ill-fated New Orleans trip, Richie and

Nanette had bought a house. Naturally, this prompted another move. The only question was when the move would take place. Richie, the master manipulator, took care of that little detail.

"How about the weekend of September 15–16?" Richie suggested.

"That's fine with me," replied the gullible Nanette.

The plot thickens.

The move took place as planned, but without Richie! He was in Mississippi for a business meeting. He left Georgia on September 14 and arrived back home conveniently the night of September 16, *after* Nanette had handled the move.

Here's the kicker. Nanette has now learned that Richie knew about the Mississippi meeting ten days *before* he suggested the moving dates.

"I'm seriously thinking about killing him," she said.

Should she do it I don't believe there are twelve people in Georgia who, given the facts, would convict her.

The ERA Goes Both Ways

For years the feminists of America fought tooth and nail polish for the passage of the Equal Rights Amendment but failed to get it passed. People on both sides of the question had strong feelings. Some were very vocal about it.

Support for the passage of the ERA seemed to be strongest in the North and Northeast, but slowly the pendulum also swung south. Inasmuch as it is my established policy to keep the reading public informed on matters of vital interest, I conducted a survey and took the public's pulse on the ERA subject. I went to the man on the street, businessmen, housewives, husbands, and others for their opinions. Some were most revealing.

"ERA?" questioned one bearded soul as he debarked from his pickup with a long-neck Bud in hand. "What th' heck do we need with that? The dern women already control most of the money, all the sex, and are fast takin' over ever'thing else. I can't hardly even keep beer in th' house no more f'r my ol' lady drinkin' it. And you got any idy how it feels t' come in after playin' poker all day Sunday, look in th' 'frigerator an' find nothin' but skimmed milk, orange juice, an' maybe a Diet Coke? I say to heck with the ERA!"

In conducting my survey, I hit ten homes at random. I just knocked on the door and introduced myself, which strikes me as pretty scientific. Some recognized my name but permitted me to enter anyway. I purposely made my contacts at various times of the day—some in the morning, some in the afternoon, some in the evening—so as to get a good cross section of opinions. I like to be fair, unless it is in my best interests to be otherwise.

My first stop was at the home of Howard and Gertrude Miltkin, a retired couple. Gertrude answered the door.

"Good morning, ma'am. I'm doing an ERA survey. Is your husband at home?" I asked.

"Yes, he's down in the basement upholstering a chair for my mother," she said. "Feel free to go on down and introduce yourself. His name's Howard. I have to hurry and get to my bridge club. The girls get furious if one of us is late."

I found Howard bending over, knee-deep in upholstery nails and material, attempting to hammer a nail under the seat cushion. I interrupted him long enough to introduce myself and explain my mission. He was very receptive.

"ERA?" he asked through a mouth filled with upholstery nails. "What's that?"

"The Equal Rights Amendment," I informed him. "You mean you haven't heard about it on the news or read about it in the newspapers?"

"Nope. Don't listen to the news or read the newspaper. Don't have time for that. Spend all my time down here in the dungeon, and my wife has never told me anything about it," Howard explained.

"Well, would you like to know about it?"

"Darn right! Last news update I got was after Truman beat Dewey in '48."

"O. K. The Equal Rights Amendment grants only that 'equality of rights under the law shall not be denied or abridged by the United States or any state on account of sex.' And that's it," I told him.

"Well now, young fellow, I understand the part about being denied quite well, but what does that *abridged* mean?" he asked, placing his little hammer on a bench.

"Abridge simply means 'to make less, diminish, or curtail.' No more, no less," I explained.

Howard studied for a moment, then asked, "You're saying then that if this ERA thing passes, that me and Gertrude would have the same rights?"

"Precisely. That's right."

"O. K. Put me down. Where do I sign?" he asked with a gleam in his eye.

My next stop, after lunch, was at the bungalow of Ralph and Marlene Thorgel where Ralph answered the door, cooking spoon in hand and wearing a lovely flowered apron featuring daisies.

I went through my spiel and waited for the invitation to come in. It wasn't forthcoming.

"Sorry, don't have time for you today," Ralph said. "Got six quarts of butterbeans and four pints of tomatoes on the stove. Got to watch 'em and be sure to put 'em up when they're just right. Overcook 'em they're not worth a darn. I ruined a whole batch of squash and okra last summer talking to a vacuum cleaner salesman, and Marlene—that's my wife—really pitched a hissie fit."

"But I only want a few minutes of your time," I persisted. "Can't your wife watch the butterbeans and tomatoes while—"

"She's not here. She's playing in a golf tournament this afternoon," he said.

"What about tonight? Could I come back tonight and—"

"Nope, sorry. It's Marlene's bowling night, and I'll be baby-sitting with the four kids. See you," he said before he closed the door.

I stood there on the steps for a minute before leaving. The butterbeans and tomatoes smelled great.

On my way home I thought about Howard and Ralph, and this story that I'd heard several years previously came to mind:

An obedient husband, Henry, died and went to heaven,

whereupon he was greeted by Saint Peter who checked his name and ID.

Henry observed two lines leading up to the Pearly Gate, a very long line with a sign, "For Henpecked Husbands," and a very short line with a sign, "For Husbands Who Ruled the Roost."

Henry promptly stepped in the short line, joining two other men there and completely disregarding the hundreds of men standing in the other line.

Within a matter of minutes Saint Peter saw Henry and inquired, "Why are you standing in that line, Henry?"

"Beats me, Pete," Henry replied. "My wife told me to stand here."

A Husband's Nightmare

I have no doubt that the invention of the telephone ranks near the top of the pile of inventions that have contributed to the tremendous progress that makes America the great nation it is. No longer the luxury it once was, it is now an absolute necessity in homes and business offices.

Possibly what happens in the little scenario that follows has happened to you at one time or another. Just follow the *bzzzzy* signal and see.

Charlie Chauvinist, the man of the house, has showered, shaved, and enjoyed a delicious breakfast prepared by the woman of the house before walking to his "second car" and driving to the office. Once there, he enjoys a second cup of coffee and a newspaper before digging into the business of the day.

He has no sooner finished his coffee and put his newspaper aside when his intercom sounds and his secretary says, "The gentleman from General Purchasing is here, Mr. Chauvinist."

"Who?"

"The gentleman from General Purchasing. The man you said was considering placing a $200,000 order with us."

Charlie negotiates the combination lock on his briefcase

with the expertise of a seasoned safecracker as he listens. Looking inside, he panics. All the paperwork for the possible order from General Purchasing is missing! Total recall sets in. It is at home, strewn all over the dining room table, right where he left it when he kissed his wife goodbye two hours earlier and patted his daughter on the head and his little boy on the fanny.

Charlie, the problem solver, slams the briefcase shut and barks into the intercom.

"Stall him, Charlotte! Stall him! Get him some coffee and a newspaper. I left the paperwork at home. I'll call Christine and tell her to bring it. I'll need about twenty minutes."

No problem, he thought to himself as he dialed his home telephone number. His fingers weren't walking, they were sprinting. "Another problem solved," he mumbled. "Christine will just cruise on down here in nothing flat with the papers."

He was already figuring his commission on $200,000, but shortly he heard the worst sound a man can hear when he's trying desperately to call home: *Bzzzz! Bzzzz! Bzzzz!* He dialed again and again, and again. Same sound: *Bzzzz! Bzzzz! Bzzzz!*

Poor Charlie never got through to Christine, but thank goodness Charlotte was able to turn on the charm and reschedule the appointment for the next morning. All was not lost, thanks to Charlotte.

Somehow he made it through the day. When he pulled into his driveway on Mortgage Circle late in the afternoon, a tired and bedraggled breadwinner, he was greeted by Christine, who was all smiles.

"Hi, honey! Did you have a good day?" she asked.

"Oh, I've had lots better ones. How about you?"

"Busy, busy, busy," she said.

"You can say that again!"

"What do you mean by that?"

"Oh, nothing. Nothing at all, Christine. What did you do today?"

She recounted her activities of the day as she set the table for dinner:

"Well, let me see now. Took the kids to school; stopped

by the library; took your clothes to the cleaners; bought Mama a birthday card; took Snuffy to the vet for shots; returned the stepladder to the Wilsons; went to the beauty shop; bought groceries; went to the dentist and had my teeth cleaned; stopped by the bank and cashed a check for you; went to a meeting at the school; picked up Bobby's Boy Scout uniform; and shelled peas. I guess that's about it."

The lines of doubt on Charlie's face depicted his disbelief. How in the world could Christine have done all that and still have been on the telephone all day? He said nothing, but couldn't figure it out. Maybe I can.

You see, I have the same luck trying to call people that Charlie had, and the only explanation I can imagine in this: All housewives have a twelve-mile-long telephone cord which they keep hidden in the cabinet underneath the telephone until they get ready to use it after the man of the house has gone. They then pull out the cord, attach it to the telephone, and start dialing. And they take the phone with them all day, wherever they go: to the supermarket, library, beauty shop, school, vet, and so on. They stay on the phone all day, and they are indeed *Bzzzz, Bzzzz, Bzzzz, Bzzzzy* all day!

If you think men have problems trying to call home, just look at what happens when the woman of the house is gone for a few days. Things that men take for granted all of a sudden go haywire.

Just for the heck of it, let us assume that she has gone to visit her Mama for a week. This could happen to you:

It is Saturday morning, and you are getting ready to go to the golf course and would like some toast and coffee. Simple? No! The toaster won't work, and you can't find the cord to the coffee pot. You search every nook and cranny but . . . no cord. The telephone rings. She is calling to see how you are getting along without her.

"Hello, Charlie! I just wanted to check and see if everything is going all right."

"Fine, Christine. Just fine," he lies. "Getting ready to go to the golf course. Going to have some toast and coffee first. By the way, I think the toaster is broken. It—"

"No, honey. It's not broken. Just do this. Open the cabinet door right below the toaster and slam it real hard. Then stand on the third red square on the floor in front of the refrigerator and jump up and down on it two or three times, real hard. It'll work then."

Charlie felt like an idiot, and he looked like one as he jumped up and down on a red tile in front of the refrigerator. But it worked, and the toaster lit up.

"O. K. Now, can you tell me where the cord to the coffee pot might be?"

"Sure. It's under the sink in the bucket that I keep the cleaning supplies in," she says matter of factly.

"In the bucket?"

"Right. I always keep it there, honey."

Charlie doesn't question her. He is out of breath from jumping.

"Well, I have to go now," Christine says. "Just call me if you need anything, O. K.?"

"Right. I'll do that."

With that, Charlies proceeds to bump his head several times on a pipe under the sink while digging in the bucket filled with sponges and rags searching for the cord to the coffee pot. No luck. He gives up and stops at a Waffle House for breakfast on the way to the golf course.

Did Charlie call Christine at her mama's? He tried, many times in the next few days. Did he talk to her? No. Why? *Bzzzz . . . Bzzzz . . . Bzzzz . . . Bzzzzy!*

There is a central thought here in this bit of by-play on housewives, and that is: Let us never take for granted the many things they do daily to make the lives of their husbands more comfortable.

Learning a Lesson of Life—The Hard Way

Some lessons in life we learn early, if we're fortunate. How true is the old proverb, "We are too soon oldt, and too late schmart."

I learned a great lesson in 1955: never interfere in a domestic argument. I was living in Houston, Texas, and driving home from work when I came upon a man beating a woman with his belt. It was brutal. He had her by the hair with one hand and was applying the belt with the other. She was bleeding from the nose and screaming. He was a giant, and she was no bigger than Twiggy. A classic mismatch.

Seeing a man beating a woman riles me no end, and I did a dumb thing. I stopped and got out of my car. The man never missed a lick. The woman continued to scream. She was drunk, but that was of no consequence. Drunk women hurt, too, when beaten.

I reached for the belt to protect her, and she fell, but got up immediately and attacked *me*! They *both* attacked me! There was no reasoning with either of them. It was their altercation, and I was an intruder. The man shoved me and the woman, sporting long fingernails, went for my eyes. Me? I went for my car and got away from there.

I arrived home with numerous scratches on my face, a bloody suit coat, a torn shirt, and I smelled of cheap perfume.

To this day I remember what the woman yelled as I drove away: "You mind y'r own d—n business, mister!"

The scene returned with reality recently as I sat in a roadside cafe near Pineville, North Carolina, late at night. I was en route to Charlotte and had stopped to eat.

It was quiet for the first few minutes, but then, "Wham!" It sounded like a freight train was coming through the door. I turned and saw a man and woman, both awesome, big, and inebriated. The woman was fuming. Daggers streaked from her eyes, venom rolled from her lips, and the aroma of cheap perfume assailed me from all over.

The hostess—undaunted—inquired of the couple, "Smoking or nonsmoking section?"

"Smokin'," grumbled the woman. "And fightin', too, honey!"

She led them to a back table, and the woman dropped a shoulder bag the size of a guano sack on it. Filled to the brim, it held most of the essentials for a fine garage sale.

The woman exploded. The man said nothing. He never got the chance. I learned that her name was Lucille and that his was Harvey. I got enough of the conversation to determine that they had been to a dance at some club earlier.

"I seen how ya' wuz daintzin' with her, up rail close an' all," the woman roared. "I seen y'r ramblin' hands, too! You think I'm blind?"

"But Lucille—"

"Jus' shut up! Ever'body wuz talkin' bout how y'all wuz daintzin', and her ole man not yet dead a month!" Lucille yelled. "Whut wuz it, Harvey, th' miniskirt or that big ole Cadillac she bought with th' insurance money that caught y'r eye?"

"Look, Lucille—"

"Shut up! I'm doin' th' talkin'." And she was, too. "Y'orter be 'shamed o' y'sef. We bin married eleven years, got five young'uns, an' you go chasin' a miniskirt an' a Cadillac. It'uz downright vulgar the way y'all wuz carryin' on, an' in a dark corner o' th'daintz floor at that! Ya' ain't nevah daintzed like that with me. An' ya' kep buyin' her them moggariters like they's on sale. Know whut ya' bought me, Harvey? A lousy beer! *One #%&*!$ lousy beer!*"

At this point a brave man, ignorant in the ways of family disagreements, joined Lucille and Harvey to make an attempt at mediation. I went to the men's room, and when I returned both were yelling at him. Shades of Houston after an absence of thirty-five years.

I paid my check and left, but true to form, as I pulled out of the parking lot, I saw Lucille and Harvey walk out arm-in-arm and get in a pickup. And they were sitting real close.

They Let the Flame Die along the Way

I stopped off at the Macon Mall on a recent trip to Atlanta to eat lunch at Morrison's cafeteria. It was raining when I arrived in the parking lot, so I decided to wait it out for a few minutes before entering. I've never owned an umbrella, and both my raincoats were hanging high and dry in my closet in Dublin.

As I sat in my car listening to the radio, I saw an older

model pickup truck pull in and park across from me. It was occupied by a man and a woman, both obviously on the shady side of seventy. The man was driving.

I watched as the man got out of the pickup and began walking in the rain toward the mall entrance while the woman, presumably his wife, remained in the pickup to tie a plastic rain cover over her hair. When she finally stepped out and started walking, her husband was almost to the sidewalk in front of the mall. He never looked back. He opened the door and entered, and his wife followed suit a few seconds and many steps later. I decided it was my turn. I walked in behind the woman.

The man walked through Penney's, never breaking stride. His wife followed but was many paces behind, and both disappeared from my view somewhere in the vicinity of the escalator. I kept thinking about them as I browsed around the store.

When did it happen? How long ago? Surely there was a time when he would have crawled over the hood of his pickup to open her door; would have taken her by the arm and guided her through the busy, wet parking lot; would have held the mall entrance door open for her and walked by her side through Penney's. But not this day. I got the definite impression that he would have much preferred to be seated in a dentist's chair undergoing a root canal than to be in the Macon Mall.

My suspicions were confirmed a short time later as I sat on a bench in front of Radio Shack and heard this exchange between the man and his wife:

"You go where you want to go, and I'll go where I want to go," she said.

"I'll be sitting right here," he said. "Just hurry up."

"You ain't got nowhere to go and nothing to do, and I ain't neither. So I ain't in no hurry," she said. "You could go look at some pants for yourself."

"I don't need no pants," he grumbled.

"Suit yourself. I'm gone."

She left, and he walked back toward Penney's, slowly. It was obvious that his feet hurt, and he was barely out of the starting gate. He was in for a long afternoon.

I went to Morrison's and ate lunch. Finished, I walked through the mall. Like the woman, "I wasn't in no hurry."

I strolled through a few shops, browsed through a bookstore, bought a Baskin-Robbins ice cream cone (vanilla, naturally), and casually walked back to the parking lot to get in my car and head north.

As I walked across the parking lot, I saw the pickup truck from Crawford County still parked there. The man was seated behind the steering wheel reading something. The rain had stopped. I watched him for a few minutes, then backed out of my parking space to leave. But I saw something in my rear-view mirror that caught my attention: The little woman was walking across the parking lot toward the pickup truck and was struggling with a double armload of packages. Her husband remained behind the steering wheel.

Did he get out and help her? No. Did he open the pickup door? No. He just sat there while she inched a large package up under her chin in order to free a hand with which to open the door. She dumped the packages inside the cab, climbed inside, and thereafter followed a one-sided conversation that I'm glad I couldn't hear.

Again I asked myself as I drove out of the parking lot, When did it happen? How long ago? Surely there was a flame at one time that burned brightly enough for the two of them to join hands and say, "I do." They just ain't happy no more, and that's sad.

As I drove along toward Forsyth, I thought about a couple that had been married for more than forty years. They were riding along when the wife, seated over by the window, looked at her husband who was driving and asked, "What's happened to us, George? We used to sit real close to each other when we rode along like this. Now look. You're way over there on your side, and I'm way over here by the window on my side. What's happened to us, George?"

George sort of grunted and answered, "Well, I ain't moved."

Part 5

On the Wild Side

You think southern girls won't party? If so, you'd best change gears and start over. They invented it!

A prime example is a trip I made to Knoxville, Tennessee, in October 1986. I was accompanied by my full-time public relations person and part-time driver, Robbie Nell Bell, from Alma, Georgia (Robbie Nail Bail, fum Almer). I was invited to participate in a book fair along with about fifty other authors. The purpose was to raise money for Knoxville's Lawson–McGee Library. The first day—Halloween—I signed books all day at the West Town Mall, finishing at 6:00 P.M.

Let me point out here that Robbie Nell was twenty-two at the time, tall, willowy, and beautiful. The only thing that has changed is that she is now twenty-six and drives a four-wheel pickup instead of my Lincoln.

Priding myself on having at least a smattering of common sense, I concluded that a twenty-two-year-old beauty would not be the least bit interested in curling up in a chair in a Holiday Inn room five hundred miles from home and watching television on Halloween night. So I told her I would take her wherever she wanted to go, back off, and let her do her thing. I think she appreciated that, so off we went in search of a fun and frolic place.

Inasmuch as neither of us had ever been in Knoxville, we just sort of cruised around for a little while. Then it dawned on me that Knoxville is home to the University of Tennessee, and I stopped and asked directions, then drove toward the campus knowing full well that there had to be an "in" place nearby. I had no trouble identifying it. A young couple walking on the side of the street didn't hesitate when I asked the question. "Rumors," they said. "That's where everybody goes to party."

They were right. Everybody goes there, and on this Halloween night the lighted sign cried out in giant letters, Halloween Special! Margaritas, Two for One!"

"All right!" Robbie Nell yelled. "Looks like my kind of place!"

The giant parking lot was filled and I thought I was in luck as I pulled into a vacant parking place near the entrance. It was dark, and, as we exited the car to go inside, the voice of a parking lot security guard boomed through the night air. "Hey! Are you folks handicapped?"

Before I could say a word, Robbie Nell yelled back while pointing to the sign, "I ain't now, but if you'll give me 'bout two hours inside, I guarantee ya' I will be!"

I moved the car, but she was right. Was she ever right! Rumors will never be the same. Within minutes after making her grand entrance, Robbie Nell was transformed from a full-time public relations person to a full-fledged party animal. She inhaled margaritas and Salem Light 100s, danced with everybody there except the janitor, and would have danced with him had it not been for the mop and broom he held all night.

Any excuse for a party will suffice for women in Dixie, and should anybody chance to be blocking the parking lot entrance at 5:00 P.M. on Friday, watch out! They'll run over you and never look back. I know this because I have a pretty, vivacious daughter, Lisa, who works on the top floor of a sixteen-story office building.

Another thing, and I can't for the life of me figure out how they do it, the girls can pull a Superman stunt and change from a business suit or conservative skirt and blouse to a miniskirt or short shorts in the elevator on the way down and be ready to party when the elevator door opens on the ground floor. This I know, too, because I've seen them hit the street on the run.

The rage in northern cities and Atlanta—one and the same—is the singles bar. It's sort of a female cattle market where the girls listen to the lies of yuppie braggarts and take their choice. Some go to the highest bidder.

Not so out in the boondocks where I hang out. Instead of singles bars, it's juke joints, but the results are the same. Every female is fair game, with no bag limit, and you can shoot 'em on the ground without a hunting license. After all, that's why they're there, to be eyed, lied to, and coaxed.

Just say the secret word, and the party is on.

But, know what? I can't recall any permanent relationship that began in a singles bar or a juke joint. They are nothing more than preludes to party time for macho types and welcome oases for out-of-town businessmen. There is no shortage of players and no age limit.

And the hors d'oeuvres are free. So is the rock music, if you can stand it.

I sat in such a place in an Atlanta hotel, a singles gathering place, and sipped on something sour. The man next to me, a senior citizen from Monroe, Louisiana, watched the couples go through various gyrations that chiropractors encourage.

"What do you think of that?" I asked him.

"Well, son, all I can say is that if'n my Daddy's bird dogs had a-done that, he'd a-wormed 'em!"

Anytime Is Cocktail Party Time In Dixie

If you by chance have labored for years under the false assumption that parties are reserved for birthdays, weddings, anniversaries, graduations, and promotions, forget it. It just ain't true in the South. Cocktail parties are big.

I know women who will throw a cocktail party to celebrate the groundhog seeing his shadow in February, or that he didn't. If he's single, they'll invite him to the party.

I also know a woman in South Carolina who threw a party

because her roses bloomed three weeks early. Another woman threw one because hers died.

The favorite party of partygivers is, of course, the cocktail party. That's where sandwiches and people are cut into little pieces and devoured with complete abandon.

I've been to a few (thousand) cocktail parties along the road, plus a few cane grindings, peanut boilings, and a candy-pulling or two, but cocktail parties are my favorite for my premier pastime: people watching.

Nobody wants to be the first to arrive at a cocktail party. People hide behind the shrubbery and trees to avoid being there first. Not me. If the invitation says 6:30, it means 6:30 and that is precisely when I push the doorbell. That could, and often does, pose a problem for the unsuspecting hostess who doesn't expect anyone to show before at least 7:15.

It doesn't bother me in the least to browse in the den, munch on cashews, cheese straws, and midget sandwiches, and be the first to drag a potato chip through the avocado concoction or clam dip while the hostess finishes zipping and teasing.

Many facets of cocktail parties are universal in nature. Like why does everybody stand in the doorway? Throw a shindig for twelve people in the Superdome, and eight of 'em will camp in the doorway for the evening. The other four will be in the restroom.

Also-rans never attend cocktail parties. Just take a look around when you attend your next one. You'll find no second-string halfbacks, PFCs, or fourth runners-up. Everybody's a star at a cocktail party, especially out of town where nobody knows any better.

It's always the halfback who ran ninety-three yards in the final minute to score the winning touchdown for the state championship; the captain who blasted the Germans to kingdom come with his very own machine gun to single-handedly win World War II; and Miss Priss of 19?? But never any also-rans.

There are no failures either. Only the successful attend cocktail parties, and business is great. "Best year ever, and planning to add on next year." That is, unless the hostess happens to be a sadist and invited an IRS agent. Then, it's backpeddling and Bankruptcyville for everybody.

Another thing about cocktail parties: guests demand the best. Like ole Roy, who chugalugs Early Times at college football games but will settle for nothing less than Crown Royal, Jack Daniel's, or Chivas Regal at the free bar. And his wife, Polly, a dedicated and frequent Mad Dog 20/20 guzzler who turns up her nose at the mere suggestion of Riunite, Liebfraumilch, or Mateus Rosé while posing the question to the bartender, "What year is it, Dahling?"

What difference does it make? If it bubbles, she'll down it. And if the hostess really wants to turn Polly on? Just slip a little cake coloring in it to make it pink and a couple of Alka-Seltzer tablets for bubbles. Two glasses will have Polly on top of the piano doing her rendition of "Hard-Hearted Hannah, the Vamp of Savannah."

Just once I'd like to hear the hostess take microphone in hand and announce, "For those of you who would like to dance, the bus to the American Legion Club is loading out back and will be leaving in five minutes."

Of course, there are always two types of people at cocktail parties: those who want to leave early and those who want to stay late. Unfortunately, they're usually married to each other.

The legendary Groucho Marx probably delivered the best line ever to a hostess as he was leaving her cocktail party, saying, "Madame, I've had a wonderful evening, but this wasn't it."

Ludlow Porch, popular radio talk-show host at WSB-AM in Atlanta, comes in a close second with this concerning a guest at a New Year's Eve party at his home.

"It was nearing midnight and Jack, a fellow worker and two-fisted drinker, had imbibed to the point where he was lap-legged," Ludlow recalls. "Seated on a stool, but barely, he turned to my wife, Diane, and said in a very low voice, 'This is a great party. I wish I was here.'"

Sometimes It's Better to "Just Say No"

Let me make one thing clear. Perrier-water clear, if you please. This is not a dissertation on the pros and cons of imbibing. Rather, it is a discourse on the problems some teetotalers experience when making every effort to decline the juice at cocktail parties, receptions, and convention city lounges.

First, a look at what can and does happen at receptions.

Has this ever happened to you? You arrive promptly at six, and immediately the hostess is all over you like a cheap suit.

"Harry and Helen! So nice of you to come! Here, let me take your coats while you name your poison," she says. "Just tell Roscoe, the bartender, over there and—"

"Not a thing, thanks. We just—" says Harry.

"Oh, nonsense! You must, Harry!" she insists. "We're celebrating!"

The hostess, unknowingly, has just afforded ole Harry the opportunity to chart his course for the evening if he plays his cards right. Here's what he should do:

"Well, I'd really like some of that white stuff in the clear bottle; but the last time I tried it I ended up doing a Russian dance, breaking all the crystal, and throwing a bulldog through a grandfather's clock. They finally got the rifle away from me, but only after I'd put three slugs dead center in a Churchill portrait and knocked the antlers off a deer head hanging over the fireplace in the den. The hostess was real nice about the whole thing, though, and dropped the attempted rape charge after I replaced her party dress and had the headboard repaired. My doctor at the psychiatric clinic said something about body chemistry and a low alcohol tolerance rate during my exit interview before I was released."

If the hostess is still within earshot or arm's length, Harry should then fire the big gun:

"But that was over a year ago, and I'm willing to give it another try. What do those doctors know anyway? How 'bout a double shot of that stuff in the bottle with the turkey on the label? It looks harmless and . . ."

That should do it for Harry. At that point he couldn't *buy* a drink if he was a HUD contract coordinator or Donald Trump's brother. Perrier water? Maybe, but only in a paper cup.

So much for Harry. Now it's Helen's turn at the reception.

The wedding's over and pictures are being taken of the bridal party—thousands of pictures of the bridal party. It's time to move on to the reception at the country club.

The line has formed to sign the bride's book with a white feather. Champagne and hors d'oeuvres await the onslaught by guests who will eat the miniatures like they're going to the electric chair in the morning. How does Helen handle the champagne issue? Take heed, all you Helens out there.

Limp slightly, but noticeably, as you thread your way through a myriad of hugs and handshakes to the long table replete with triangular pimiento cheese and chicken salad miniatures. Waiters in white jackets will glide through the hall balancing champagne-filled trays, Las Vegas style.

The mother of the bride will spot you sooner or later with this probable exchange taking place:

"Helen! You look so pretty! Here, have some champagne."

"Thank you, no, Hortense," you reply, limping noticeably in the direction of the miniatures, melon balls, and simmering sausage lumps surrounded by pastel toothpicks and no place to discard them.

"Oh, come now! You simply must toast my baby and . . . say, are you limping, you poor dear?"

"It's nothing, really. I had a little accident at Ralph and Margo's wedding reception last Saturday. I'm fine, really I am, Hortense," you tell her.

"What happened, Helen? Please tell me."

"Well, to tell you the truth, I tripped over a cheese ball, fell in a punch bowl, and dislocated my kneecap," you inform her.

"My goodness! What in the world was a cheese ball doing on the floor?"

"Oh, it wasn't on the floor," you tell her. "It was on the hors d'oeuvres table. I was doing a Go-Go dance there after a couple of glasses of champagne. Next thing I knew, I tripped over the cheese ball, hit the punch bowl, and was lying prone on the floor with a busted kneecap. But the photographer got some great shots, Hortense! In fact, he's scheduled another session with me for next Thursday if my knee's all right. He says I have real potential as a photographer's model, and he's going to furnish the champagne.

"And, guess what? The Hahira Shriners have invited me to their convention next year in Las Vegas and . . . oh, what the heck! I might as well have a glass of champagne even though the stuff does bring out the primitive woman in me."

"Yes, I see," says Hortense. "Ahem . . . let me get you a cup of punch, dear. I made it myself, and it's delicious. Pineapple juice and Pepsi."

"But I hate to be a clod, Hortense," you tell her. "After all, it is little Jill's wedding day. I think I can handle a few glasses of champagne. I'll give it the old college try just for her."

That should do it, Helen, you little ole teetotaler you. And there's no way Hortense is going to let you near the champagne and ruin Jill's wedding reception. Just rest easy and sip along on Hortense's punch. Cheers!

Finally, there's the matter of conventions. Here's a scene that is undoubtedly familiar to thousands of teetotalers. It is played daily in convention city lounges from Miami to Montreal, Los Angeles to New York City.

Harry and Helen have checked into their hotel after a loud and boisterous flight. Helen kicks off her shoes, flops face down on the king-size bed, sighs long and hard, and says, "Oh, Lord! If Walter had yelled 'How 'Bout Them Dogs' one more time, I'd have jumped out of the airplane."

"Ole Walter lives and dies with the Dogs," Harry says as he hangs up his coat and removes his tie.

"He's mighty loyal for a guy with only a GED diploma and a certificate from a ten-day insurance seminar," Helen sneers. "And who the heck is this Herschel What's-His-Name that he keeps talking about, Harry?"

"Let's just pretend that you didn't ask that question, Helen," Harry says as his face turns ashen. "And, for God's sake, don't ask Walter! After all, he *is* the company president, you know."

"I know, Harry. The whole world knows," Helen grumbles.

Helen somehow makes it through the reception with the time-honored "Just a Coke, please."

At the awards dinner, the regional manager presents plaques for everything from Most New Accounts to Best Convention Bartender. Harry didn't win in either category.

Helen is two hours ahead of schedule when she turns to Harry at 8:30 P.M. and whispers, "I've got a headache, Honey." Before Harry has a chance to offer his rebuttal, the rafters ring with a familiar cry, "How 'Bout Them Dogs!"

The echo is equally as long, "Go You Hairy Dawgs!"

That was the straw that broke the Tiger's back. Helen, an Auburn graduate and unable to resist, mounts the table, tilts her head back, cups her hands around her mouth, and let's go with, "Waaaaarrrrr Eagle!"

The dinner over, nine to twelve is scheduled as free time. You know, do your own thing. It was to be TV for Harry and *Ladies Home Journal* for Helen, but one telephone call changed that.

"That was Ray, the new regional manager," Harry said. "He wants us to join him in the lounge. So get your duds on and—"

"Oh, Harry! Do we have to?"

"You know I'm being considered for promotion, Helen, and Ray *is* the regional manager."

"All right! I *know* who Ray is," Helen barked. "Let's go get it over with."

They weren't three feet out of the elevator when the voice bounced off the wall leading to the Paradise Lounge. "Yahoooooo! How 'Bout Them Dawgs!"

Walter? No, Ray.

Hang in there, Helen. You can handle it. Here's one way.

When the cocktail waitress appears at Ray's table to take orders, just chime right in when your turn comes around. It goes like this:

"Gin and tonic," says Ray.

"Piña colada," says Rita, his wife.

"Gimme' a whiskey sour on the rocks," orders Sharon, Walter's wife of the moment.

"Beer!" growls Walter. "Long-neck Bud in a bottle. An' some pork skins."

Harry orders Scotch on the rocks.

You're next, Helen. And remember to keep a straight face.

"How 'bout you, Honey?" asks the platinum bombshell.

"I'd like a Scotch and Gatorade," you say with authority.

"Any special brand?"

"Orange or lemon will be fine."

"No, Sugah. I mean what brand of Scotch?"

"I don't care what brand. I can get loaded on Scotch tape, rye bread, blended fabric, gin rummy, or listening to Jimmy Buffet sing 'Margaritaville.' Do you have any Gatorade or not?"

"Of course not," says the waitress curtly. "This is a lounge, not the Superdome."

"Well, in that case, bring me a bourbon and buttermilk." (Straight face.)

"My Godamighty! I thought I'd heard 'em all! Bourbon and buttermilk?"

"Right on! I love it," you tell her.

"I'm sorry, Honey, but—"

"O. K. . . . O. K., just bring me a plain Coke, please. Do you have that?"

"Yeah, sure. One plain Coke coming up. Want some mustard or pepper sauce in it?"

"No, thank you. I always drink my Coke straight."

If you can't beat 'em, confuse 'em, Helen. And if nothing else works, you can always feign a headache. Right, Harry?

Beware of Cheri Bombs on New Year's Eve

I've never been real big on New Year's Eve parties where I have to make a reservation in February, plunk down a hundred bucks for a bottle of cheap champagne, a silly hat, a horn, loud music, and a one-minute hunting license to stalk and kiss women I hardly know whose husbands are either in the men's room or doing a little stalking of their own in the bar when midnight arrives and the time-honored kissing ritual is observed.

I did, however, break with tradition and go to such a celebration New Year's Eve 1989, a wild, noisy, silly-hat, horn-blowin', kiss-whoever's-still-standin'-and-semisober-at-midnight party in Atlanta featuring rock music that would blow out a truck tire.

I was the guest of my good friend, Ludlow Porch, who owns not only the restaurant where the party was staged, the Blue Ribbon Grill, but a big hunk of Atlanta and the North Georgia mountains as well, and a radio audience of thousands that listen to him for four hours every morning when he mans the microphone for his popular Monday–Friday talk show on WSB-AM. (AM? Right. "FM radio is the work of the devil," says Ludlow, "and it'll give you pimples if you listen to it.")

While we were eating at a front table, Cheri, a fan of Ludlow's, joined us and sat by him across the table from me. Cheri has four big and visible assets, two of them being that she is young and beautiful.

Ludlow handled the introductions and continued eating. I stopped and stared. Friend, I'd eat liver with Cheri. She's that beautiful, with Hall of Fame stats: like 17–42–24–38. The seventeen is her SAT score, but then brains ain't really a requirement in Cheri's line of work as a nude dancer at the Gold Club.

Shortly, Cheri's friend and co-worker Nancy arrived and sat next to me. Another doll and another Hall of Fame candidate. I'd eat pickled pig's feet with Nancy. I asked her to marry me right off, but the music was so loud that she didn't hear me. Susan, the waitress, did and said, "Can't right this minute, Sugah. Gotta' work til' three. Check back with me then." She tooted her horn and walked away.

Cheri introduced Nancy to Ludlow. He took it from there.

Ludlow is the undisputed king of the radio spoof and has pulled off classic ones on Atlanta radio. Here's what he did to me when introducing Nancy.

"Nancy, I'd like you to meet my good friend, Tom Turner," he said without warning. "He's Ted's older brother."

With that, he got up and walked away from the table.

Nancy was impressed. So was Cheri. So was I.

So was Susan, who overheard the introduction and said she thought she could arrange to get off a little early.

"Do you work for your brother's television network?" Nancy asked, edging closer.

"Occasionally, when I'm not traveling abroad," I said nonchalantly.

"Doing what?" Cheri asked, her foot rubbing the calf of my right leg.

"Oh, I handle Teddy's investments and review his portfolio with all his brokers. I buy and sell corporations, take care of his boat, and select the movies to be shown on television," I lied.

Susan dropped a margarita and a Miller Lite. Both Nancy and Cheri moved even closer and sat motionless in awe, with visions of $$$$ marks dancing in their pretty heads.

Ludlow watched and listened from his vantage point behind the bar. I sat tall in the saddle and tried my best to look rich and worldly.

The three of us—Cheri, Nancy and myself—were exchanging telephone numbers when Ludlow arrived back at the table at 10:30 P.M. My few moments as a male Cinderella would soon end as Cheri announced that she had to leave for the Gold Club. Before leaving, she did something, quite unintentionally, that I hadn't seen in all the years I've known Ludlow Porch. She completely broke the guy up with this exchange, revealing her SAT score in the process.

"Are you coming soon?" Cheri asked Nancy.

"In a little while. I don't go on until midnight."

"Are you driving?"

"Yes, why?"

"Well, don't drive down Peachtree Industrial Boulevard if—"

"Oh? Why not?"

"Because," Cheri explained, "I talked to Roxanne a few minutes ago, and she said state troopers are set up at Peachtree Industrial and Holcombe Bridge Road, and they're checking IUDs!"

Cheri left. Nancy left. Midnight arrived, and there I was with Ludlow and Susan—a matrimonial prospect—the only two still standing and semisober. I had a choice to make. I shook Ludlow's hand and kissed Susan, wished them a Happy New Year and left, thereby breaking our brief engagement.

Susan's silly hat was on crooked, and she tooted her horn and waved as I exited the Blue Ribbon Grill parking lot. "Goodbye, Mr. Turner! And a Happy New Year to you! Ya'll come back, ye heah!"

I smiled as I cruised by the state troopers at Peachtree Industrial and Holcombe Bridge, feeling safe and secure for two reasons, one of them being that I hadn't been drinking.

Topless Art: A Touch of Genius

It took a while for topless nightclubs to make their way into the deep Southland, but their coming was inevitable. Not only to the big cities but to the rural hamlets and villages that dot Dixie as well.

For years those in the boondocks read with considerable interest about the topless bars in New York and Chicago, but only those who traveled there had ever seen one. Then it happened. A topless nightclub opened deep in the Bible Belt, and the male inhabitants of the small town in which it chose to locate awaited opening night with great anticipation and expectation.

But pity the old reporter, Harry, who worked for the Bible Belt weekly that served the community in which the club was opening. He was assigned to go there on opening night, when some of the local talent would be afforded auditions, and write a story about it. The old editor's wife wouldn't let him go—himself.

The old editor believed in keeping abreast (no pun intended) of everything that went on in his small town, so he sent Harry and cautioned him not to use the word *breasts* or the names of any local girls in his story lest some of the readers be offended. Also, he instructed Harry to have the story—with pictures—on his desk first thing the next morning.

Harry dutifully went to the club, camera in hand, and watched the dancers perform and the locals audition before returning to the newspaper shortly after midnight to write his story.

Recalling the admonition of the old editor, he was baffled for lack of a lead. Finally, calling on his many years of experience and ingenuity, he began typing. At last, his story finished, he placed his copy, along with pictures from his trusty Polaroid, on the editor's desk and went home.

This was Harry's lead, what the editor read upon arriving for work the next morning:

"Last night, professional and local dancers at Eve's Garden were the first in the history of the county, permitted by court order, to perform with their (.) (.) bare . . ."

Part 6

In the Market Place

They'll never stay down on the farm now that they have discovered the world that awaits in the city. Women have climbed the ladder to peaks heretofore unimagined, and they're doing quite well, thank you.

There are no doors closed to women in the workplace any more. They compete, like their male counterparts, for jobs and positions previously reserved and labeled "For Men Only."

Who would ever have thought that the day would come when women would lead troops into combat, chase speeders and arrest drunks, head large corporations, report the evening news, do a regular sportscast, climb utility poles, run bulldozers, write personal newspaper columns and walk off with Pulitzer Prizes in the process, sit at the bank president's desk, run for vice president, drive emergency life-saving vehicles, perform delicate surgery, prosecute or defend law cases, sit on the highest court in the land or in the President's cabinet, head probation and parole offices, fly commercial airliners, and stand in church pulpits!

The women of the world have come a long way.

I'm still making every effort to get used to the idea that a woman cuts my hair, and she does a dang good job of it, too!

Women are out there in the marketplace for two reasons. First, two incomes are a necessity for a family to survive these days. Second, the challenge of success gnaws at them night and day, just like men.

One thing I have noticed during the great transition is that women still prefer to work for men. I did a survey on the subject once, and the results were overwhelming. The women are in the marketplace to stay, however, and you can bet the egg money on it.

Women Perform Lunch Hour Magic

The South is steeped in tradition, one being the much revered lunch hour. It is an untouchable ritual and not to be tampered with, this midday break when some working women accomplish more in one hour than during the entire workday.

The British have their tea; the Irish their beer; the French their wine; and the Russians their vodka. All are traditions. In America, it's the lunch hour.

I know office workers who perform magic on their lunch hour, who can (and do) have their car washed, pick up a birthday cake, drop off the dry cleaning, make a bank deposit, check out a shoe sale at the mall and see if "that" dress has been reduced since the lunch hour the day before, have a prescription filled, drop off a roll of film to be developed, run by the house to check on the roast, select a get-well card for a sick friend and drop it off at the post office, zip by the school to leave lunch money, and return three books to the library—all on their lunch hour.

All finished, they make one last stop at a drive-in window to pick up a hamburger and a diet Coke to eat at their desk when they return to the office. And you've wondered for years how all that mustard and catsup gets on your statements and invoices.

A case in point is a pretty secretary who works at my newspaper. I once saw her rushing back to the office with a bag filled with hamburgers. It was raining, and she was almost out of breath.

"On your lunch hour, Cheryl?" I asked as we met.

"Already had it," she replied, never breaking stride.

"Oh? Well, what's in the bag?"

"Hamburgers!" she yelled over her shoulder. "I went shopping with my Mama on my lunch hour. Now, I've gotta' get back to my desk and eat!"

It's the old lunch hour ripoff. It, too, is an American tradition with the eat-on-the-run girls. The fast food drive-in window is as familiar to them as the latest dress sale.

Here are a few short shots regarding the lunch scene.

The beggar knocked on the door at lunch time, and when the housewife answered, he said to her, "Excuse me, ma'am, but I have no money and I'm hungry. Could you please spare me a bite to eat?"

The housewife pointed to a pile of wood and said, "All right, I'll give you lunch if you will just chop up that pile of wood."

The beggar eyed the pile of wood, thought a few seconds, and said, "Let me see the menu first."

A woman came out of a very expensive restaurant after having had lunch and was confronted by a dirty, unkempt man in ragged clothing.

"Here, you poor man, is a nickel," she said to him. "By the way," she added, "how on earth did you ever get into such a lowly and miserable state?"

"I guess I was just too much like you, lady, always giving large sums of money to the poor."

A Job Makes a "Heap o' Difference"

One of the first things that impressed me at my first high school reunion was how much some of my classmates had changed. Oh, some of them had been just waiting to get out of the house and away from Mom and Pop so they could be their own men and women. Others had "blossomed" after high school and had come into their own. None of us thought they had it in them, but they did, and they were obviously well on their way to success.

But there were those few—actually, every class seems to have them—who changed so drastically they were almost beyond recognition. They had landed jobs nobody had ever suspected they would get, and somehow the jobs made new men and women of them.

A few come to mind right now.

Anna Acne. Remember Anna? She's the one who sat in the back of the bus alone and read movie magazines all the way to school. Anna read the same magazine on the return trip, in the same seat—alone.

Anna read about the life and loves of Gina Glamour, Barbara Beautiful, and Sophia Silicone, but nobody on the bus paid any attention to her or noticed that she read a lot. (Unless there was a job to be done that nobody wanted to do. Then the spotlight fell on Anna Acne.)

She graduated and sort of dropped out of sight, but that was of no particular concern to her classmates. However, Anna didn't let all her reading go to waste. No, sir!

Shortly after graduation, she sat on her back porch at home out on Route 3, after having fed the chickens, and filled out a coupon in the back of one of her magazines. She then enclosed $4.98, plus postage, for her one-pound jar of Clear-Plex, guaranteed to give her a Barbara Beautiful complexion or "double your pimples back!" Anna had no doubt that Clear-Plex would work because she had seen it advertised on "Hee-Haw" once. What the heck. If it'll work for Dolly Parton, it'll work for Anna, but only above the neck.

Sure enough, the package arrived twelve days later, and Anna, filled with confidence, removed it from the mailbox. She had every right to be confident. The rust on the mailbox flag was beginning to disappear after only forty-five minutes' exposure to the miracle cream, Clear-Plex.

Anna immediately buried the jar in the chicken yard next to the hen house. For the next seventeen nights she stole away and slipped out to her secret place and liberally applied Clear-Plex to her face. She even ate a dab or two. What happened? Sure enough, in eleven days the acne began to disappear and by the twenty-first day it was gone.

"See, I told you that you would grow out of it, Anna!"

The plot thickens. Anna packed her Clear-Plex, along with a few personal items, boarded a bus in McIntyre, and headed for the city. She got a job in a department store in the cosmetics department where she works with Molly Manicure and Rita Rinse.

You would never recognize her now. Anna Acne is a new woman thanks to Clear-Plex. She doesn't spell her name "Anna" anymore. Her name tag reads:

Anyah
Beauty Consultant

Her mail-order gingham dress is gone. She gave it to the Salvation Army shortly after going to work, along with her lace-up shoes, high-neck blouses (she now keeps the top three buttons unbuttoned), un-slit skirts, and plain jeans.

Anyah now reports for the daily fashion parade in shoes with heels that come equipped with a half dozen Dramamine, enough make-up to do a long-running Broadway musical, and more "things" hanging around her neck than the Anheuser-Busch Clydesdales! Her hair? It's twisted to one side like she had just walked out of Hurricane David! And frizzly.

She spends thirty-five minutes of each hour at work tugging at her blouse and skirt, twelve minutes checking her hair and make-up, and seven minutes parading back and forth past the triple-sided mirrors in the ladies' wear department. The remaining six minutes she spends tabulating on preprinted tab sheets how much she hasn't sold.

Nope, the folks back on Route 3, McIntyre, would never recognize old Anna Acne. She is now a full-fledged member of the department store parade and daily fashion show.

How about Stella Sapphire? She used to be in the egg business with her husband, Clyde, near Soperton. No more, Sweetheart. Ole Stella has done flew the coop. She's in the jewelry department now, right next to Anyah. Her name tag? "Stehlagh." What else?

She came to Dublin, shed forty-three pounds and a husband, and hasn't had a birthday since 1966. Stehlagh's still thirty-four. Ask her.

Rings? Stehlagh's got 'em! One on every finger and a couple on some.

You really can't blame her, though. Up until she left Clyde and the chickens, the only one she ever had was Clyde's army ring with the blue stone that he won in a crap game in Okinawa in '44. She made him replace it with a wedding band in '52.

Earrings, bracelets, and necklaces? Boy! Each one could be a novel, but I'll try and complete the picture.

Her earrings hang down to her hip bones, very prominent since she dropped the excess forty-three pounds. Bracelets and necklaces? She's got single strands, double strands, serpentines, plaited ones, long ones, short ones, eighteen, twenty-four, and thirty inches.

Ole Stehlagh exists on diet bars and an occasional salad but makes regular payments to Laura Layaway on her jewelry. First things first!

Yep, ole Stehlagh has joined the fashion feud, competing against girls like Linda Lingerie, Gwenda Girdle, Henrietta Housewares, and Laura Layaway. Each is trying to catch the eye of Jack Jock in sporting goods or Harvey Haberdasher in men's furnishings.

Morris Manager just sits back, relaxes and enjoys the show, every day.

Lest I leave the impression that only women are sometimes affected by a change of jobs and environment, let me hasten to record my thought about Harvey ("Just call me Harv") Haberdasher and ole Jack Jock.

Ole Harv, from New Jersey originally, fell off the back of a carnival wagon eight years ago up near Dudley. His only previous legitimate employment was as a stock clerk in men's furnishings at Macy's across the river in New York. He worked there for three weeks, quit, and joined the carnival. His main jobs with it were putting up and taking down tents, plus sweeping up after the elephants and horses.

Harv walked on into Dublin behind a guy pulling a little red wagon, and stopped in the Huddle House for coffee. While there, he read the want ads. Afterward, he shaved his beard in the men's room, borrowed a comb, and headed for a job interview.

He's been at the job for six months now and what a change! A gold chain adorns his neck where a ring of dirt used to be. (Long since removed with soap at the Huddle House.) He wears three-piece suits, ruffled shirts, stacked heels, and red jockey shorts. His hair is combed forward and, with a lot of help from hair spray, sticks up like a ski jump. His little finger sports a turquoise ring.

Ole Jack Jock? Same ole Jack. Wore Keds to his daughter's wedding and listened to a Falcon–Redskins game through an earphone.

"Ain't got time for none of them floozies! Not with the World Series, football, and Hawks' exhibition games on TV. No way, man!"

Ole Jack may say that, but I know a secret. Sarraugh Sachet in notions has her eye on him, and she recently borrowed the remaining half-jar of Clear-Plex from Anyah!

And the parade goes on. Every day.

Secretaries: Cream of the Corporate Wine List

No book on women, southern or otherwise, would be complete without at least a few pages spotlighting the mint juleps of the office. There is no doubt in my mind that secretaries run the offices in America. They merely tolerate those who administer the companies for whom they work, sometimes called bosses. Who are these bosses and secretaries anyway?

The bosses are those who arrive early when the secretary arrives late, and late when she arrives early. The secretary is the woman the boss pays to learn how to spell while she looks for a husband.

At the top of the corporate ladder is the executive. And what is an executive? He's about halfway between what his wife thinks he is and what his secretary knows he is.

Bosses and executives are as helpless as a baby when

their secretaries are out of pocket. Think of what would probably happen in her office should her boss be forced to make it on his own for a week.

Had the secretary been on the job, a simple letter could have been dictated, typed, proofed, corrected, signed, and mailed in less than an hour. It would have looked like this:

Somewhere, Alabama
March 7, 1990

Mr. John Anderson
Acme Products, Incorporated
1253 Williams Street
Chattanooga, Tennessee 37401

Dear Mr. Anderson:
This will acknowledge receipt of your order received today. It is appreciated very much and will receive expeditious handling.

My secretary has gone on her holiday and will be away from the office for ten days. While I do have a typist available, she has also gone on a spree for her holiday to Las Vegas and may never return.

I just wish that both would return soon, as I am handling the secretarial and typing duties in their absence.

Meanwhile, thank you for your order. You may rest assured it will be shipped at the earliest possible opportunity.

Very truly yours,

Bo Whaley
Sales Manager

P.S. I don't type very well. Please overlook all errors. Thank you.

Simple, right? No, not when the secretary is away and the sales manager is wearing the secretarial hat. When that happens, the letter could look like this:

Subware, ALLavvama
mock 7.1)90

Mr. Johb Amdestin
Avne Ptodiuvttts
12%# Wiliiiiimaspnn Stret
Charrniggaaa,Tenmesdee 3'$0!

Deat Mrrrrr Admetin:
   Tjis wilackmowlefgr rev ei t of yout odor reCivVeddd
tody. It id aprexisatd bert micj a nnnd wil reCive eXX-
ptduuuss hamflibk.
   Mi secrterri hax gon ob hir hilifat ans wil b gon fir a
wekk. whil i do hab a typish av albel shee hab akso gon
ob a sprii fir hr hilifat two Lag Viggus an mat nebbber
rittun.
   i jussss wisj mi secrterri od typish wuld huddy ad com
bak tu wokk.
   menwidde, tjabk yout fot yuut odor. yu may ressssstt
adduted id wil b slipd ad tHee eatiestt oppodumItty.

vRet trilly yoird,

Boooooo wJakey
sailes mabbafer

pS: Idon't tippe viry wale. plise obbelokk al errrrrros.
thAbk yout.

So much for the typing. How about the dictation? Sup-
pose the secretaries wrote down and typed *exactly* what
some bosses dictate? The next morning Mr. C. J. Squizz,
President, Squizz Soap Company, Detroit, Michigan, could
receive the following letter as dictated to Phyllis by her
boss:

All right, Phyllis. Take a letter, and this time take it
exactly the way I say it because it's damned important.
Ready? O.K. Here we go . . . Mr. O., or A. J., or some
fool initials . . . look it up . . . Squizz . . . God! What a

name! . . of the Squizz Soap Company in Detroit . . . That's in Michigan, ain't it? . . . Dear Mr. Squizz . . . Hmmm, let me see now. What do I want to tell that old fool . . . Yeah, the last shipment of soap you sent us was of inferior quality . . . Inferior quality? Hell, it wasn't worth a damn, Phyllis! . . . And I want you to understand . . . No, scratch that out, Phyllis . . . I hope you understand . . . Hmmmmmmm . . . Unless you can ship . . . furnish . . . ship . . . no dammit, furnish us with your regular soap, you needn't ship us no more, period . . . Or whatever the grammar is. You fix it, Phyllis. Now, where was I? Oh, yeah. Paragraph. Your soap wasn't what you said . . . Hah! I'll say it wasn't. Them bums really tried to pull one on us, Phyllis . . . What the hell, do they think we're some sort of morons? . . . We're sending back your last shipment . . . Sure we're gonna' send it back! . . . I'd like to feed it to 'em with a spoon and make 'em eat it! . . . *Buuuuuurrrrrpppp!!* . . . Excuse me, Phyllis . . . O. K., now read it back to me . . . No, don't read it back to me . . . We've wasted enough time on them crooks! . . . Just fix it up and sign my name and then we'll go to lunch. O. K.?"

Waitresses Must Live with Don Juans

Sometimes I think I must spend more time in restaurants than Duncan Hines. Being a bachelor and never having had any desire to learn to cook, it follows that I come to know a lot of waitresses. And I respect what they do, the long hours they put in, and some of the people they have to put up with.

I was already seated, drinking coffee and reading my newspaper, when the self-styled Don Juan came in. He wasted no time going into what was obviously his established restaurant routine, propositioning one waitress, insulting another, and embarrassing a female customer before seating himself up front near the cash register.

A pretty, neat little blonde waitress, not more than eighteen and obviously new on the job, drew the unpleasant assignment of waiting on Don Juan. In waitress parlance, "It was her turn." It was like throwing a lamb to the wolves, a classic mismatch.

I'll never understand how some men come up with the mistaken idea that the waitress comes with two eggs over light, grits, sausage, toast, coffee, and a twenty-five-cent tip.

The guy came on strong with all the old and worn-out clichés that every waitress who ever asked the question, "More coffee, sir?" has heard repeatedly.

"Are you ready to order, sir?" she asked.

"Yeah, Baby, but I don't see what I want on the menu," Don Juan answers.

She tries to ignore the insinuation, be nice and maintain her composure.

"What would you like, sir?"

"What's your home telephone number? I'll call you after you get off tonight and tell you." (Good Lord! He's at least thirty years older than she is!)

Although young and inexperienced in dealing with scum, she remained calm and unruffled and stood her ground with order pad in hand. She waited for his order, took it, and moved on, well aware that she would have to return.

In the meantime, Don Juan was joined by three more men, providing him with an audience. When the little blonde brought his breakfast, she had to blush through his barrage of double-meaning comments while his three buddies laughed at his sick humor like the jackasses they were.

As I watched Don Juan go through his routine, I couldn't help but recall this little story about waitresses that seemed to fit the occasion.

The customer, very demanding and rude, remarked to the waitress just before leaving the restaurant, "Tell me, why is it that I never get the treatment I deserve when I dine in this establishment?"

"Perhaps, sir," the waitress replied, "it is because those of us who work here are too polite."

It is no breeze to be a waitress. They work long and hard for little pay. So the next time we are enjoying breakfast at 7:00 A.M. on a cold morning, we might do well to remember that the waitress who brings it to the table has been up and at 'em since about 3:30 A.M. More than likely, she has two youngsters waiting at home with a sitter. She needs snide and insulting remarks about like we need chocolate syrup on our eggs.

Don Juans? They're a dime a dozen, and overpriced at that.

Never Interfere with a Woman's Soap Opera Schedule

Some things are sacred to southern women. One is "their" soap operas. To interfere with their favorites is a worse transgression than eating Cream of Wheat or moving up North.

I well remember when, in June 1981, CBS changed the air time of one of the most popular soap operas, "The Young and the Restless," from 12:30–1:30 P.M. to 1:00–2:00 P.M. Mutiny was the war cry from the women viewers.

I learned about the time change when I overheard a conversation between two employees in my office, Ruby and Debbie. Age is not a factor when it comes to soap opera loyalty. Ruby is a senior citizen, and Debbie is just past thirty.

Ruby was frantic when she called out to Debbie, "What are we going to do? They've changed our story!"

"I don't have any idea. What are you going to do?" Debbie asked.

"I honestly don't know, but I do know that I'm in a mess," Ruby said. "I know that for sure."

Within minutes I encountered yet another employee on her way to see her supervisor. She stopped long enough to answer a question.

"Where are you going in such a hurry, Pat?"

"To see Mr. Roberts and get my lunch hour changed," she said.

"Oh? Any particular reason?"

"Yes, *one* particular reason," she answered. "I watch "The Young and the Restless" on my lunch hour and CBS has changed the time it runs."

"And what if Roberts won't change your lunch hour?"
"I'll quit."
"Would you really?" I asked.
"You can bet on it," she claimed. "I dropped out of college for one quarter when I could only get Accounting I during the time my story was on the tube, and I'll quit my job. I'm *not* going to miss 'The Young and the Restless!' I grew up with it."

I was beginning to get the message that these people were serious. So was my own daughter. I learned that when I stopped by her apartment to see her the next day, around noon.

I found her seated on the sofa—barefooted—with a saucepan perched on its arm, her feet curled under her with toes flexing and squinching. That's when I got my first glimpse of Mrs. Chancellor.

"How're you doing, Lisa?" I asked, thinking it was a logical question for a daddy to ask his daughter.

"Shhhhhh!" she grunted between letters of the alphabet soup she was eating from the pan and never taking her eyes off the TV screen. She could have stuffed her nose with ABCs and never known it.

I stood mute for the next twelve minutes while Mrs. Chancellor, Derek, Jill, and Suzanne did their thing on the television screen. When they all faded into oblivion, until "tomorrow," I spoke again.

"You doing all right?"

"Fine. Just had to watch my story. [She explained that it took her six minutes to drive home from her job, run inside her apartment, turn on the TV and stove, heat the soup, and watch "my" story.] If I miss part of it on thirteen at twelve, I can get it on twelve at one."

If you think that's confusing, watch the soap sometimes.

"And what happens if you miss it completely?" I asked.

"Oh, I just ask somebody what happened when I get back to work," she said matter-of-factly. "Everybody watches it, you know."

No, I didn't know, but I was learning.

I realize that there are those who may not be totally familiar with America's Number One daytime soap opera. Therefore, I feel an obligation to brief you, even though by the time this book comes out, it will be out of date. It's very simple:

Mrs. Chancellor is an older woman and wealthy. She was married to Phillip, but he died. She is now married to Derek, a hairdresser. She has a son, Brock, by a former marriage and Derek has an afflicted child.

Vanessa is the mother of Lance and Lucas. Mrs. Foster is Mrs. Chancellor's maid and the mother of Jill, Snapper, and Greg. Suzanne is Derek's ex-wife and lives with Mrs. Chancellor. Jill is in love with Derek but is married to Mr. Brooks, who is very wealthy and is the father of Laurie, Chris, Leslie, and Peggy, his children by a former marriage. Mrs. Foster is in love with Mr. Brooks.

Phillip, Mrs. Chancellor's deceased husband, is the father of Jill's baby. Mrs. Chancellor's son, Brock, is in love with a girl named Casey, who is the sister of Nicky, who is in love with Mrs. Foster's son, Greg.

All clear? Good.

I now know two things about women for sure: they are going to watch their story, and they are going to get their hair done once a week, even if they have to slip out of intensive care at the hospital to do it!

A Marriage Counselor's Nightmare

In the previous chapter I attempted to shed light on the popular daytime television program, "The Young and the Restless," for the benefit of the uninitiated. While the show is extremely popular with women, I'm not satisfied that I completely enlightened their men. Permit me to continue.

I was in a Dublin, Georgia, restaurant for dinner and well into my second cup of coffee when I heard a mother, Grace, and daughter, Betty, conversing at a nearby table. The subject was, naturally, "The Young and the Restless." Both are addicts.

"Did you see what happened to Mrs. Chancellor today, Mama?"

"No, I missed it. Had a hair appointment," the mama said. "What happened?"

"Oh, that Suzanne got herself all dressed up in Mrs. Chancellor's nightgown and jewelry and started harassing Mrs. Chancellor. She told her that she was—"

"Bah! That Suzanne! I simply can't stand her," the mama said. "If I were Mrs. Chancellor, I'd have kicked her out long ago."

"Me, too," the daughter concurred. "Well, anyway, Suzanne got herself all dressed for bed and kept telling Mrs. Chancellor that she was going to entice Derek to go to bed with her and—"

"I knew it! I just knew it was going to happen as sure as the world!" the mama said. "Mrs. Chancellor ought to shoot her, and that Derek, too!"

I finished my coffee and made what I considered to be a normal inquiry.

"Excuse me, Betty, but who the heck is Mrs. Chancellor?"

Both Betty and her mother reacted as though I had asked of an Englishman, "Who is Elizabeth?"

"What? Who is Mrs. Chancellor?" both cried out in unison and disbelief. "She's the old lady in 'The Young and the Restless,'" Betty said. "Everybody knows that."

Yes, everybody but me.

I respectfully asked if I might join them for yet another cup of coffee. They were gracious and said I could.

"Betty, I wonder if you and your mother would do me a favor?"

"Sure, if we can."

"Oh, I'm sure you can," I said. "You see, I'm somewhat familiar with the names of the characters on 'The Young and the Restless; but I'd like to know something of the plot."

"Oh, sure! No problem," Betty said, her eyes lighting up. "It's very simple."

Yeah. And so is Rubik's Cube and nuclear fission.

"I'll just tell what happened yesterday," Betty said. "Mrs. Chancellor paid Suzanne, who is Derek's ex-wife and Mrs. Chancellor's current husband, a huge sum of money to stay away from Derek. Well, Suzanne started blackmailing

Mrs. Chancellor for more money and told her if she didn't get it, she was going to take Derek away from her."

"That's right," said Grace, "but Mrs. Chancellor has nobody to blame but herself if she loses Derek. Heck, she's been wearing that same black dress for three weeks and—"

"Mama! What do you mean?" Betty chimed in. "That Suzanne is just downright conniving and mean."

"Well," said Grace, "I wanted Lance to marry Leslie. He's real good looking! And you can bet on this: that Suzanne is going to run her crazy."

And you can bet on this: the shenanigans that take place on "The Young and the Restless" would cause a marriage counselor to have nightmares.

When I left them, they were debating the final outcome of Mrs. Chancellor, Derek, and Suzanne hot and heavy. I heard Betty say, "Well, I'll just bet that Derek and Suzanne . . ."

I considered what Betty and Grace had told me while driving home and concluded that I still had not the faintest idea just exactly who is married to, in love with, sleeping with, enemies of, mother and father of, son and daughter of, or divorced from whom.

It only seems fair that those of us who are ignorant of "The Young and the Restless" know what a majority of the fairer sex is doing every day at noon. You can find out if you'll consult your wife, daughter, maid, secretary, or any woman sales clerk.

In the meantime, good luck to you, Mrs. Chancellor, wherever you are. America needs you. At least a vast majority of the women do.

Redneck Roosters Welcome Women with Open Arms

When I want to get the straight skinny about something, I head south on U. S. 441 to Mel's Juke, about a six-pack north of Broxton, Georgia.

It was at Mel's that I first got the straight scoop about Ollie North and the Iran-Contra mess, the pros and cons of

Jim Bakker and Jessica Hahn, and the lowdown (no pun intended) on Jimmy Swaggart's tumble from glory following the revelation of his clandestine trysts in a fleabag motel in Louisiana with Debra Murphree.

I understand that through contact with Mel, Princess Diana first learned that Prince Charles sucks his thumb. It was Mel, also, who clued Nancy Reagan that Raisa Gorbachev eats chitlins like President George Bush eats pork skins. And would you believe that the president of Timex learned from Mel that John Cameron Swayze wears a Rolex, or that the *National Enquirer* scooped the media world when Mel revealed to that tabloid that Barbara Walters is the sister of Charlie McCarthy, the Edgar Bergen dummy?

With such illustrious credentials, who else but Mel could set me straight on the Supreme Court ruling that private, all-male clubs with more than four hundred members could no longer keep women out? I bought a six-pack and drove just north of Broxton to talk with the man.

I arrived in midafternoon and found Mel sitting at the lunch counter overhauling an outboard motor. Mel's handy with motors and things.

"Hey there, newspaper man," he said. "Want somethin' to eat?"

"Hi, Mel. No thanks."

Me? Eat at Mel's Juke? The only thing I'd even remotely consider eating there would be a boiled egg or a coconut.)

"Lookin' f'r Robbie Nell? (Robbie Nail Bail, fum Almer, head—and only—waitress at Mel's, guardian of the jukebox, and whatever.)

"Nope. Came to see you this time, Mel."

"Oh? What's on y'r mind?"

"I want to get your thinking on the Supreme Court ruling that says previously all-male clubs with more than four hundred members can't keep women out no more," I told him. "I know you belong to the Redneck Roosters, and ya'll have more than four hundred members, I know. But never any women members, right?"

"Nope, never had no women members," he sighed, "an' we got more'n four hundred members all right. More like four thousand, ever'body what's been kicked out o' th'

Moose, Elks, Klan, AmVets, VFW, and done time in Jackson or Reidsville prisons."

"Do ya'll still meet down at th' river?"

"Right, at Moccasin Landin' ever Friday an' Sat'dy night. And we got us a new clubhouse, too," Mel said. " 'Scooter' Blasingame, who owns Scooter's House Trailer Sales ovah' roun' Hahira, let us have a repossessed double wide, an' Second Story Simpson made arrangements f'r a air conditioner. It keeps th' trailer real cool, but th' air conditioner itse'f is a li'l hot," Mel said with a wry grin.

"And the Roosters still have no women members?"

"Right, an' I'm real glad t' hear 'bout th' new rulin', too."

"Yeah?"

"Dang right! But don't think we ain't tried. Our problem ain't keepin' women out, but gittin' 'em in. We almos' had one las' summer when Bobwire Miller bought two quarts o' Mad Dog 20/20 and a twelve-pack o' Bud 'fore he picked up 'Skinny' Swanson, th' night waitress at Big Mama's Grill out fum Pearson, when she got off at midnight."

"Yeah, go on."

"Well, they set in Bobwire's pickup behin' Cool Springs Church, lissened to George Jones tapes, and drunk that wine an' beer til' dang near daylight when Bobwire cranked up an' headed f'r th' trailer."

"Did he have a wreck or what? What happened?"

"Didn't nuthin' happen," Mel said with a sly laugh. "When they got to the Rooster's trailer, ole Bobwire stepped out o' th' truck an' passed out cold as a mack'rel. Skinny left him there an' went on home with Buddy Barfield, seein' as how th' nex' day was Sunday an' her day off n' all. An' that, newspaper man, is as close as we ever come t' gittin' a woman in th' Rooster trailer," Mel told me.

"Do you think the new Supreme Court ruling will help you get women in?"

"Well, lemme put it to ya' this a' way. We're workin' at it hard as we know how."

Part 7

Mothers Are Special

It is no great secret that in order for a woman to become a mother she must bear a child. That is the way God intended it, thank goodness! Should the roles have been divinely reversed, there is absolutely no doubt in my mind that kids would come one to a family, and those preoccupied with planned parenthood and the world population explosion would be out of business.

Should men bear the responsibility of birth, there would be no need for advocates of birth control, either. They could close up shop and look for another cause around which to rally.

I have never known a man who could go through what a woman must go through to bring a child into the world. But they pass out cigars and boast like they had done something great.

I don't think a man would make it through the delivery room door. He'd first fight—doctors and nurses. And he'd scream and cry.

The big thing going these days is for the husband to accompany his wife into the delivery room and then stand there while the baby is being born. Those promoting such madness lay claim to the fact that this is a procedure of love and support.

Friend, let me go on record right here and now that I ain't about to do that. Furthermore, not only would I not go into the delivery room, I wouldn't even want to be in the same

building. That's the coward I am. Just yell down to the park-
ing lot and say "Boy!" or "Girl!" and that all is well. I could
handle that.

Mothers are very special people. I know. I have one, God
bless her, who has been in a nursing home for eleven years.
After two broken hips, a broken nose, and a broken knee,
she doesn't walk any more and can't go out with me to eat
like she used to. I see her every day when I'm in town, and
the best we can do now is a milkshake. I never leave home
to go and see her without one, usually chocolate.

The amazing thing about this lady is that she has seen
more ups and downs than a yo-yo but never fails to ask two
questions when I visit her: "Are you feeling all right, Bo?
Are you eating right?" Yes, an eighty-eight-year-old lady in a
wheelchair wants to know if her only son is all right and
eating right. Does she complain? Never!

Maybe it would be well if we paused just long enough to
consider what mothers are, anyway:

• A mother is a nurse, teacher, counselor, mediator, con-
fessor, arbitrator, cook, seamstress, maid, taxi-driver, book-
keeper, laundry woman, programmer, censor, banker,
planner, referee, umpire, cheerleader, and general Mrs. Fix-
it. She is all these and more.

• What does a mother do? She wipes away a tear, shares a
laugh, spanks a bottom, cries when you fail, and laughs
when you succeed. She prays with you and for you. She
cooks your food, makes your bed, cleans your room, picks
up after you, and takes you places.

You know about those things. But there is yet another
dimension that you just may not think about. Remember?

Like the time when you were six years old and she
watched you walk into that school for the first time, proba-
bly cleaner than you've ever been since. And I ask you, is
there a prize for the mother who presents the cleanest first
grader each September? When you walked in that school-
house that first day, you had been scrubbed from top to bot-
tom, and your mama probably took a final swipe behind
your ears as you walked through the door.

A mother can take a dainty hankie and a dab of saliva and
clean the Empire State Building.

And don't think for a minute that the outfit you wore that first day was just something she happened to pick up at a yard sale the day before. Oh, no! She had shopped for it for months, and it made no difference that after that first recess you looked like a chimney sweep. When you walked in that first day, you were Mr. Spic and Span.

In addition to being very special, mothers are a strange breed. So tough, yet so tender. We break their hearts a thousand times over in the span of a lifetime, and they keep bouncing back.

Has there ever been a woman who experienced the miracle of childbirth who didn't harbor the hope that "this one is going to do something great"? I doubt it. And who can identify the mother who has ever said, "I know this one will never amount to a hill of beans"? Not I.

Mothers have a special way about them. They have a way of solving seemingly impossible problems, accomplishing the unbelievable. They know just the right thing to say when you feel bad and it seems that the whole world is caving in around you. Who never heard a mother say, "Well, maybe it's not all that bad. We'll find a way." And they do, magicians that they are.

What about the hours she spends on bended knee asking God to help you be the person she hopes you'll be? Or the hours she spends rubbing an aching stomach and then spends more hours watching as you sleep? What about the untold miles she's spent rocking you because she loved you and knew that you felt safe and secure nestling up close to her bosom from which she fed you?

Finally, no matter how many chores she had to do or the fact that the days didn't have enough hours for her to finish, she always seemed to find the time for you.

Mothers are tough.

The Joys of Becoming a Mother

For thirteen years since January 1978, I have written three columns a week for a daily newspaper. At least twice a year

I offer my space to a high school student planning to pursue a career in journalism. Nora Cordell Hatchett is one of those. She wrote three guest columns while a student at Dublin, Georgia, High School.

After her marriage to Tommy Hatchett and the birth of their first child, I invited Nora to write another column on motherhood. What follows are Nora's thoughts on the subject of motherhood.

The Joys of Motherhood

Was it just yesterday the world was silent? I wondered as my alarm blared at 5:00 A.M., and the snooze button no longer worked. The sound that wakes me now comes from my baby monitor, which my husband calls "crying in stereo."

I well remember the first time I heard that sound, minus a few octaves. Everything moved in slow motion, like a movie. Masked people and sterile gloves hovered over me like some show on surgery I'd seen on television. The clicking of instruments and the bright aluminum lights fit together in perfect harmony, and everything was icy cold although I was quite warm—and nauseous.

The first cry was so anticipated. I lay there for what seemed like hours waiting, holding my breath, praying silently to hear that all important yelp—"the cry of life." A chill swept over my body when I heard it. Nothing could have sounded more beautiful until I heard it again . . . and again . . . and again.

I've decided all alarm clocks should have recorded baby cries instead of buzzers and bells. But then, no one would ever sleep!

I still never really think of myself as a mother. I keep waiting for her parents to come and pick her up and pay me. I guess that comes from years of babysitting. But every now and then reality strikes and certain events spark my motherly instincts, like the first time I changed Collier's diapers.

I had been looking after children since I was thirteen and had changed quite a few bottoms, but this time it was different. Suddenly brands became important, and questions clogged my mind. Like, should I use Pampers, Huggies, or Luvs? Should I scrimp and go with the cheap brand that might cause diaper rash or splurge and go for the prestige label? Am I being a terrible and lazy mother for not using cloth diapers? How much alcohol do you actually dab on the umbilical cord? And how much is a dab anyway? What would Mama do? And where the heck is she when I need her? I had never felt so alone.

Her temperature lit my concern like neon. Just what *is* the proper temperature for a baby? Her first day home I changed her outfit seven times, used the rectal thermometer five, and spent the rest of the day reading Dr. Spock. But no matter how many times I read him or how much I memorize and quote him, when a crisis strikes, I run all over the house looking for my Dr. Spock book while carrying a screaming baby in my arms.

All my life I had dreamed of the moment I would discover that I was pregnant. I knew exactly how it would be, too. An elderly and gentle nurse, dressed in a crisp snow-white uniform, would walk over to me gracefully wearing an angel's smile, take my hand in hers, squeeze it gently and lovingly, and whisper softly, "You are with child, my dear." Then I would blush, and my face would glow blissfully as I walked from the doctor's office with my secret buried deep within my heart to tell my beloved husband the good news.

It didn't happen exactly like that. The day I found out I was pregnant I had fallen from a fourteen-foot deer stand and landed on my head in twenty-five-degree weather at 4:30 A.M. The nurse was young, fat, and wore yellow pants and a pink shirt. She walked like an elephant and didn't look me in the eye, and her voice had two volume levels: loud and off.

"It's positive," she said matter-of-factly.

I threw up.

I continued to throw up—morning, afternoon, and night. I was tempted to paint a mural in the bottom of my toilet because that's what I looked at morning, afternoon, and night.

After five months of "re-tasting my food," I decided the final four were make-up months and that a milkshake a day would cure any ailment. I was right, with the exception of obesity.

My sister Rennie was married in the eighth month of my pregnancy. Originally, I had been scheduled to be matron of honor, but when my Mom started looking for a bush large enough for me to stand behind, I decided to bow out gracefully.

Finally, the time came, and just like Lucy Ricardo I woke Tommy at 3:00 A.M., standing by the bed with labor pains and a packed suitcase. Inasmuch as I was three weeks overdue, everything in my suitcase had to be ironed before I could wear it. The suitcase had been packed since the day the young, fat nurse with the yellow pants and pink shirt announced to the world, "It's positive!"

And little Collier was born.

When Collier was but three weeks old, I was celebrating my birthday a week late at the Dublin Country Club when my best buddy, Bo Whaley, stopped by my table, gave me a big hug, and asked me to write yet another column for him. He suggested that I write on being a new mother, and the only title I could come up with at the time was "The Jokes of Motherhood." You see, it has taken a little while for me to understand just exactly what a mother is, and the true meaning of joy.

Collier was born in July. I tiptoed into her room one night the following December and sat by her crib. Just the two of us. She smelled so fresh and clean, as only a baby can, with her clothes line-dried. Her tiny feet were tucked snugly under her bottom, resembling a frog. One arm rested by her side, the other above her head. I smiled and whispered, "Just like your Daddy." I thought she grinned at that, but maybe she didn't.

My heart felt so full, like the grinch when he realizes that Christmas is not about presents or turkeys or ornaments or stockings, but rather the spirit within every person that brings the true Christmas. It was at that moment that I realized why I shouldn't write an article about "The Jokes of Motherhood" because being a mother is not really about early morning alarms, diapers, clothing, pregnancy, or labor pains. No, instead I would write about the joys of motherhood and rediscovering the wonder and excitement of experiencing life for the very first time.

God doesn't just send us children to sustain or perpetuate the human race, but rather that they might recapture our spirit, enlarge our hearts, and make us aware of what a truly awe-inspiring world surrounds us. He sends us children to prevent the sterile preoccupation with material goods that prompts alienation from His everlasting love and strength.

If I could be granted but one wish for the children, it would be that their eyes would always be open to the wonders that surround them and that their ears would always be tuned to the sounds of nature.

I thank God that my world is no longer silent.

Why Mothers Get Gray Early

I know of no group more versatile than mothers, and I'm constantly amazed at what one can accomplish in a single day. Mothers are really miracle workers with aprons.

If there is an underrated segment of the American society, it has to be mothers. It's not so much that we don't appreciate them as much as it is that we don't tell them often enough that we do.

There are many reasons why I could never be a mother, other than my physical makeup. Foremost is that I don't have enough patience to be one, not when I look back on the years my own mother spent trying to guide me in the right direction. Let's face it, I was not a good little boy and hated vegetables. She saw to it that I ate them.

If I had to name the one thing that would cause me to blow my top if I were a mother, it would be meal planning and food preparation. I think this is the prime reason why mothers get gray. Let us take a hypothetical case that may not be as hypothetical as it seems.

You—mother and wife—have done the laundry, picked Judy up from baton class, delivered Evelyn to cheerleader practice, taken Robert to Boy Scout camp, attended your study group, picked up the dry cleaning, bought groceries and fought the checkout line, returned three books to the library, and engaged in a long and not so pleasant conference with little Ralph's teacher.

You walk in the back door, dog tired, put the grocery bag that contains the necessary ingredients for Sloppy Joes that you plan to prepare for dinner on the kitchen table, and steal four minutes in the recliner with a glass of tea before slipping into that beat-up, but comfortable, housecoat to cook supper.

The time is now 6:45 P.M., and you are well into the Sloppy Joes when the telephone rings. Howard, your dutiful breadwinner, is calling.

"Hi, Anne! Just thought I'd call to tell you that six men from the home office, including the company president, are here, and I invited them to have dinner with us. I'll pick up the wine. You take care of dinner. O. K.? Nothing fancy. See ya' 'bout 7:30. Love ya', Honey. Bye."

He loves you? Then how could he do that to you? It's good for fifteen gray hairs, and the urge to kill, or divorce, is upon you. But, wife and mother that you are, you race back to the supermarket and start all over, with a 7:30 P.M. deadline. But being a miracle worker, you make it.

Now, let's reverse the situation.

You have spent an entire afternoon preparing a great meal for the husband and kids. You have taken special pains to cook just what they like: roast beef, rice and gravy, potatoes, butterbeans, candied yams, homemade biscuits, and your very own prize-winning apple pie with vanilla ice cream. At the last minute, you rush out and buy a quart of milk for Judy and Robert. Your husband, Donald, will have his usual coffee while the rest of the flock will drink iced tea, sweetened, of course.

You are gone no more than fifteen minutes and return, milk in hand, to hear the telephone ringing. It's Robert.

"Hi, Mom! I won't be home for supper, I'm at Jimmy's, and we're gonna' cook hot dogs and build model airplanes. Bye!"

Then, a repeat call. This one from Evelyn, sweet and considerate Evelyn.

"Won't be there for supper, Mom! I'm going to the gym

with Linda to help decorate for the Junior–Senior Prom.
You can fix me something when I get home. Bye!"

You are into your second glass of iced tea, sweetened, of
course, when hubby Howard calls.

"Hi, Anne! I'm going to Gene's after work to help him
work on his boat. You and the kids go ahead and eat. I'll just
grab a hamburger on the way. Love ya'! Bye."

So, what do you do? You do what any good and neglected
housewife and mother would do. You find yourself a com-
fortable, secluded spot and sit and cry . . . and cry . . . and
cry.

And when you've finished crying, you can count gray
hairs. You should have a bumper crop.

Mothers Are Very Special People

Mothers really are very special people, a rare breed.
They're strong as an ox and tender as a dew drop. No one
has ever determined just how many burdens their frail
shoulders can bear; how many heartaches and disappoint-
ments their hearts can sustain; or just how many times they
will go that second mile.

Down through the years, recognized authorities of the
written word have penned varied thoughts on mothers, who
and what they are. This is the light in which I see them.

A mother is in reality a composite, a combination of many
things. Above all she is a human being, but there are times
when she surfaces as an almost superwoman. And a mother
is as tough as she is tender. She has to be. Here are but a
few things that a mother must be:

• A mother is a magician. She finds lunch money when
there is seemingly none to be found. She makes tears disap-
pear with a kiss and mends broken hearts with a hug. And
she loves you when you least deserve to be loved, knowing
that's when you need it most.

• A mother is a physician. She knows just where and how
hard to rub when it hurts and kisses more stumped toes,
bumped heads, scraped elbows, and cut fingers than anyone

else in the world. She wipes dirty faces and runny noses, diagnoses from experience, treats with loving care, and heals through diligence and prayer.

• A mother is a detective. She needs no polygraph to decipher your answers. She knows when you've done right or wrong and weighs the evidence fully before rendering a verdict.

• A mother is a confidante. She listens to the details of a broken love affair, a disappointment, errors in judgment, the consequences of a bad decision, and offers advice that you never dreamed of.

• A mother is a judge. She listens to the evidence presented by both sides before rendering such monumental decisions as who gets to ride in the front seat, who gets the end piece of the chocolate cake, who gets the white meat, which television program to watch, whether or not you can go swimming, who hit whom first, and whether you can spend the night at a friend's house.

• A mother is a chef. She can do more with a pound of hamburger meat, a smidgen of cheese, a can of tomato paste, and a few slices of bread than Betty Crocker. And at the supermarket she can stretch a dollar from the canned vegetables to the meat department, and still manage to have enough left over to buy a few goodies.

• A mother is an athlete. She plays catch when she doesn't feel like it, pushes you in the wagon when her back is killing her, and fills in at shortstop when you can only come up with seven other baseball players. She'll take her turn at bat although her feet ache to the bone and there's dinner to be prepared or clothes to be washed.

• A mother is a chauffeur. She drives thousands of miles each year to make sure you're on time for majorette practice, a Little League game, cheerleader practice, piano lessons, a Boy or Girl Scout meeting, and school. She comes back again to pick you up.

• A mother is a person who can find things. She can find the baseball glove you left under the kitchen sink, the earring that has been behind the sofa for months, the composition book that was left behind the commode, the shoe that somehow ended up on top of the garage, the record album

that nobody put in the stack of newspapers she's saving for
the church, the knife that wound up in the laundry, the bas-
ketball that came to rest at day's end in the garbage can, and
the tennis racquet that joined the lawnmower, rake, axe,
gasoline can, and hedge trimmers at the end of summer. A
mother can even find the tennis balls that rolled underneath
the storage house all by themselves or the belt you said
you'd never need again in a cardboard box in the storage
room that also holds the deflated football that you'll ask her
to find next week.

• A mother is a teacher. She teaches things like "Now I
lay me down to sleep . . ." "Thank you God for the food
that we are about to eat. . . ." "The Lord is my shepherd, I
shall not want. . . ." "Thou shalt not steal. . ." "Do Unto
Others . . ." "Jesus loves me this I know, for the Bible tells
me so. . . ." "One-Two-Three-Four-Five-Six. . . ." "I
pledge allegiance to the flag of the United States of Amer-
ica. . . ." and "Oh, say can you see, by the dawn's early
light. . . ."

And what does she expect in return? Nothing really, but it
would be nice if sometime soon you took her in your arms
and said, "Thanks, Mother. Thanks for everything. I love
you."

Conclusion

I should have known better.

It is no more possible to conclude a book on women than it is to sit down in front, back up and go ahead, or hurry up and wait. Why? Because the antics of the delightful darlings are so unpredictable that even they can't forsee them. We men don't stand a chance!

The word *conclusion,* of course, means "the end," and to characterize the completion of this book the end of the subject would be misleading. Let me call it an intermission, an interlude if you will.

I've had a barrel of fun writing this book, primarily because of my love for women and an abiding admiration for ladies. There's a difference, you know.

I know of nothing more enjoyable than the company of a lovely lady, and I have been extremely fortunate to have known many, ranging in age from ten to ninety. As of this writing, I enjoy the friendship and love of two young ladies. One, Misty Lei Scott, is fifteen and loves me; I am teaching her how to drive. I've been in love with her since she was eight, and she knows it. The second, Mandy Yates, is eleven, and she also loves me. A hug from Mandy would solve all the problems in the Middle East, and a smile would melt all the world's prejudice and hatred.

How does a man write a book on the subject of women? It

takes a good memory and a wild imagination. While many of the stories in this book are true, some are the figments of a sixty-two-year-old bachelor's imagination coupled with delightful fantasies. I have drawn upon my years of association with the fair sex (is there an unfair sex?) and thousands of hours of thinking about them.

What was it the doctor told the old gentleman during an office visit in the middle of which he complained of blurred vision and frequent headaches? "Well, Lem, you're just going to have to give up at least half of your sex life," thereby posing a monumental problem for the old fellow.

The next day Lem told his cronies at the country store what the doctor had told him.

"Well, whatcha' gonna' do 'bout it, Lem?" asked one.

"Don't rightly know, Homer, but I gotta' make up my mind whether to give up talkin' 'bout it or thinkin' 'bout it."

One of my favorite pastimes is sitting alone on the banks of Turkey Creek or on the back porch of my country place there, thinking and fantasizing. I like to take an imaginary situation, cultivate it mentally, and record what I think could or would happen. The best part is that you can manipulate the characters as you like. I've done that with my make-believe Redneck girl, Robbie Nell Bell from Alma (Robbie Nail Bail fum Almer). No back talk or arguments from Robbie Nell. She does as I imagine she would.

So take what I've written for better or worse. I've taken all I've learned, stirred it up, and wrote it down "my way."

This book is my handiwork, and I take full credit or blame for its contents. I want it understood that I love women. I don't understand them, but I love 'em."

Remember these thoughts that have survived the test of time:

"The best way to fight a woman is with your hat—grab it and run" *(Unknown)*.

"Whenever I go out partying, all the ugly girls go home early" (Alex Hawkins, author of *That's My Story and I'm Sticking to It*).

"A handsome woman is a jewel; a good woman is a treasure" (Armand Saadi, sixteenth-century Persian poet).